V&R unipress

Geschichte im mitteleuropäischen Kontext

Band 3

Schriftenreihe herausgegeben von Renata Skowrońska

Nikolaus-Kopernikus-Universität Toruń
(Polnische Historische Mission an der Julius-Maximilians-Universität Würzburg)

Uniwersytet Mikołaja Kopernika w Toruniu
(Polska Misja Historyczna przy Uniwersytecie Juliusza i Maksymiliana w Würzburgu)

Magdalena Wiśniewska-Drewniak /
Katarzyna Pepłowska (Hg.)

Urkunden, Archive, Kontexte

V&R unipress

Bibliografische Information der Deutschen Nationalbibliothek
Die Deutsche Nationalbibliothek verzeichnet diese Publikation in der Deutschen Nationalbibliografie; detaillierte bibliografische Daten sind im Internet über https://dnb.de abrufbar.

Umschlagabbildung: Kontaktabzüge von Fotos von Lederaccessoires, die im Auftrag des Instituts für Industriedesign 1954 gemacht wurden. Bildnachweis: Fundacja Archeologia Fotografii (Archiwum Marii Chrząszczowej). Foto Magdalena Wiśniewska-Drewniak.
Wissenschaftliche Sekretärin: Marta Sikorska
Philologische Redaktion (Deutsch): Renate Schindler
Philologische Redaktion (English): Steve Jones
Übersetzung von Abstracts und Schlüsselwörtern: Steve Jones, Anu Kannike, Tomasz Leszczuk, Katarzyna Szczerbowska-Prusevicius
Druck und Bindung: CPI books GmbH, Birkstraße 10, D-25917 Leck
Printed in the EU.

Vandenhoeck & Ruprecht Verlage | www.vandenhoeck-ruprecht-verlage.com

ISSN 2701-9241
ISBN 978-3-8471-1472-7

Inhalt

Vorwort

Die Schriftenreihe *Geschichte im mitteleuropäischen Kontext* ist einem weiten Spektrum von Fragen gewidmet, die in der Region Ostmitteleuropa im Bereich der Geisteswissenschaften, zu denen auch die Archivkunde gehört, erörtert werden.

In der seit 2021 herausgegebenen Reihe sind bislang zwei Bände erschienen. Im ersten mit dem Titel *Migration – Kommunikation – Transfer* sind Beiträge zum gegenseitigen Austausch und zu ethnischen, kulturellen und religiösen Verbindungen zwischen den Ländern und der Bevölkerung Mitteleuropas versammelt. Im zweiten mit dem Titel *Gruppenidentitäten in Ostmitteleuropa* wurde das Phänomen der Nationalidentität beleuchtet, die zu den wichtigsten Merkmalen unserer Gesellschaften zählt und die im Laufe der Jahre nach verschiedenen Kriterien gestaltet wurde.

Das Buch *Urkunden, Archive, Kontexte*, in das sowohl Texte mit allgemeinem Charakter als auch Fallstudien Eingang gefunden haben, bildet die neueste, dritte Veröffentlichung innerhalb der Reihe. Die Aufsatzsammlung bringt gesellschaftliche, historische, rechtliche, organisatorische und etliche andere Kontexte nahe, die die Art und Weise beeinflussen, wie historische Quellen und Archive gebildet, verwaltet und benutzt werden. Die archivische Landschaft, die im vorliegenden Buch dargestellt wird, zeichnet sich durch Vielfalt aus und der hier behandelte Themenkreis der wechselnden Kontexte macht die spezifischen Bedingungen sichtbar, in denen ein Archiv, eine Quelle oder eine Urkunde zum Träger einer Information wird, die in einer bestimmten Realität aufgeschrieben wurde und in einer anderen gelesen wird.

Das Leitthema des Bandes wurde durch Dokumente im weitesten Sinne und ebenso komplex betrachtete Archive inspiriert, die als Objekte (oder eher gesellschaftliche Erscheinungen) in ihrem Kontext zu betrachten sind. Sie entstanden unter verschiedenen Umständen und dienten verschiedenen Zielen – zum Beispiel dem Aufbau und der Festigung von Macht und Prestige, der Sicherung einer straffen Organisation und Verwaltung bestimmter Unternehmen, der Bildung von Identität und historischer Narration in Bezug auf bestimmte

Phänomene und Gesellschaftsgruppen. Gleichzeitig mussten sie sich den von ihnen unabhängigen (beziehungsweise zum Teil unabhängigen) rechtlichen und organisatorischen Bedingungen fügen, sie wurden auch von bestimmten Traditionen und Bräuchen geprägt.

Sogar in einem einzigen, gegebenen Moment ist die Mannigfaltigkeit der Erscheinungen, Situationen und Bedingungen, die diverse, mit der Bildung und Benutzung von Archiven und Dokumenten verbundene Aspekte beeinflussen, überwältigend. Dazu kommt noch die historische Schicht – denn Kontexte wandeln sich in der Zeit und sind für bestimmte Perioden und Orte charakteristisch.

Sieht man die Frage in einer sehr weiten Perspektive, muss man feststellen, dass in die Archive Dokumente gelangen, die einen großen Differenzierungsgrad aufweisen. Für ein tiefes Verständnis dieser Urkunden ist es notwendig, über den Rahmen einer bloßen Analyse der darin enthaltenen Informationen hinauszugehen und in die Untersuchung den Blick auf den Kontext einzubeziehen, d.h. sowohl die Bedingungen, die mit dem Entstehen einer bestimmten Quelle oder Quellen verbunden sind, als auch andere Informationen, die zur Umgebung der jeweiligen Urkunde gehören, zu betrachten. Die Bewahrung des Kontextes ist darüber hinaus von zentraler Bedeutung für das Provenienzprinzip, und die archivarische Beschreibung, die die Archivare seit jeher zu leisten haben, soll ein Werkzeug sein, das den Nutzer durch die verschiedenen Kontexte leitet, die für das Verständnis einer historischen Quelle unentbehrlich sind.

Archive wiederum fügen sich (und taten dies auch in der Vergangenheit) von selbst diversen Kontexten, die darauf Einfluss nehmen, wie diese Erinnerungsinstitutionen organisiert sind, wem und welchem Zweck sie dienen, wie sie ihren Pflichten nachkommen und welcher Art diese Pflichten eigentlich sind. Die Dauerhaftigkeit archivalischer Quellen sollte nicht mit der Statik der Archive gleichgesetzt werden – das gilt sowohl für die Gegenwart als auch für die Vergangenheit. Diese Institutionen, die potenziell zum Hort des Konservatismus werden können, veränderten sich und verändern sich immer noch, indem sie willig oder widerstrebend auf ihre Umgebungen reagieren und eigene Bedingungen kreieren, die mit der Nutzung von historischen Quellen (nicht nur durch die Geschichtswissenschaftler) zusammenhängen.

Die Archivkunde ist als wissenschaftliche Disziplin und praktische Tätigkeit (beide Bereiche sind ja ohnehin immanent miteinander verzahnt) von Anfang an in diese vielfältigen Kontexte eingebunden, die sowohl mit dem Dokument und der Dokumentierung als auch mit den Archiven, die diese aufbewahren, im Zusammenhang stehen. Ein Widerhall dieser komplexen Vielfalt ist die Multidimensionalität der in diesem Band vorgestellten Texte, die die sich wandelnden Aspekte aus Geschichte und Gegenwart der Dokumentierungspraxis und der Archive behandeln.

In geographischer Hinsicht bezieht sich die Mehrheit der Aufsätze auf das polnische Gebiet, es werden darin jedoch Themen aus verschiedenen Zeiten der Geschichte behandelt, wodurch auch die geographische Spannweite größer und fließend ist. Die Sammlung wird um zwei Texte ergänzt, die von Ländern handeln, die zum weit gefassten ostmitteleuropäischen Raum gezählt werden – der eine ist in Rumänien und der andere in Estland angesiedelt.

Die Einladung zur Publikation nahmen 15 Autoren wahr. Die eingegangenen Arbeiten wurden nach dem chronologischen Prinzip angeordnet, denn der Band spiegelt, wie es bereits signalisiert wurde, aufgrund seiner Heterogenität die sich in Zeit und Raum verändernde archivische Landschaft wider.

Die Sammlung wird durch den Beitrag *The Second Life of Documents. A Study of the History of the Legal and Political Culture of Early Modern Poland* von Waldemar Chorążyczewski eröffnet, in dem der Wandel der Kontexte und der daraus folgenden, neuen Bedeutungen einer Urkunde am Beispiel der Erarbeitung der systempolitischen Grundlagen Polens in der frühen Neuzeit präsentiert wird. Der Autor vertritt den Standpunkt, dass die Einordnung der in einem bestimmten Zusammenhang entstandenen Dokumente in neuen, sich stets in der Zeit wandelnden Kontexten, die oft eine Umdeutung im Geiste der neuen politischen Herausforderungen zur Folge hatten, in den Forschungsfragen der Diplomatik und Archivkunde unzureichend berücksichtigt wird.

Das nächste Kapitel, das den Titel *Archives of the Greek Catholic Bishopric in Przemyśl and the Reform of the Uniate Church in the 17th and 18th centuries* trägt und aus der Feder von Wioletta Zielecka-Mikołajczyk stammt, stellt eine archivarische Charakteristik des im 17. und 18. Jahrhundert gebildeten Archivs der unierten Bischöfe von Premissel (Przemyśl) dar. Die Autorin, die das Augenmerk auf den weiteren Kontext der sich in der Unierten Kirche vollziehenden Wandlungen richtet und Merkmale aufzufinden versuchte, die das analysierte Archivgut mit den in anderen Diözesen vorhandenen Dokumenten verbindet, stellt fest, dass in Bezug auf die Einführung neuer Dokumentationsformen ähnliche Initiativen auch in anderen Diözesen, d.h. in Premissel, Cholm (Chełm) und Brieg (Brzeg) beobachtet werden können.

Im Beitrag *Magnates and Landowner Archives of the 18th–20th Centuries. Evolution or Revolution?* zeichnet Krzysztof Syta ein Bild der Archive großadliger Familien. Die systempolitischen Veränderungen, die während der Teilungszeit erfolgten, zwangen die Eliten des damaligen Adels dazu, sich den neuen, von den Besatzern aufoktroyierten Bedingungen anzupassen. Diese Prozesse verursachten wiederum Transformationen in den Magnatenarchiven, was in dem Aufsatz von Krzysztof Syta einer Analyse unterzogen wurde. Der Autor beschreibt die sich wandelnden historischen, systempolitischen und gesellschaftlichen Bedingungen, angesichts deren die im 19. Jahrhundert entstandenen Gutsbesitzerarchive außer ihren traditionellen pragmatischen vermögens- und wirtschaftsbezogenen Funktionen neue Aufgaben übernahmen und sich im Laufe der Zeit in großem Maße in Schatzkammern nationaler und Familientradition wandelten, die mit eifriger und fachmännischer Fürsorge gepflegt wurden.

Bei der Erforschung der veränderlichen Kontexte, die die Einordnung der erhaltenen Quellen prägen, dürfen die Aktivitäten zur Aussonderung von Archivalien mit historischem Wert nicht vergessen werden. Dieser Problemstellung widmet sich Robert Degens Text *The History of Selection. Polish Attempts to Make a Selection of Archival Materials While Preserving Their Organic Context Before 1939.* Im Fokus des Autors steht die Zwischenkriegszeit, in der polnische Archivare, die die archivarische Selektion durchführten, als Kriterium für die dauerhafte Aufbewahrung von Akten das Vorhandensein von organischen Verbindungen zwischen den archivalischen Materialien ansahen, die mit der Zeit und aufgrund des massenhaften Zustroms von Dokumenten an Bedeutung verloren hatten. Gestützt auf zahlreiche Beispiele werden in dem Beitrag Aktivitäten zur Aufbewahrung der gesamten Dokumentation vorgestellt, um in beispielhaften Registraturen die zwischen den Akten bestehenden organischen Relationen festzuhalten.

Marcin Smoczyński legt eine komparatistische Analyse der polnischen und deutschen Büroreform in der Zwischenkriegszeit vor. Im Kapitel *Polnische und deutsche Büroreformen in der Zwischenkriegszeit* widmet sich der Verfasser der Geschichte, den Grundsätzen, Autoren und Folgen der Rationalisierungsarbeiten, die darauf ausgerichtet waren, in polnischen und deutschen öffentlichen Ämtern die Effizienz im Umgang mit den Urkunden und Akten zu steigern. Marcin Smoczyński weist nach, dass die in Polen vorgenommenen Lösungen die jenseits der westlichen Grenze implementierten Maßnahmen widerspiegelten.

Einflüsse anderer Staaten oder Systeme auf den Prozess der Entstehung von Dokumenten fielen in der Nachkriegszeit in den Ländern des sogenannten Ostblocks besonders ins Auge. Dies wird in den beiden folgenden Abhandlungen hervorragend aufgezeigt. In der ersten von ihnen, *Considerations About the Soviet Influence on Archival Operations in Romania*, untersucht Bogdan-Florin Popovici den sowjetischen Einfluss auf die Entwicklung der Archivkunde in Rumänien. Bei der zweiten, *National Defence of the People's Republic of Poland in the Light of Doctrinal Documents – Discussion Illustrated by an Example from the Navy* von Robert Rybak, handelt es sich um die Beschreibung des Charakters, der Inhalte und der wechselseitigen Relationen der Grunddokumente, in denen die Fragen der Verteidigungsbereitschaft der Volksrepublik geregelt wurden, mit besonderer Berücksichtigung der Vielfalt der Doktrinaldokumente, der Kontexte, in denen sie entstanden, und der wechselseitigen Beziehungen zur Zeit des Warschauer Paktes.

Im vorliegenden Band fehlt es auch nicht an Texten, die sich auf die mit der gegenwärtigen Tätigkeit der Archive verbundenen Fragen beziehen. Marlena

Jabłońska wirft in ihrem Aufsatz *The Environment of Contemporary Archives as the Context of Their Operations. An Area of Many Dimensions* ein Schlaglicht auf die Faktoren, die die Aktivität der zeitgenössischen Archive in Polen beeinflussen, indem sie die Umgebung dieser Institutionen bestimmen und somit den Kontext schaffen, in dem sie arbeiten. Die Autorin richtet ihr Augenmerk auf fünf Aspekte: den soziokulturellen, rechtlich-politischen, ökonomischen, technologischen und internationalen und deutet an, dass jeder einzelne von ihnen den Archivraum mit Fragen, Problemen und Herausforderungen füllt und zugleich einen Bereich darstellt, auf den die Archive einwirken können.

Der Frage nach der heutigen Wahrnehmung der archivischen Tätigkeit in Polen geht auch Katarzyna Pepłowska nach. Das Kapitel *The European Union Policy Regarding the Re-use of Public Sector Information and Its Legal Impact in Poland* ist der von der Europäischen Union in Bezug auf den Zugang zu Informationen des öffentlichen Sektors, deren Wiederverwendung und die Offenlegung von Daten verfolgten Politik gewidmet, die auf die Rechtsordnungen der Mitgliedstaaten, darunter Polens, einwirkt. Der Text zeigt das Vorgehen der Europäischen Union in Bezug auf das Gemeinschaftsrecht und den Einfluss der entsprechenden Maßnahmen auf das polnische Archivrecht im Bereich der Wiederverwendung von archivalischen Dokumenten, die als Informationen des öffentlichen Sektors eingestuft worden sind und von den polnischen Archiven zugänglich gemacht werden. Dies erlaubt es, neue Bedeutungen der Unterlagen, darunter neue Kontexte für ihre Auslegung und ihre Verwendung zu erschaffen.

In den Archiven der ganzen Welt werden heutzutage Maßnahmen getroffen, die eine Annäherung zwischen dem Nutzer und dem Archiv bewirken sollen. Sie sollen auch die Gesellschaft dazu bewegen, neue Facetten der Urkunden zu erfassen. Diese Dependenzen werden im Sammelaufsatz *From Community Involvement to Research Interests: Crowdsourcing Projects of the National Archives of Estonia* beleuchtet. Die Autoren Liisi Taimre, Aigi Rahi-Tamm, Sven Lepa und Tõnis Türna beschreiben die Crowdsourcing-Projekte, die in den Archiven in Estland realisiert werden. Die vorgestellten Forschungsergebnisse aus diesem Bereich bezeugen eine breite Teilnahme der Gesellschaft an der Beschreibung archivalischer Quellen.

Zu den grundlegenden Aktivitäten der Archive zählen das Sammeln, Aufbewahren, Bearbeiten und Zur-Verfügung-Stellen der Bestände. Eine von ihnen rückt Krzysztof Kopiński im nächstfolgenden Kapitel *Die unendliche Bearbeitung und Evidenzführung (von der altpolnischen Urkunde zum elektronischen Dokument in Polen)* ins Zentrum der Betrachtung. Der Verfasser bringt darin seine Überlegungen über die Bearbeitung archivalischer Materialien und zur Evidenzführung seit dem Mittelalter bis zur Gegenwart zum Ausdruck.

Der die vorliegende Publikation abschließende Text *Archival Appraisal in Community Archives* von Magdalena Wiśniewska-Drewniak beinhaltet eine einleitende Analyse der Kontexte, in denen Sozial- und Bewegungsarchive (auch freie Archive oder Archive von unten genannt) Entscheidungen darüber treffen, welche Materialien in ihre Bestände aufgenommen werden sollen. Die Autorin richtet ihre Aufmerksamkeit auf verschiedene Stufen der archivarischen Selektion, denkt darüber nach, wie die archivarische Selektion von den Sozialarchivaren betrachtet wird, und reflektiert über das Gewicht des menschlichen Faktors im Rahmen dieser Tätigkeit sowie die Art und Weise, wie der Dokumentation ihr Wert zugesprochen wird. In dem Beitrag werden Ergebnisse der Forschung und der zahlreichen, zu dieser Problemstellung durchgeführten Interviews dargestellt.

Die in diesem Band versammelten Texte erschöpfen mit Sicherheit nicht das breite Spektrum der Forschungsprobleme, an denen die gegenwärtige Archivkunde interessiert ist. Die Vielfalt der in dem Buch angesprochenen Fragestellungen macht es zu einem Forum für den Austausch von Wissen zu den neuesten archivbezogenen Forschungen im weit gefassten ostmitteleuropäischen Kontext.

Der vorliegende Band wie auch die früheren Publikationen innerhalb dieser Reihe verdanken ihre Entstehung dem Engagement vieler Personen: Es waren daran Vertreter und Mitarbeiter der Fakultät für Geschichtswissenschaften der Nikolaus-Kopernikus-Universität in Toruń und der Polnischen Historischen Mission in Würzburg sowie Autoren, Herausgeber und Übersetzer beteiligt. Allen, die an der Gestaltung des Buches mitgewirkt haben, wollen wir unseren herzlichen Dank aussprechen. Wir wollen auch den Autoren danken, denn es sind die Forschungsergebnisse eines jeden von ihnen, die die vorliegende Publikation ausmachen.

Dr. Katarzyna Pepłowska
Dr. Magdalena Wiśniewska-Drewniak

Waldemar Chorążyczewski

The Second Life of Documents. A Study of the History of the Legal and Political Culture of Early Modern Poland

Abstract
In diplomatics and archival science, the role played by pre-existing documents in new contexts in a constant state of flux has been insufficiently researched. This variability is clearly observable in the development of the political foundations of Poland in the early modern period. The belief in the sufficiency of ancestral systems gave many documents from the past a new lease on life. Others needed to be reinterpreted in line with new political challenges.
Keywords: early modern Poland; documents in political life; modernisation of the state; the cult of old law

Classical diplomatics tries to successfully answer a number of questions relating to the process of creating documents, such as: the initiative to write a document, its form and dictate, and the means of authentication. It meticulously examines the relation of the document to the legal action it certifies, and thus plays an important role in the discussion on the orality and literacy of human culture. It feels competent in determining the status of a legal document. It is very effective in tracking all formal and substantive repetitions. It is less likely to deal, and copes less well, with the individual features of documents, including the authorship or origin of non-formulaic fragments – breaking conventions and archetypes – of the text of documents recognised especially through their narratives and dispositions. They are often the works of scholars who remain anonymous to us, which leads to laborious research despite uncertain outcomes.

Diplomatics has even less to say about the fate of the documents after they have left their office and been deposited in the recipient's archives. And these fates are often not simple, but confusing, full of unexpected twists and turns. From information scattered throughout various studies not connected with diplomatics, we learn about "burying" or putting documents "to sleep", about

Assoc. prof. Waldemar Chorążyczewski, Nicolaus Copernicus University in Toruń, ORCID: https://orcid.org/0000-0002-0063-0032.

their unexpected discovery sooner or later, reminiscent of their exhumation or resurrection, their return to the issuer and deletion, and finally about a planned extermination resembling an ancient *damnatio memoriae.*

Archival science, a product of modernist thinking, helps us to perceive a different dimension of the second life of documents. Its basic research model, the reconstruction of the archive-making process, refers, in its classic version, to the category of an archival fonds. An archival fonds is created by selecting and processing the entirety of files produced by one systemically individual creator. It would appear to be consummate work, featuring an inventory and handed over to users. It may be safely assumed that in the future, due to changes in information needs, the study may be resumed, furnished with new search characteristics. Recently, there has been increasing talk about environmental and social changes that may endanger archives and actually herald their death. The concept of a life cycle of archives, from creation until their final annihilation, creeps forth. This life span of documents may include multiple hibernations and awakenings, and thus the second life of documents may become their third, fourth life, and so on, including after the annihilation of the original record.

Throughout its life cycle, a document finds itself in different contexts, sprouting new meanings. Each document sooner or later leaves its creator. It wanders through the world, is ignored and disappears or catches someone's interest and finds itself in a context different from the previous one. In this context, each object that makes up a collected whole also acquires a new meaning ascribed by the collector. But he, too, is not the final instance for giving meaning to the text. Coming into contact with interested parties for various, unpredictable reasons, it becomes something new, with a significance unknown to previous creators and administrators. Those who read the texts create new texts on their basis, and when the texts used finally fade, their trace will remain in citations and uses, possibly in full or partial copies.

The above-mentioned issue of who authored a document text, which is relevant in source studies, provides a valuable clue indicating familiarity with documents, which is crucial for their second life. A good illustration is the narrative formulas of the incorporation documents of Podlasie, Volhynia and the Kyiv region.[1] At the Lublin Sejm[2] of 1569, before the conclusion of a real union between Poland and Lithuania on July 1, three territories previously included in the Grand Duchy of Lithuania were incorporated: Podlasie (March 5),[3] Wołyń

1 Chorążyczewski / Degen 2017, pp. 201–208.

2 Sejm – parliament in the Polish-Lithuanian Commonwealth, composed of two chambers – the Senate and the Chamber of Deputies (representatives of the nobility), as well as the King. None of these bodies could make laws without the participation of the others.

3 Ohryzko 1859 (2), pp. 77–80.

with Bracławszczyzna (May 26),[4] the Kyiv region (June 5).[5] In our present opinion, these were incorporations, whereas the documents accompanying these legal actions clearly speak of the restoration of these so-called eternally Polish lands to the Kingdom of Poland. The thesis about the restoration of Podlasie, Wołyń and the Kyiv region required appropriate argumentation. This is contained in the narrative formulas of the relevant acts. Someone must have constructed this argument, and clues about this person may be found in the narratives. Despite the understandable differences, the similarities are striking. Podlasie and Wołyń already belonged to Poland in the pre-Jagiellonian era. We do not know from when, but they belonged continuously until the reign of Casimir Jagiellon, who illegally incorporated them into Lithuania. Argumentation in the case of the Kiev region is the most artificial, the weakest, and yet the most valuable in terms of seeking out the author. Ruthenia was incorporated into the Kingdom in the 14th century by King Casimir the Great, and Kyiv was, after all, the capital of Ruthenia. The bad king here is Władysław Jagiełło, not his son Casimir Jagiellon. The withdrawal during the separation of the Kyiv region corresponds well with the feeling of Poland's weaker rights to this land. The immaturity of the disquisition is a clue for establishing the author. The sources cited by the author are equally valuable. First of all, these are privileges in the royal treasury, followed by old chronicles.

In the second half of the 1560s, in accordance with the constitution of the Warsaw Sejm in the years 1563–1564, a commission was established to revise the resources of the Crown Archives. It was composed of Stanisław Górski, Szymon Ługowski and Jan Zamoyski. The royal secretary was considered to be the most active member of this team, and the inventory created at the end of the work in 1567 is commonly known as "Zamoyski's inventory" to this day. Looking at the political career of the future Chancellor and Grand Hetman of the Crown, it must be admitted that the organisation of the Crown Archives could have been an event of immense importance in his life. It gave him first-hand knowledge from which he drew arguments in the political struggle.

The interregnum that immediately followed this work, or rather interrupted it, resulting from the death of the last Jagiellon in 1572, allowed Zamoyski to shine with his freshly won preeminence. By organising the Crown Archives, Zamoyski became an unparalleled expert in Polish law. Zamoyski considered himself a mere translator of old laws, just like other noble activists of the 16th century. They did not feel like they were creating something new, but only reconstructing.[6]

---

4 Ibid., pp. 80–84.
5 Ibid., pp. 84–87.
6 Sobieski 1978, p. 146.

It was Zamoyski who, using old formulas, drew up the decree of the election of King Henry III of France. He provided senators with information about Poland's foreign alliances. From the privilege of Alexander Jagiellon from 1501 he drew an article *de non praestanda oboedientia*, according to which it was possible to break allegiance with the monarch if he had violated the law. He always had copies of documents from the Crown Archives to hand. He brought them on journeys, including to Paris while participating in the delegation to Henry III, elected king of Poland in 1573. Here, thanks to his proficiency, he composed letters on behalf of the delegation. No wonder it earned a reputation as irreplaceable in public affairs.[7]

The most outstanding example of Zamoyski's use of old documents, which may be considered today an example of great manipulation, is the way he had the *viritim* election recognised as a way of choosing a Polish monarch – i.e., through the personal participation of the entire nobility in the selection of the king. Given the cult of ancestral laws at the time, we understand that this concept could not have emerged as something new. Zamoyski interpreted a document of the Ruthenian nobility from 1436 in such a way that the principle of viritim election arose thereof as a noble duty. The act of confederation of 10 July 1436 involved the Ruthenian, Podolia and Bełz voivodeships. Zamoyski revived it during his work at the Crown Archives, and also translated it into Polish. Then he revealed it to the nobility gathered at the regional assembly of the Chełm region in Krasnystaw. The resolution of the assembly referred to this act of "sedition", agreeing with Zamoyski's interpretation whereby, upon pain of penalty as stated in the act of 1436 for those who did not take part in regional assembly (just as those who avoided military campaigns) all citizens were obliged to appear at the election. It did not matter that in the act of confederation of 1436 it was about regional assemblies (*sejmik*), not a general assembly (Sejm).[8] Zamoyski's representation and the resolution of the Chełm nobility were of great relevance for shaping the concept of *viritim* election.

The instrumental treatment of the legal legacy of the previous centuries is evidenced by the fact that Zamoyski found a historical and legal basis for a free election at the moment when he abandoned his outlook on election by representatives of the nobility.

The cult of antiquity at the threshold of modern times was a common phenomenon, leading straight out of the Middle Ages. Indeed, in the common perception of medieval Europe, the source of law was primarily a custom sanctioned by antiquity. Antiquity was a desirable value, and the law at the time

7 Michalak 1986, p. 28.
8 Sobieski 1978, pp. 93–99; Chorążyczewski 2006, pp. 71–72.

existed independently of people.[9] Liberation from this feature of modern public life has not always been favoured by the currents of humanism. For a long time in Renaissance Italy, innovation was considered undesirable in terms of both state and art. After all, the art of revival was supposed to be a return to old patterns as opposed to modern gothic. It must be admitted, however, that over time a reevaluation began, heralding the conviction of the positive nature of innovation so dear to us. Furthermore, even the most sincere declarations of attachment to old forms did not exclude actual innovation.[10]

The legal culture of the Polish nobility of the 16th century was thus characterised by traditionalism – i.e., the cult of old law, which Wacław Uruszczak rightly considers to be the legacy of the Middle Ages. This researcher even noticed that it was the attachment to old laws that underpinned the concept of enforcing laws,[11] a key political movement in early modern Poland that shaped the political system of the Republic of Poland almost until the end of its existence. Representatives of this movement postulated, inter alia, reforms in the judiciary, treasury and army, the return of royal lands to the crown treasury and the limitation of the rights of the Church. The middle-nobility enforcement movement not only grew out of the cult of antiquity, but also bolstered this cult. Senatorial opponents of enforcement were also forced to refer to arguments from the past. Nobody wanted to be accused of wanting to violate the existing order.[12]

Enforcement activists granted themselves the right to interpret legal acts. This interpretation was necessary in a political culture that made reference to laws established by ancestors. Originally, however, the interpreter of the old laws was the king. Therefore, Sigismund Augustus was indignant when the nobility dared to invoke the old laws. Indeed, their interpretation was "a matter of office".[13] Meanwhile, when in 1562 the king convened a Sejm, announcing that he would not be present, the nobility objected, considering that it would be against the old customs.[14] This was not entirely true. Sigismund the Old, father of Sigismund Augustus, ruling in the years 1507–1548, created many precedents in this respect. However, recognising their legitimacy, with an awareness of how inefficiently the Sejm and the legislative process progressed in such circumstances, was not beneficial for the nobility. Therefore, they referred to another group of events from the past-namely, they threatened to assemble all the nobility, similar to the former general assemblies. Referring back to the old form of parliamentary life

9 Uruszczak 1979, p. 11.
10 Burke 1991, p. 162.
11 Uruszczak 1979, pp. 48–49.
12 Marciniak 1983, pp. 130–131.
13 Czapliński 1984, p. 42.
14 Ibid., p. 43.

turned out to be an effective deterrent for the king.[15] It can be clearly seen that, despite the king's reluctance, the right to interpret the old law became an attribute of the Sejm as a whole, in the sense that one element of it could not act without the other three: the king, the senate and the chamber of deputies. The ancient custom became a sanction of the constitutions passed at the Sejms of the 16th century.

The ancestors left the archives at the head of the Cracow Crown Archives. While referring to them, in the second half of the reign of Sigismund Augustus, many forgotten acts were discovered. They formed the basis for developing new acts, such as the act of the Polish-Lithuanian Union (1569), the act of the General Confederation after the death of Sigismund Augustus (1572), the act of the Warsaw Confederation introducing religious tolerance (1573). The political foundations of the Polish-Lithuanian Commonwealth were created thanks to what was called the exhumation of documents, and should be regarded as their resurrection, giving them a new lease on life.

For the politicians of the 16th century, the legacy of previous generations was a treasure trove of models and solutions that only needed to be cut to fit the present day. This treasure trove was used selectively, electing not to recall inconvenient customs and laws, and at times giving the value of precedence to unexpected acts that suddenly gained new gravitas and, in the shifting political circumstances, practically new content. One thing is certain: the adherence to the principle of the primacy of the old law in political life required adequate knowledge of the text of this law, and it also allowed experts and interpreters of the old law to pretend to be political leaders. The application of the principle of interpretation was conducive to an interest in old laws and models of behaviour recorded in the acts.

The cult of the old law was conducive to extracting documents from hiding, awakening, exhuming or resurrecting them. Situations in which documents stood a chance for a second life can be divided into two groups. The first is the reinterpretation of documents whose records no one questioned, no one pulled out of the void, no one recalled, but only reread their meaning. The second is the use of a text or fragment of a forgotten document, and not necessarily with reference to this borrowing.

The chronologically most vibrant example of such a reinterpretation is the tolerance privilege for Jews issued by Bolesław, prince of Poland, in 1264. But Bolesław was a Polish prince in its 13th century meaning, when Poland was identified with the later Greater Poland, and it was only this district that was originally granted the privilege. Meanwhile, in the collections of legal acts in force in the modern era, this document still functioned without literal changes. It was understood, however, that it concerned the entire Polish-Lithuanian Common-

15 Ibid.

wealth, treated at the time as Poland, and not just two voivodeships in Greater Poland.

For the middle-nobility movement, as for Polish politicians in general, there was no doubt that the acts from the beginning of the Jagiellonian era incorporated Lithuania into the Crown and then they simply had to be enforced, and so the Grand Duchy had to be subordinated to Polish offices.[16] In their opinion, the real union with Lithuania was not a novelty. Characteristic of the legal relationship between Lithuania and Poland is the position represented by Hieronim Ossoliński at the Sejm of 1553. He stated that in Horodło in 1413, Jagiełło and Vytautas transferred their rights to Lithuania to the Crown. This act was additionally sworn in by the lords and nobility of the Grand Duchy. The Act of Horodel was observed until the beginning of the reign of Sigismund the Old. Now it was only necessary to convene a parliament common to both Poles and Lithuanians in order to make the union a reality.[17]

The same was true of the attitude of noble politicians to the realisation of Royal Prussia and, consequently, the liquidation of the autonomy of this district. The first executive Sejm in Piotrków formulated a new interpretation of the legal grounds for the seizure of assets, i.e., the acts of 1440–1454, and above all of 1504. It turned out that the statute of Alexander prohibited the king from disposing of the crown's assets without the consent of the other two elements of the sejm in the territory of the entire Crown within its borders at that time, including Prussia and the Duchy of Zator and Oświęcim, which after all remained under one seal and royal sceptre. Thus, the donation, fiefdom and sale of royal goods in Prussia in the years 1504–1562 were considered contrary to the law.[18] Therefore, based on the observance and even exercise of the old law, it was enough to recognise Prussia, notwithstanding the Prussians, to be an integral part of the Crown under that old law, and therefore not to acknowledge the Prussian autonomy that had actually functioned since the Thirteen Years' War. For the Prussians, it meant, of course, a breach of their national privileges, separate from those of the Crown. So, two interpretations of the law contradicted each other. The victor would be the one who had more political clout to back him up – i.e., the alliance of the nobility and the king. The second executive Sejm in Warsaw from 1563–1564 confirmed the interpretation of the previous Sejm.[19] However, as far as the Prussians could count on the support of at least some crown senators in defending themselves against enforcement on the basis of the common fate of the aggrieved, all elements of the Sejm supported a tighter union between Prussia and

16 Cynarski 1988, p. 108.
17 Kaniewka 1979, p. 396.
18 Szczuczko 1994, p. 68.
19 Ibid., pp. 169–170.

the Crown, just like in the case of Lithuania. The act issued during the Lublin Sejm of 1569 this time contained an interpretation of the privileges of Casimir Jagiellon for Prussia, namely the provisions that the king would consult Prussian councillors in important matters concerning Prussia. According to the Prussian interpretation, this meant that the Prussians did not have to sit in the Crown Senate and participate in the general assemblies, but only in the Prussian Sejm. However, it turned out that, they had interpreted the provisions of the privileges based on a misunderstanding. Indeed, Prussian councillors were also Crown councillors, and the privilege only guaranteed that in matters important to Prussia they would be able to decide with their participation, which could also take place at the Crown Sejm. Prussians could not excuse themselves from sitting in the Polish Sejm. Nor should they claim that they were not summoned to the Crown Sejms in the past when the royal chancellery had evidence to the contrary. Even old arguments from the period of battles with the Teutonic Order were recalled, saying that Prussia was the land of the Polish Kingdom, formerly taken from the kingdom, and then returned to join it.[20]

The exhumation of a document presupposes that it has been previously buried – in practice, by placing it in an archive and, at least temporarily, forgetting about it. The most stunning example is the so-called Statute of Jan Łaski – i.e., the codification of Polish law made by the Crown Chancellor in 1505 and formally published in the following year. It officially aimed to "make knowledge of the law universal rather than exceptional".[21] Łaski conducted a thorough search through archives and old manuscripts, and if he did not include something, this was not by accident. He could not have been unaware of files that he himself had edited a few years earlier – specifically, two documents from 1501, issued in Mielnik: the act of the Polish-Lithuanian union and an act known as senatorial, which gave wide-reaching authority in the kingdom to the senate. Łaski left them out on purpose, so that they would not perpetuate and would fade from human memory and be finally buried. Printed copies of the Statute, certified with the crown seal, were sent to church chapters and coffers – i.e., land archives – and unsealed ones were sold freely.[22] The practice of political life in the following decades proves the effectiveness of this procedure. Hieronim Ossoliński, during the Sejm of Piotrków in 1562–1563, while preparing a response to the bishops regarding tithing, was to prepare an overview of the state privileges of the nobility, which was indeed based on the Statutes of Łaski.[23]

20 Bodniak / Skorupska 1979, pp. 226–227; Chorążyczewski 2006, pp. 69–70.
21 "[…] znajomość prawa z wyjątkowej stała się powszechną." Pappe 1999, p. 104.
22 Ibid., pp. 104–105.
23 Chorążyczewski 2006, p. 67.

Jan Łaski had an outstanding master – Krzesław Kurozwęcki, his superior, protector and predecessor in the office of the Crown chancellor. He was the initiator of the Mielnik act known as the senatorial act, whereby the senior senators gained the decisive vote in the sejm court, and offices would be distributed not according to the free decision of the king, but according to a fixed order, the Cracow starosta would have to be the castellan or the Cracow voivode. However, the most important provision was the possibility of refusing allegiance to the king if he wronged the dignitaries or acted against the law.[24] Kurozwęcki took this last decision from the Golden Bull of Hungarian king Andrew II of 1222. He encountered it in 1494 when he accompanied Polish king John Albert on his trip to Hungary. He then had it entered into his chancellor's book.[25]

However, the meticulously prepared and then carefully hidden Mielnik acts in 1501 survived in the archives and were revived at the right moments. One of the provisions of the Henrician Articles that constituted a kind of basic legal act prepared in 1573 and presented to be sworn in by elected Polish kings, was an article *de non praestanda oboedientia* that Jan Zamoyski derived from this 1501 privilege of Alexander Jagiellon, condemned to oblivion.[26]

On the other hand, the Mielnik act of the Polish-Lithuanian union gained importance during the efforts to finally establish a real union, successfully completed in 1569. First, in March 1502, despite the existence of an act from October the previous year, earlier acts from the years 1433 and 1434 were sought in the archives of the Cracow chapter.[27] Nevertheless, when the Mielnik Act itself became antiquated, despite its formal non-validity, it was exhumed in 1564, when the negotiations for the union gained momentum.[28]

An example of a clear re-use of a text from an earlier document, forgotten and then recalled, is the act of confederation after the death of Sigismund Augustus. This act, designed to ensure peace throughout the state, was passed "seeing our ancestors decision in which they forbade such evil and wanton things."[29] More specifically, the Nowy Korczyn Confederation of 1438 was referred to, summarising or even citing many of its provisions translated into Polish, namely those relating to ensuring internal peace for the country. On the other hand, the passages targeting heretics-Hussites were completely omitted.[30] This is not surprising, since the act of confederation was also adopted by heretics to a large

24 Michalski 1984, p. 50.
25 Papee 1999, p. 53.
26 Michalak 1986, p. 28.
27 Frost 2018, p. 529.
28 Ibid., p. 544.
29 "[...] widząc przodków naszych to postanowienie, w którym takich złych, a swawolnych rzeczy bronili." Ohryzko 1859 (2), p. 123.
30 Idem 1859 (1), pp. 63–64; idem 1859 (2), p. 123.

extent, and ensuring internal peace seemed to require the cooperation of those of different faith. The act of confederation of the Lesser Poland voivodeships after the death of Stephen Bathory could already refer to:

> The customs of our glorious ancestors and old lists and confederations that were made in such and such cases, namely the confederation in the new town of Korczyn made by our ancestors in 1438 and us in Cracow after the death of the well-renown King Sigismund Augustus, in 1572 [...] restored and strengthened.[31]

It is odd that the same Nowy Korczyn Confederation was soon to serve slightly different purposes, but also in accordance with the principle of invoking the laws of ancestors. Proving the invalidation of the Warsaw Confederation in 1573, the Catholic camp referred to the still valid anti-heretical confederation, this time according to their interpretation, directed against the Hussites.[32] However, political pragmatism tended to suggest that the authors of the confederation act were right. Their deliberate literal omission of the anti-Hussite articles of the confederation from 1438 was in line with the spirit of this act, whose purpose was to preserve public peace.[33]

Observation of the political life of that time from perspectives other than Lesser Poland shows that the establishment of a confederation for the interregnum period and the very need to ensure a peaceful functioning of the state was more primary and more vital than the laws of the ancestors, whose binding force was announced with pomp and ceremony. The Greater Poland Confederation, an institution identical to the Lesser Poland Confederation, was supposed to be the result of a completely different legal act, namely the confederation established in Radomsko in 1382. After two centuries, there was nothing left for the nobles but "to devise a method and course of action ready to execute this privilege".[34] Because it must be remembered that according to the understanding of that time, patterns were not drawn from old acts at all. It was simply assumed that these acts were legally binding from the time of the king's death.[35]

The facts cited above indicate an important feature of archives. Acts located there for safe keeping, even if they remain dormant for a long time, can come back to life, step into the limelight and join in shaping a new reality. The docu-

---

31 "[...] do zwyczajów chwalebnych przodków naszych i do starych spisów i kapturów, które się w takowych i innych przypadkach czyniły, ten mianowicie kaptur, który jest w nowym mieście Korczynie od przodków naszych anno 1438 czynionych i od nas w Krakowie po zejściu króla sławnej pamięci Zygmunta Augusta, roku 1572 [...] ponowiony i utwierdzony." Ohryzko 1859 (2), pp. 224–226; Chorążyczewski 2006, pp. 70–71.

32 Korolko 1974, p. 117.

33 Chorążyczewski 2006, p. 71.

34 "[...] tylko sposób i postępek gotowy egzekucji tego przywileju obmyślić." Dworzaczek 1957, p. 5.

35 Chorążyczewski 2006, p. 71.

ments in question have an interesting life in and as of themselves, relevant for our understanding of the world around us. On the other hand, the sciences dealing with documents (diplomatics) or entireties consisting of documents (archival science) enrich their subject matter with the cultural and social functioning of documents, which are in a constant state of flux.

[Translated by Steve Jones]

Bibliography

Literature

Bodniak, Stanisław / Skorupska, Zofia: *Jan Kostka kasztelan gdański, prezes Komisji Morskiej, rzecznik unii Prus z Koroną*. 1979.

Burke, Peter: *Kultura i społeczeństwo w renesansowych Włoszech*. 1991.

Chorążyczewski, Waldemar / Degen, Robert: *Przyłączenie czy przywrócenie? (na marginesie aktów inkorporacyjnych Podlasia, Wołynia i Kijowszczyzny z 1569 roku)*, in: Skep'ân, A. A. (ed.): *Vâlìkae knâstva Lìtoŭskae: palìtyka, èkanomìka, kul'tura. Zbornìk navukovyh atrykulaŭ v dzvûh častkah*. 2017/1, pp. 201–208.

Chorążyczewski, Waldemar: *Dokument w życiu politycznym Polski wczesnonowożytnej*, in: *Studia Archiwalne*. 2006/2, pp. 61–72.

Cynarski, Stanisław: *Zygmunt August*. 1988.

Czapliński, Władysław: *Dzieje sejmu polskiego do roku 1939*. 1984.

Dworzaczek, Włodzimierz (ed.): *Akta sejmikowe województw poznańskiego i kaliskiego*. 1957/1/1.

Frost, Robert: *Oksfordzka historia unii polsko-litewskiej*. 2018/1.

Kaniewka, Irena: *Ossoliński Hieronim (zm. między 1575 a 1576)*, in: *Polski słownik biograficzny*. 1979/24, p. 396.

Korolko, Mirosław: *Klejnot swobodnego sumienia. Polemika wokół konfederacji warszawskiej w latach 1573–1658*. 1974.

Marciniak, Ryszard: *Acta Tomiciana w kulturze politycznej Polski okresu odrodzenia*. 1983.

Michalak, Halina: *Jan Zamoyski – propaganda i autoreklama*, in: *Przegląd Historyczny*. 1986/77, pp. 25–43.

Michalski, Jerzy (ed.): *Historia sejmu polskiego*. 1984/1.

Ohryzko, Józefat (ed.): *Volumina legum*. 1859/1. (1)

Ohryzko, Józefat (ed.): *Volumina legum*. 1859/2. (2)

Papee, Fryderyk: *Aleksander Jagiellończyk*. 1999.

Sobieski, Wacław: *Trybun ludu szlacheckiego. Pisma historyczne*. 1978.

Szczuczko, Witold: *Sejmy koronne 1562–1564 a ruch egzekucyjny w Prusach Królewskich*. 1994.

Uruszczak, Wacław: *Próba kodyfikacji prawa polskiego w pierwszej połowie XVI wieku. Korektura praw z 1532 r.* 1979.

Wioletta Zielecka-Mikołajczyk

Archives of the Greek Catholic Bishopric in Przemyśl and the Reform of the Uniate Church in the 17th and 18th Centuries

Abstract

This article represents an attempt to examine the archives of the Uniate bishops of Przemyśl from the 17th and 18th centuries in the broader context of the changes taking place in the Uniate Church and to seek features that might link them with documentation produced in other dioceses. Despite the serious obstacle posed by the state of preservation of the legacy of eparchies other than Przemyśl, it can be stated that similar initiatives to introduce new types of production took place in the dioceses of Przemyśl, Chełm and Volodymyr-Brest.

Keywords: archives; reforms; Uniate Church; Orthodox Church; eparchy of Przemyśl

The Archives of Przemyśl-Sambor bishops, currently kept in the State Archives in Przemyśl, are the largest preserved archival fonds containing materials on the history of the Uniate Church in the 17th and 18th centuries. The sources contained therein are so significant that they have often formed the basis for valuable considerations by historians and archivists.[1] However, no questions have been asked so far about the relationship between the history of the eparchial archives and the modernisation trends present in the Uniate Church in the 17th and 18th centuries. In the aforementioned period, the bishop archives underwent an interesting development path, becoming highly developed indeed during the 18th century. It is worth asking whether the reform movement in the Church, aimed at strengthening the power of the eparchs, and the development of diocesan institutions and church administration, left its mark on the Przemyśl archives. Were the documents collected by Przemyśl bishops only a local initiative, or did they fit within a wider practice applied throughout the entire Uniate metropolis of Kyiv? Due to the current scant knowledge on the operation of eparchial archives and diocesan institutions of Eastern Churches in the modern era, it

Dr Wioletta Zielecka-Mikołajczyk, Nicolaus Copernicus University in Toruń, ORCID: https://orcid.org/0000-0001-6100-0563.

1 Lakota 1939; Nabywaniec 1992/1993; Lorens 2005; Krochmal 2016.

would seem justifiable to tackle this topic, which may have relevance in the broader context of research on the history of the Kyiv metropolis, whose task is to answer to what extent it was a coherent organism, functioning according to a specific model.

An attempt to compare the organisation of the Przemyśl archives with the system in other dioceses of the Kyiv metropolis is difficult for several reasons. The first is the complicated history of the Uniate metropolis of Kyiv in the turmoil of the 17th century during which some of the Uniates' legacy was lost. The Przemyśl archives suffered losses in the 17th century during the intense rivalry between Uniates and Orthodox Christians for power over the diocese, while the vast majority of archives from the 18th century have survived. Fragments of materials from the Lviv and Chełm eparchies have survived to our times. On the other hand, the archives of the Volodymyr-Brest and Lutsk dioceses are considered lost.[2] It is difficult to study the processes taking place simultaneously in the archives of Kyiv metropolitans and in the archives of Przemyśl bishops. Regarding the pontificates of some Kyiv metropolitans, we generally have few sources confirming the size of the archives and the nature of the documents stored there. For example, metropolitan Hipacy Pociej (1599–1613) secured the documents confirming the granting of privileges to the Orthodox and Uniate Church in two chests.[3] Metropolitan Józef Welamin Rutski (1613–1637) rarely visited his residences in Nowogródek and Vilnius; therefore, he made use of a personal office supplied with a collection of the most necessary documents.[4] Metropolitan registers of entries were kept during his time, at least periodically. He seems to have attached more importance to the archival activities of the Basilian order, whence he came, as he commissioned monasteries to archive foundation documents and the legacies made for them.[5] The legacy of Rafał Korsak (1637–1640) is known to a limited extent. At the end of the 17th century, the archives of the Uniate metropolitans were in disarray, and in 1699 metropolitan Leon Ślubicz-Załęski commissioned them to be put in order. Thanks to the implementation of his guidelines, the bishop archives was elevated to the standards of archiving at that time.[6] Regulations intended for the eparchs of individual dioceses regarding the keeping of archives have not survived, except for the decision of the Zamość synod (1720), which ordered bishops to hire a notary (chancellor). Similar archival solutions may be observed both in the metropolitan archives and in Przemyśl, such as entry books and the accumu-

2 Dovbišenko 2001, pp. 14–15.
3 Pazdnâkoŷ 2014, p. 155.
4 Ibid., p. 158.
5 Ibid., p. 159.
6 Ibid., p. 169.

lation of church privileges.[7] However, it is difficult to discern any relationship. Most likely, the rulers of Przemyśl, Włodzimierz, Brzeg and Chełm acted on their own and created eparchial archives, guided by the need to secure documents confirming bishopric rights and stipend.

During the 17th and 18th centuries, the archives of Przemyśl-Sambor bishops – regardless of their ritual affiliation – were kept, like the offices of secular authorities, on the basis of a book of entries, which was a well-established system in the territory of the former Republic of Poland. The content of documents issued and those sent from outside were entered therein, as well as, more importantly, reports on legal acts performed and on the actions of third parties acting before the office to give them legal force.[8] Chronologically (with some exceptions to this rule), the entries included the place where they were drafted, the year, month and day when a particular action occurred, followed by a presentation of the merits of the case – when a claim was made, the testimonies of witnesses were quoted, and the court verdict was given where applicable.[9] On the basis of random data, it may be assumed with high probability that the same was also the case in other dioceses of the Kyiv metropolis – for example, the neighbouring Chełm and Volodymyr-Brest eparchy.[10]

Regarding the Przemyśl Church, the book of entries was certainly kept during the pontificate of the first Uniate bishop, Atanazy Krupecki.[11] However, the scale of this phenomenon remains unknown. Residual data indicate that court documentation was prepared in Polish. Nevertheless, we know that the Ruthenian language was also used in the bishop's office. Certainly, the Uniate Przemyśl eparchs who tried to keep the diocese in their hands after the death of Bishop Krupecki (1652), when rivalry with the Orthodox flock turned into an armed conflict, faced serious difficulties in keeping this type of documentation. This would be indicated by the situation in 1662, when Uniate clergy from the Oleszyce and Tarnogród deaneries doctored the books of the Latin consistory in order to authenticate the declaration of the census of the faithful.[12] They probably did because the office of Prokop Chmielewski was largely suspended. He fought against the Orthodox Church, although it is known that he used the services of the writer Genadiusz Mitkiewicz.[13] We know almost nothing about the office of the

7 Skočilâs 2010, p. 453.
8 Olczak 1995, p. 15; Krochmal 2016, p. 263.
9 Zielecka-Mikołajczyk 2019, p. 100.
10 Archiwum Państwowe w Lublinie: *Chełmski Konsystorz Greckokatolicki* (hereinafter: APL: ChKGK), sig. 3, p. 1; Lietuvos valstybės istorijos archyvas (hereinafter: LVIA): f. 634, op. 3, sig. 18, fol. 3.
11 Archiwum Państwowe w Przemyślu (hereinafter: APP): *Akta Miasta Przemyśla*, sig. 589, pp. 11–13.
12 Archiwum Archidiecezjalne w Przemyślu: sig. 47, fols. 1181–1181v.
13 Krochmal 2015, p. 190.

last two Uniate bishops from the period of co-rule in the Przemyśl diocese, i.e., until 1691, of Antoni Terlecki and Jan Małachowski. Undoubtedly, however, from at least 1661, the court registers based on the book of entries were kept by the Orthodox side, led at that time by Antoni Winnicki, and then by Jerzy Hoszowski.[14] Innocenty Winnicki, assuming power in the diocese, took over the archives, which contained the court books and the manner of running the office, from his predecessors. After the announcement of the union in the Przemyśl diocese during the synod of 1693, Bishop Innocenty Winnicki, in order to confirm and organise the legal and material affairs of churches located in the diocese, ordered that the descriptions of the churches and benefices prepared by the governors during the visitation be transferred to the bishop archives.[15]

The preserved court books prove that even during the reign of the Orthodox bishops of Przemyśl until 1667, the language of the church court was primarily Ruthenian, while entries in Polish began at that time. When Innocenty Winnicki took over the diocese, and after the announcement of the union in the diocese, the books were kept in Polish. Ruthenian was used in documents confirming the privileges of brotherhoods, gifts for parishes in episcopal estates or regulations concerning indulgences. During the 18th century, Ruthenian was marginalised in court books in favour of Polish and then Latin. From 1741, on the basis of the Zamość reform announced in the Przemyśl diocese a year earlier, Latin was introduced as the language of church court reports, as it was in the bishop's curia. In fact, during the pontificate of Onufry Szumlański, and then the rule of the diocese of the last bishop of the pre-partition era, Atanazy Szeptycki, Latin had a position similar as in the Latin Church. This change was possible thanks to the partial replacement of the staff of the Przemyśl consistory with better qualified personnel in the first half of the 18th century. At that time, the bishops employed quite well-educated writers, authorised by the Holy See as public writers. Some were educated in Lviv in the papal seminary, where, thanks to the foundation of Bishop Jerzy Winnicki, clergy candidates from the Przemyśl diocese could study. They included Jan Narolski (until 1701), Bazyli Zubrzycki (1699, 1704–1705), Jan Chryzostom Bernakiewicz (1732, 1758, 1765, 1769), and Jan Babtista Kafillewicz (1759, 1761, 1765).[16] The documents prepared by them did not deviate from the office standards of the time.[17]

While attempting to define the status of Latin in the court records of other Uniate dioceses, it should be stated that in the case of the Chełm eparchy this language was used since the 1740s, as evidenced by the files of notary Jan Wa-

14 APP: *Archiwum Biskupstwa Greckokatolickiego w Przemyślu* (hereinafter: ABGK), sig. 1supl, p. 1.

15 Zielecka-Mikołajczyk 2019, p. 99.

16 APP: ABGK, sig. 15supl, 16supl, 17supl, 18supl; Zielecka-Mikołajczyk 2019, pp. 102–103.

17 APP: ABGK, sig. 33supl, p. 41.

silkiewicz from the years 1645–1669.[18] This practice resulted from the staffing capability of the diocese, served by Jan Wasilkiewicz, who was authorised by the Holy See as a public notary. The entries he prepared did not differ in terms of structure from other documents of this type during this era. On the other hand, court books in the 1780s were kept mainly in Polish, Latin being rarely used.[19] Fragmentary data from the 18th century show that in the diocese of Chełm, Latin was used in court records, similarly to the diocese of Przemyśl. However, due to the poor preservation of the archives of the Chełm eparchs, it would appear impossible to accurately indicate the extent to which it was used in court files.

The language used for entries in court books as well as the rhetoric therein corresponded in principle to that used in secular offices in various regions of the Polish-Lithuanian state. Claims were usually made because the wrongdoer had forgotten "the fear of God" or "the dignity of the priesthood".[20] An act of physical or verbal violence or an attack on the victim would always be committed "without reason given" or "in a manner unknown".[21] In 1729, the consistory writer noted the claim made by the nobleman Andrzej Kopysteński against some Uniate parish priests from Strzelce

> that, against common law and noble freedom, the accused blocked my way as I was riding from a church fete held at the monastery of St. Spas, and there they beat me and wounded me to their liking, as a post-examination performed *per generalem regni ministerialem* testifies.[22]

Similar rhetoric was used in the Volodymyr-Brest Consistory.[23]

The employment of better educated staff in the chancellery, combined with the necessity to implement the provisions of the Zamość synod of 1720, led to the appearance of new types of books kept in the archives of Przemyśl bishops. One of them contained lists of diaconate and presbyterate orders made from 1723.[24] Three books from 1723–1731, 1741–1758, and 1758–1775 have survived.[25] The first one was written mostly in Polish with Latin interjections. The remaining two were written in Latin. The information contained therein is an obvious testimony to the reform carried out in the diocese, consisting not only in the general

18 APL: ChKGK, sig. 91.
19 Ibid., sig. 1, pp. 216–220.
20 APP: ABGK, sig. 10supl, pp. 91, 101; Frick 2010, pp. 15–18.
21 Ibid., sig. 10supl, p. 136.
22 "[...] o to, iż pozwani przeciwko prawu pospolitemu i wolności szlacheckiej zastąpili na drodze wolnej jadącemu mnie z odpustu z monasteru św. Spasa, i tam mnie według swego upodobania bili i poranili, jako obdukcja per generalem regni ministerialem uczyniona świadczy." Ibid., pp. 122–123.
23 LVIA: f. 634, op. 3, sig. 18, fol. 2v.
24 Śliwa 2017, p. 501.
25 APP: ABGK, sig. 80, 78supl, 79supl.

registration of men ordained as priests, but also in admitting persons who met the relevant requirements for candidature as priests. They were expected to come from a legal marriage and a suitable social status (priestly or noble). An important criterium was that the priest be free from any accusation of bigamy, which closed the door to the priesthood. Usually, these entries included the name and surname of the new priest, the names and surnames of his parents, his town of origin, the date and place of the diaconate, subdiaconate and presbyterate ordination. Another aspect of the reform of the Przemyśl Church visible in the books of newly consecrated priests is that they were assigned a specific parish benefice at the time of their ordination. At the beginning of the 18th century, one problem facing the Uniate Church was the practice of ordaining people without taking care to secure a parish for them where they might perform their ministry. As a result, sometimes priests only after receiving ordination applied to patrons to be granted a benefice. Were such efforts to end in failure – as sometimes happened, whether it was because of the reluctance of the patron, the community or the paucity of the parish's stipend – the priest was left without a source of income and was forced to look for another job. There were cases of them turning to vagrancy. Such incidents lowered the prestige of the Uniate priesthood in the local society. Therefore, in fact, even before ordination to the priesthood, a candidate to the clergy should have already been granted a benefice from a patron. An appropriate entry in the book of newly consecrated persons was the only confirmation that this obligation had been fulfilled. The grants for parishes themselves began to be registered in the Przemyśl consistory during the rule of the diocese of Bishop Onufry Szumlański. From 1754, a book was kept that registered particular benefices.[26] This practice continued in 1773, after the diocese had come under the rule of the Habsburgs as a result of the first partition of the Polish-Lithuanian Commonwealth.

While in Przemyśl the registration of new presbyters was a consequence of the implementation of the Zamość synod, this practice was applied much earlier in the neighbouring Chełm eparchy. Bishop Gedeon Woyna-Orański (1692–1709), whose pontificate witnessed the revival of the conciliar eparchy life,[27] providing the legal basis for the modernisation of the Chełm Church and the organisation of church funds, in January 1703 ordered that registers be kept of ordained priests. These books were written continuously until 1759. The first of them, covering the years 1703–1730, was written in Ruthenian.[28] However, another one from the period 1730–1759 was in Polish with Latin dating.[29] During the tenure of Bishop

26 Zakład Narodowy im. Ossolińskich we Wrocławiu: rkps. 9540/II.
27 Gil 2005, pp. 97–98; Skoczylas 2008, p. 41.
28 APL: ChKGK, sig. 634.
29 Ibid., sig. 635.

Maksymilian Ryłło (1756–1784), the themes of the books were expanded and, in addition to newly ordained priests, grants for parishes were also entered there. They were conducted in this formula until the end of the Commonwealth.[30] There is no information about lists of newly consecrated persons in the Volodymyr-Brest diocese. In 1730, Teodor Krokowski was consecrated to parish in the Volodymyr-Brest diocese and recorded in the Chełm eparchy documentation.[31] This probably happened exceptionally because of the vacancy at the Volodymyr-Brest cathedral after the death of Korneliusz Lebiedzki on 22 January 1730.[32] The practice of applying for ordination from another eparchy when there was a vacancy of the episcopal throne of the mother diocese was an ordinary practice of the Church – both Orthodox and Uniate. It can be considered very likely that lists of newly ordained priests were also kept in the Volodymyr-Brest diocese, but they have not survived.

Another type of documentation related to the reform of the clerical status of the Przemyśl diocese are the bishop's orders (mandates) for governors (deans) regarding the conduct of a community inquiry with regard to candidates for the priesthood. The practice of the authorities of the diocese investigating the social position and morality of those applying for the priesthood was known to have happened earlier. However, it was not until the mid-18th century that appropriate documentation was drafted in this respect. The bishop sent a letter to the governor announcing candidature for a priest to fill a church vacancy and ordering an investigation to discover the origin and level of morality of the candidate. The governor was obliged to check his origin as well as question the local population about his decency, sobriety, and possible attempts at bribery in exchange for support for his candidacy. In addition, he was to decide whether the stipend assigned to the church was sufficient for the priest to maintain an adequate standard of living, or whether the staff of the parish was too large.[33] It seems that during the pontificate of Atanazy Szeptycki, forms were sometimes used on which the name of the person concerned was entered.[34] A response to the bishop's instructions was a comprehensive account of the activities carried out by the governors, containing the testimonies of witnesses, verifying the suitability of the candidate for the priesthood. Ultimately, this ended up in the diocesan archives.[35] On the basis of individual documents, it is known that such a practice also existed in the Volodymyr-Brest diocese, but in the 1780s.[36]

30 Ibid., sig. 636.
31 Ibid., sig. 634, fol. 42.
32 Wereda 2006, pp. 93–94.
33 APP: ABGK, sig. 33supl, pp. 1–3.
34 Ibid., p. 45.
35 APP: ABGK, sig. 70–75.
36 LVIA: f. 634, op. 1, sig. 401, pp. 79–80, 275.

In addition to organising control over the flow of people to the priesthood, bishops strove to expand their knowledge on the activities of the clergy and faithful in the parishes. Such an opportunity was provided by pastoral (general) visitations whereby the ordinaries might discover the needs of the diocesan clergy and the faithful, monitor their purity of faith, and provide information about the material and financial condition of the parish. In terms of administrative issues, they strengthened the borders of dioceses, deaneries and parochia. Their need was noticed by Uniate hierarchs from the beginning of the 17th century. The frequency of visitations to the diocese was one of the problems of the Uniate Orthodox Church even in the 18th century. The example of the Przemyśl diocese shows that the visitation rate of the bishoprics in Kyiv metropolis was reasonable. The eparchs had a system of viewing their canonical territory, but its weak link was the lack of practice in drawing up visitation reports. The bishop was informed about the state of parochia by his envoys present at the deanery councils, operating in a system of so-called "triads".[37] However, in some dioceses of the Kyiv metropolis, an eparchy monitoring system was applied based on visitation reports as early as at the end of the 17th and the beginning of the 18th century. Visitation reports from the Volodymyr-Brest diocese have survived, as well as fragments from the Turów-Pinsk and metropolitan diocese.[38] In the Chełm eparchy, the first traces of visitation reports date back to 1715.[39] During the "pre-Zamość" period in the Przemyśl diocese, no visitation reports were drafted.

An attempt was made to solve the problem of organising visitations by the fathers of the Zamość Council in 1720, who, taking into account their experiences so far, arranged the visitation process and defined detailed guidelines for the bishops and their plenipotentiaries who carried them out. Within the 117 points, the major focus was the clergy and its discipline. Visitors were also advised to monitor deacons, church fraternities, shelters, nuns and monks, the condition and equipment of churches and chapels, the state of church goods, indulgences and the manner and circumstances in which the sacraments were administered. The implementation of the synodal recommendations brought a reform program for the functioning of the Kyiv metropolis. The questionnaire developed during the Zamość synod became the basis for carrying out visitations in the following decades of the 18th century.[40] This can be seen in the diocese of Lviv, where reports from 1726 have been preserved, as well as in Volodymyr-Brest and

37 About the characteristics of the visitations system of Uniate dioceses during "pre-Zamość" period, cf. Skočilâs 2010, p. 490; Skoczylas 2008, pp. 28–32.

38 Gil / Skoczylas 2012, pp. LXV and 3–228; Wereda 2014, p. 49; Walczak 2012, tab. 13; Lisejčykaŷ 2009, p. 14.

39 APL: ChKGK, sig. 100.

40 Wereda 2013, p. 261.

and Chełm. In the Przemyśl eparchy, this type of documentation began relatively late, starting from 1738 and the beginning of the 1740s.[41]

In the 1740s, the Przemyśl visitation form usually contained six items concerning the functioning of the parochia, 1) data on the patron, church privileges, land borders, funds for the renovation of the church; 2) liturgical utensils; 3) priestly clothes and cloths; 4) books; 5) belfry; 6) information about the paroch, about the receipt of grants and installations in the parish by the bishop or his envoy. Nearly 20 years later, the inspectors were required to fill in a form containing ten points: 1) data on the patron; 2) foundation documents; 3) the paroch's monitoring of its land; 4) interference on church grounds of troops, patrons and Latin clergymen; 5) ongoing legal action concerning church grounds; 6) number of parishioners; 7) paroch income obtained from parishioners; 7) the amount of crops in the fields belonging to the church; 9) relations with the Latinists, conversion to the Latin rite; 10) information about the personalities and morals of the parish priest.[42] The change resulted directly from the bishop's expectations regarding the type of information he needed about the diocese. The first visitations provided basic data about the churches, while those from the 1760s were focused on obtaining information about the material status of the churches, parishes and parochs. These data were to be used to eliminate abuses committed by priests, such as benefice debt and keeping people unrelated to the church service on them. Likewise, it was possible to tackle inappropriate conduct by priests.

Attention should be paid to the structure of the visitations made at the end of the 17th century and in the period until the Zamość Council in the 18th century. The preserved descriptions for the Volodymyr-Brest and Chełm dioceses are linked by an almost complete omission of issues related to the documentation of individual churches, i.e., the foundation acts that provided the basis for a church's construction or precise information on the paroch's stipend. In 1698, the Brest official, January Ohurcewicz and the Chełm bishop Józef Lewicki (in the years 1720–1723) focused primarily on the following data: 1) data on the patrons of the church; 2) the condition of the building and interior furnishings (church utensils, books); 3) land used by the paroch. January Ohurcewicz's descriptions were more detailed. Information about the parish clergy was limited to an absolute minimum – i.e., the name and surname of the paroch, and Bishop Lewicki sometimes gave their age.[43] In addition, January Ohurcewicz provided quite detailed information – unheard of in 18th century visitations – about the ceremonies accompanying the visits. The Brest official always noted the presence of

41 APP: ABGK, sig. 19, 20, 26, 30, 32, 49; Zielecka-Mikołajczyk 2020, p. 48.
42 Zielecka-Mikołajczyk 2020, p. 57.
43 APL: ChKGK, sig. 100, fols. 16–19v.

the "court", parishioners and the parish priest during his visitations. During the visit, services were held and confessions were heard.[44] The contents appear to be the personal contribution of the visitor to the layout of the diocesan monitoring form.

The above-described visits to Brest and Chełm differ to a great extent from the forms used in the Uniate dioceses after the Zamość Synod, especially those written from the mid-18th century. From that later period, visits to parts of the Volodymyr-Brest diocese have been preserved: the deanery of Mielnik, Prużański, Kobryń, Polesie, Kamieniec, Włodawa from 1759, Brest 1773, as well as parts of the Chełm and Przemyśl eparchy.[45] They are characterised by a different, i.e., higher, standard of handwriting, with a tremendous level of detail and development of form. The Mielnik visitation from 1759 includes as many as 15 issues to be checked. Some of them are already familiar from the old type of visitations, but they have been included in more detail, while new elements have been included in the form – i.e., descriptions of the sacristy, church service, and cemetery. A significant feature of these descriptions are entire tracts of information devoted to parochs and parishioners. With regard to the former, priests' personal data, information about the grant received, sometimes regarding its legality, the year of ordination, documents confirming the introduction to the parish and the person making this act, as well as the paroch's financial obligations towards the bishop were given. Finally, the priests' living quarters were described in detail, illustrating their standard of living, and sometimes the level of care devoted to the household and commitment to its development. A peculiar novelty of these visitations is the block of data devoted to parishioners, including information on the number of the faithful in the parish, the number of people who have the right to receive the sacrament of penance, go to Easter confession, and able to learn catechetics.[46] The opinion of parishioners about the parish priest, i.e., his decency and fulfilment of priestly duties, was also noted. The records in the above visitations stand as a testimony to the change that took place in the Uniate Church in the 18th century and expressed in the eparchs' quest to deepen their knowledge about life in the parishes and to strengthen their influence over the diocesan clergy and the faithful. Importantly, the faithful in these visitations are no longer just a margin of interest for officials visiting the eparchy, but they have the right to express their opinion, which gives them a kind of subjectivity in the entire church organism.

44 Gil / Skoczylas 2012, pp. 32–41.

45 LVIA: f. 634, op. 1, sig. 48, 50; Buczyło 2014, p. 15; APL: ChKGK: sig. 112, 113, 114; APP: ABGK, sig. 23–42.

46 Lietuvos mokslų akademijos Vrublevskių biblioteka: f. 41, sig. 394, p. 539–569; APP: ABGK, sig. 19, pp. 78–116; APL: ChKGK, sig. 115, fols. 4v–7v.

Another aspect of visitations from the second half of the 18th century, which distinguishes them from earlier sources of this type, is the attention paid to the need to regulate the formal matters of the Uniate parochia and to obtain documents confirming their affiliation to the Uniate Church. Hence, the forms began to include information on the foundation documents of the church, the stipend assigned to them and the legates obtained.[47] It also seems that greater importance was attached to the reform decrees indicating areas of action in which the parochia required improvement. It should be emphasised that the problems considered by the inspectors might appear in a different order, with varying levels of detail and diligence as well, but the extramural visits to the dioceses of Volodymyr-Brest, Chełm and Przemyśl presented the idea of striving for a reform of the Uniate Church at the level of parish life. In the case of the Przemyśl diocese, this reform is confirmed by a peculiar source in the form of lists of the faithful from 1767, made during the reign of Bishop Atanazy Szeptycki.[48] In the Uniate diocese of Lviv, a similar list of the faithful was drafted in 1763.[49]

The state of preservation of the legacy of the archives of the Uniate bishops of the Kyiv metropolis presents a serious obstacle in the study of the flow of reform trends between the central archives of the metropolis and the diocesan archives, and among the latter. For this reason, the archives left by the Uniate bishops of Przemyśl – though very extensive and containing a great deal of data on the changes taking place in the territory of the cathedral of St. John the Baptist in Przemyśl – can only be compared with fragments of the legacy left by other eparchs. The data arising from these comparisons show that, at least in part, the documentation kept in the eparchial archives was related to the reform of the Uniate Church, and the Przemyśl archives contain elements similar to those present in other archives. However, changes did not always occur at the same time. Local needs and solutions adopted in individual dioceses were not without significance. The connection with the reform of the Uniate Church is most evident in visitation reports from the second half of the 18th century.

[Translated by Steve Jones]

47 LVIA: f. 634, op. 1, sig. 50, p. 12; APP: ABGK, sig. 19, pp. 1–75, 78–118; ibid., sig. 54, pp. 5–27; ibid., sig. 38, pp. 1–115; APL: ChKGK, sig. 115, p. 3.

48 APP: ABGK, sig. 66.

49 Cf. Central'nij deržavnij istoričnij arhiv Ukraïni, L'viv: f. 201, op. 1, sig. 13–14, 16, 20–22, 26, 28–33, 36–37, 39–44.

Bibliography

Archival Sources

Archiwum Archidiecezjalne w Przemyślu: sig. 47.

Archiwum Państwowe w Lublinie: *Chełmski Konsystorz Greckokatolicki*, sig. 1, 3, 91, 100, 112, 113, 114, 115, 634, 635.

Archiwum Państwowe w Przemyślu:

- *Akta Miasta Przemyśla*, sig. 589;
- *Archiwum Biskupstwa Greckokatolickiego w Przemyślu*, sig. 19–20, 23–42, 49, 54, 66, 70–75, 80, 1supl, 10supl, 15supl, 16supl, 17supl, 18supl, 33supl, 78supl, 79supl.

Central'nij deržavnij istoričnij arhiv Ukraïni, L'viv [Центральний державний історичний архів України, Львів]: f. 201, op. 1, sig. 13–14, 16, 20–22, 26, 28–33, 36–37, 39–44.

Lietuvos mokslų akademijos Vrublevskių biblioteka: f. 41, sig. 394.

Lietuvos valstybės istorijos archyvas: f. 634, op. 3, sig. 18; op. 1, sig. 48, 50, 401.

Zakład Narodowy im. Ossolińskich we Wrocławiu: rkps. 9540/II.

Printed Sources

Gil, Andrzej / Skoczylas, Ihor (eds.): *Wizytacje generalne cerkwi i monasterów unickiej eparchii włodzimierskiej końca XVII – początku XVIII wieku: księga protokołów oraz inne opisy*. 2012.

Lakota, Grigorij [Лакота, Григорий]: *Tri sinodi peremis'ki j eparhial'ni postanovi valâvs'ki v 17–19 st.* [*Три синоди перемиськи й єпархіальні постанови валявські в 17–19 ст.*]. 1939.

Lisejčykaў, Dzenis [Лісейчыкаў, Дзеніс] (ed.): *Vizity uniâckih cèrkvaў minskaga i navagrudskaga saboraў 1680–1682 gg.* [*Візіты уніяцкіх цэркваў мінскага і навагрудскага сабораў 1680–1682 гг.*]. 2009.

Literature

Buczyło, Andrzej: *Kształtowanie się sieci parafialnej Kościoła unickiego na terenie brzeskiej części diecezji włodzimierskiej w latach 1596–1795*. 2014 (typescript).

Dovbiŝenko, Mihajlo [Довбищенко, Михайло]: *Ukraïns'kì cerkovnì arhìvi litovs'ko-pol'-s'koï dobi. Istorična dolâ ta perspektivi rekonstrukcìï* [Українські церковні архіви литовсько-польської доби. Історична доля та перспективи реконструкції,], in: *Arhìvi Ukraïni* [*Архіви України*]. 2001/6, pp. 10–23.

Frick, David: *"Słowa uczczypliwe", "słowa nieuczciwe". Język sporów sądowych i ruska polemika*, in: *Terminus*. 2010/2, pp. 15–35.

Gil, Andrzej: *Chełmska diecezja unicka 1596–1810*. 2005.

Krochmal, Anna: *Archiwum historyczne eparchii przemyskiej*. 2016.

Krochmal, Jacek: *Unia kościelna w eparchii przemysko-samborskiej za czasów biskupa Prokopa Chmielewskiego (1652–1664)*, in: *Miscellanea Historico-Archivistica*. 2015/22, pp. 169–202.

Lorens, Beata: *Bractwa cerkiewne w eparchii przemyskiej w XVII i XVIII wieku*. 2005.

Nabywaniec, Stanisław: *Diecezja przemyska grecko-katolicka 1772–1795*, in: *Premislia Christiana*. 1992/1993.

Olczak, Stanisław: *Kancelarie kościelne w okresie staropolskim*, in: *Archiwa, Biblioteki i Muzea Kościelne*. 1995/64, pp. 15–24.

Pazdnâkoў, Валерий [Паздняко ў, Валерий С.]: *Arhiў pravaslaўnyh i grèka-katalickih mitrapalitaў Vâlikaga Knâstva Litoўskaga ў. XVI–XVIII stst. (gistoryâ, struktura, sklad)* [*Архіў праваслаўных і грэка-каталіцкіх мітрапалітаў Вялікага Княства Літоўскага ў. XVI–XVIII стст. (гісторыя, структура, склад)*]. 2014.

Skočilâs, Igor [Скочиляс, Ігор]: *Галицька (Львівська) єпархія XII–XVIII століть: організаційна структура на правовий статус* [*Galic'ka (L'vivs'ka) єparhia XII–XVIII stolit': organizacijna struktura na pravovij status*]. 2010.

Skoczylas, Ihor: *Sobory eparchii chełmskiej XVII wieku. Program religijny Slavia Unita w Rzeczypospolitej*. 2008.

Śliwa, Tadeusz: *Okruchy z historii Kościoła obrządku greckiego*. 2017.

Walczak, Wojciech: *Unicka eparchia turowsko-pińska w XVII–XVIII wieku. Struktura organizacyjna*. 2012.

Wereda, Dorota: *Biskupi unickiej metropolii kijowskiej w XVIII wieku*. 2013.

Wereda, Dorota: *Stołpowicki-Lebiecki (Lebecki) Kornel (Korneliusz), h. Ościa (1689–1730)*, in: *Polski słownik biograficzny*. 2006/44, pp. 93–94.

Wereda, Dorota: *Unicka diecezja włodzimiersko-brzeska (część brzeska) w XVIII wieku*. 2014.

Zielecka-Mikołajczyk, Wioletta: *Między trzema językami. Pismo i pisarze w środowisku biskupów przemyskich obrządku wschodniego w latach 1679–1762*, in: *Rocznik Przemyski*. 2019/1, pp. 93–105.

Zielecka-Mikołajczyk, Wioletta: *Wizytacje z "Tek Podolińskiego" przechowywanych w zbiorach Muzeum Narodowego im. Andrzeja Szeptyckiego we Lwowie jako źródło do badań nad dziejami unickiej diecezji przemyskiej w XVIII w.*, in: *Klio. Czasopismo poświęcone dziejom Polski i powszechnym*. 2020/4, pp. 41–64.

Krzysztof Syta

Magnates and Landowner Archives of the 18th–20th Centuries. Evolution or Revolution?

Abstract
At the turn of the 19th century, magnate archives of the elite class of the nobility began to undergo a process of transformation. This was due to the fact that their erstwhile creators and owners had to adapt to the new political and social and economic conditions imposed by the administration of the partitioning states as well as general civilisational changes. Landowner archives, developed in the 19th century on the basis of magnate archives, in addition to their traditional, pragmatic economic-material role and organisational principles, were largely transformed into treasuries of national and family tradition, overseen by zealous and professional care.
Keywords: private archives; family archives; magnate archives; landowner archives; private archival materials; Poland in 18th–20th centuries

Introduction

Archival fonds of private provenance currently kept in the holdings of historical archives, and sometimes in the collections of libraries and museums too, often in a fragmentary or residual form, due to the nature of their authors, should be considered exceptional.[1] In Polish lands, basically until the middle of the 20th century, their creators were mainly representatives of the nobility, which during the 19th century transformed into the landed gentry. Bourgeois archives were relatively poorly represented. The genesis of family and property archives, and thus those constituting the most numerous category of private archives in the period in question, can be traced back to the 14th century. However, there is no doubt that their peak development, paradoxically, occurred during a period

Assoc. prof. Krzysztof Syta, Nicolaus Copernicus University in Toruń, ORCID: https://orcid.org /0000-0002-9466-1525.

1 The typology of archives of private provenance and private archives in the Polish literature has been most thoroughly presented by Teresa Zielińska; cf. Zielińska 1971, pp. 71–88. On the criteria of dividing family and property archives into archival fonds; cf. eadem 1978, pp. 127–129.

that was not particularly happy for the Polish state and nation.[2] Indeed, in the 18th century, during which the Republic of Poland was partitioned, **magnate archives**[3] flourished, alongside a large group of archives belonging to the middle nobility, and some of these were transformed into landowner archives during the partitions (1772–1918). They partially retained their former feudal character, and partially underwent significant transformations. These changes were especially noticeable in terms of the organisation, holdings and function of the archives. Unfortunately, not many survived the turmoil of World War I or its painful consequences related to military operations, or the wake of the Bolshevik revolution in the eastern territories of the former Republic of Poland.[4] Fortunately, however, partly through the strength of tradition, but also via the conscious action taken by the owners of surviving family and property archives, a considerable number of them still survived in the interwar period, as demonstrated by Antoni Chwalewik[5] and Karol Buczek[6] in their publications. The death knell for archives – not only those of landowners, but essentially all kinds of archives previously in private ownership – was sounded by World War II and its immediate aftermath, when remaining archives were taken over by the state archival administration through nationalization.[7]

Undoubtedly, the turning point that affected all areas of the social life of the Polish-Lithuanian Commonwealth and led to its collapse was marked by the partitions and their consequences following 1772. Transformations of a political, economic and social, cultural and educational nature also left their mark on the history of family and property archives. The archives of great magnate families – such as the Czartoryski, Lubomirski, Potocki, Radziwiłł, Sapieha and Zamoyski families – began to undergo various transformations, similarly to their creators and owners, while adapting to the new reality of the partition, as well as various social, political and economic ideas and challenges. In order to capture these changes, it is necessary to conduct a comparative analysis of magnate archives with those of the landed gentry. Areas that can and should undergo such an analysis include the status of archives (understood in terms of organisation, place and role in the structure of a magnate latifundium in the 18th century, and landed estates in the 19th–20th centuries), staff, and holdings. Due to the synthetic ap-

2 A synthetic approach to the history of family and family-property archives in Poland; cf. Tomczak 1989, pp. 238–243, 301–306.

3 Magnate archives in the 18th century awaited their own monograph; cf. Syta 2010, which also lists literature on the subject.

4 On the destruction of landowners' residences in Lesser Poland and Red Ruthenia during World War I, where the holdings of family and property archives were also collected; cf. Szydłowski 1919.

5 Chwalewik 1926–1927/1–2.

6 Buczek 1927, pp. 1–97; idem 1930, pp. 1–85.

7 Górski 2009, pp. 23–24.

proach to the subject matter, a basic method of analysis and logical construction, as well as analysis and criticism of the literature, was applied to a limited extent in order to achieve the research objective.

1. Archives of magnates in the 18th century

Archive status

Magnate archives of the 18th century were not a homogeneous group in terms of organisation and functionality. In a way, this was related to the fact that they belonged to the magnate class of families that differed from each other, for example, in terms of origin and history, financial status, level of participation in public life, economic activity or, finally, reproduction. The latter played a particularly important role. The more reproductive families that created their own lines and branches fashioned – theoretically, at least – the largest holdings-rich archives located in their main residences.[8] These and other factors not mentioned above had a significant impact on the shape of the archives, which today we might categorise as family archives or family property archives. There was no hard and fast rule, but we can assume that the family that created a particular archive could demonstrate their long-standing aristocratic status in most areas defining their inclusion within the elite of the nobility going back at least several generations, and so their archive, and sometimes even network of archives, even adopted an institutional form, constituting an important, albeit not always appreciated by contemporary researchers, component in the organisational structure of the manor. In the case of at least a few magnate families, one might claim that in the 18th century they created their own archive networks, which usually consisted of one central archive, characterised as a historical and family archive, usually located in the most representative family residence. The second level of this archival structure consisted of archives located in individual property complexes that comprised the magnate's latifundium. Here, the following rule applied: the more territorially fragmented it was – in other words, not one compact complex of landed estates – the more archives were created. This kind of extensive archival network was created by the Sanguszko family in the middle of the 18th century, at the behest of Paweł Karol Sanguszko (died 1750) and later his sons. This network included archives in Dubno, Lubartów, Ozierce in Belarus, Sławuta in Wołyń,

8 On the one hand, examples include the Lubomirski, Potocki, Radziwiłł and Sanguszko families. At the turn of the 18th century, each of them, within individual lines and branches, created several large family and property archives. On the other hand, there were families with few births, such as the Branicki family of the Gryf coat of arms, or the Zamoyski family; cf. Syta 2010, pp. 229–231, 250–252.

Tarnów, Wiśnicz, Zasław in Wołyń.[9] The Ruthenian voivode August Aleksander Czartoryski (died 1782) created an even more extensive archival network on his estate. Structurally, it consisted of two central archives housed in Lublin and Warsaw, the Podenhoff archive in Wołożyn (transferred to Lublin in 1736), as well as local archives, mainly of an economic nature, kept in Brzeżany, Dzików, Grzymałów, Klewanie, Lviv, Międzybóż, Mysz, Oleszyce and Szkłów. The largest of these was the Międzybóż archive, which functioned as a collective legal, material and economic archive for the Podole and Ukrainian estates.[10]

In the 18th century, magnate archives functioned within the structure of the magnate manor's organisation as an integral part of its office and registry.[11] However, the archive holdings were kept in separate rooms at the owner's residence – palace or manor house – and sometimes in separate buildings of a residential complex. This remark, of course, applies primarily to historical and family archives, because economic-financial and legal-material documentation, as mentioned above, was often stored in the administrative centres of individual estates. At this point, it is worth mentioning the common phenomenon of combining the archive holdings with library collections – i.e., the simultaneous presence of both literary and typically archival manuscripts in a library collection.[12] The principle of linking archival materials with library collections was practiced by the Radziwiłł family from Nieśwież basically from the end of the 16th to the 20th century.[13] On the basis of archival registers from the 18th century, one might venture that an archive could contain books and library manuscripts more often than the other way round. However, there are known cases of storing archival materials in libraries in the 18th century. This was the case with the Radziwiłł family in Nieśwież, where selected correspondence, bound in the form of books, was kept in the palace library.[14]

In the 18th century, magnate archives mainly functioned to support the pragmatic activities of the magnate, primarily those of a legal-material, economic-financial, and finally political nature. Other than acquiring, preserving,

9 Gorczak 1902, p. IV, VI.

10 On the history of the Czartoryski archives in the 18th century; cf. Buczek 1938.

11 Syta 2016 (2), pp. 96–99.

12 The difficulties in distinguishing between a library manuscript and an archival manuscript have been mentioned in the Polish literature, especially in the 1950s, when archives from private sources, especially magnate ones, became the object of practical interest for archivists working on their collections. Additionally, at that time a serious dispute arose in Poland between librarians and archivists over the right to keep this type of manuscript. This topic has been covered by: Stebelski 1951; Horodyski 1956. From more recent publications it is worth mentioning a work devoted to materials of public life, including archives of private provenance, in handwritten books between 1660–176; cf. Matwijów 2000.

13 Jankowski 2018, pp. 190–191.

14 Barwiński 1909–1913, p. 4.

arranging and querying, magnate archives rarely seemed to manifest other needs related, for example, to maintaining the historical traditions of the family, state or nation. In addition to the above-mentioned functions of magnate archives, the formation and the disposal of archives should also be discussed. The former occurred in two ways. On the one hand, it offered supervision over the records-creating process that took place in what may be broadly understood as the magnate's office. Universal control over clerks and magnate officials, inter alia, through the obligation to document their activities, significantly bolstered archival holdings in terms of the mass production of economic and financial documentation in the 18th century.[15] Another major area where the holdings of magnate archives developed were inquiries carried out at the behest of magnates in the offices and archives of public offices and, more rarely, private ones. The result of these archival searches were mainly extracts, i. e., excerpts and registers of files and entries made in books. In the 18th century, these copies, as it were, "flooded" the holdings of magnate archives. The disposal of archives in this period, if anything, was rather inductive. The disposition of Izabela Branicka, contained in her will of 1805, in which she instructed her officials that "all papers to be found in desks [...] be gathered up for the archives, and all letters be burnt" should be considered the exception rather than the rule.[16] Generally, efforts were made to keep the entire documentation in the magnate archives, but certain principles of evaluation applied, as evident in the descriptions of documentation contained in the archival registers of the period.

Archivists

Magnate archives in the 18th century, in most cases, did not have their own permanent caretakers. The full-time Radziwiłł archivists in Nieśwież, including Aleksander Goffoux, Józef Wessel and Antoni Kałakucki[17] as well as the archivists employed in the archives of August Aleksander Czartoryski – Szymon Cerenowicz, Jędrzej Sienicki, Michał Drużbacki and Jan Józef Witoszyński – may be regarded as exceptions to the rule.[18] Interestingly, some of them took an oath when they accepted employment at the archives, which significantly raised their status among other court officials; sometimes they were instructed on the

15 On the economic and financial documentation produced in connection with the administration of Jan Klemens and Izabela Branicki's estates in the second half of the 18th century; cf. Syta 2018 (2).

16 "Papiery wszelkie w stolikach znajdować się mogące [...] wspólnie pozbierawszy do archiwum oddadzą, a listy wszelkie popalą." Kupczewska / Łopatecki 2016, p. 118.

17 Jankowski 2000 (1), pp. 35–36.

18 Buczek 1938, pp. 58, 62–63, 65.

principles of their work and the order in which they were to maintain the archives entrusted to them. However, archives were usually under the supervision of magnate officials, such as marshals, treasurers, secretaries or plenipotentiaries. A perfect reflection of this situation was the entrustment of tasks related to securing and maintaining order in the Branicki Archives in Białystok in the second half of the 18th century to three people who performed various functions at the court of Izabela Branicka.[19] The persons responsible for the magnate's archives had to demonstrate a sound understanding of archival holdings, tended to organise them sporadically, prepared various archival registers, conducted archival inquiries, and lent files.

Holdings

The holdings of magnate archives in the 18th century partly arose from the collection of documentation from an earlier period, although the vast majority increased in size over the course of that century. As indicated by the chronological structure of the *Archives of the Zamoyski Estate in Zwierzyniec* (*Archiwum Ordynacji Zamoyskich ze Zwierzyńca*), developed from the end of the 16th century until 1944 and currently stored in the State Archives in Lublin, relatively little has survived from the 16th and 17th centuries compared to the following century.[20] Disregarding the specificity of this archive, which is definitely of an administrative and economic nature, it can certainly be assumed that magnate archives at the end of the 18th century mainly contained documentation created during that century. This remark applies not only to economic, financial or legal-material archives, but also reflects the public activity of the authors of the archives as well as their private lives. This is evidenced both by the current state of the magnate archives and their general registers prepared in the 18th or early 19th century.[21] Most of the files included in these lists are dated to the 18th century.[22]

19 These people were Branicka's general plenipotentiary Stanisław Karwowski, her treasurer Wojciech Matuszewicz and one of the secretaries Piotr Piramowicz; cf. Syta 2016 (1).

20 Based on the data contained in the records of this fonds on the website, the number of archival units with 16th–17th century archives is close to 150, while 1808 have survived from the next century. These numbers do not include plans and maps as well as some of the holdings not fully registered, but it can be assumed that these proportions largely reflect the statistics of the real holdings of the archive from the end of the 18th century; Archiwum Państwowe w Lublinie: *Archiwum Ordynacji Zamoyskich ze Zwierzyńca* [2021].

21 Among the large number of archival registers of magnate archives from this period, one might mention general summaries of the *Potocki Archive from Krzeszowice* (*Archiwum Potockich z Krzeszowic*) drafted in the years 1739, 1762, 1825 (sig. 13–18) and general summaries kept in the collection of the *Tarnowski Archives of Dzików* (*Archiwum Dzikowskie Tarnowskich*) from

When assessing the extent of the magnate archives, it can be estimated that they could have included several hundred archival units (fascicles, books), which in turn contained from one to several dozen individual documents, sometimes taking the form of several-page gatherings.[23]

During this period, the archives were stored in the form of fascicles – i. e., loose bundles of documents secured with a paper cover and probably bound with string. Archival materials in the form of books, with various formats and bindings, were a definite minority. The files eventually organised as books were originally in the form of loose documents, sewn and bound at a later stage. Only various types of movable and immovable property registers as well as collective economic and financial statements were given the form of a manuscript book from the very beginning.

Finally, it is worth mentioning the organisational work performed in the magnate archives during the 18th century. Based on the source material, it can be assumed that this type of work was carried out in individual archives at least several times during this century.[24] Usually, the impetus for such activities were important events in the history of the owner's family – e. g., his death, property divisions, family alliances.[25] Organisational work was usually conducted by people trusted by the owner of the archive, often its officials. Archives were organised into categories and subcategories, and the main criterion for their arrangement was the structure of the landed property of the owner of the archive. Archival materials other than those pertaining to legal and material matters were described in a more general way, and often divided based on the criterion of

1776, 1779, 1800 (sig. 187–192) kept in the holdings of the National Archives in Cracow (Archiwum Narodowe w Krakowie, hereinafter: ANK). The collection of the Central Archives of Historical Records in Warsaw (Archiwum Główne Akt Dawnych, hereinafter: AGAD) contains at least a dozen such general registers in the *Radziwiłł Warsaw Archive* group (*Archiwum Warszawskie Radziwiłłów*) (sig. 5, 7, 12, 21–22) or in the *Plater Archives from Antuzów* (*Archiwum Platerów z Antuzowa*) where the general summary drafted in 1792 has been preserved (sig. 1).

22 On selected holdings of magnate archives in the context of the contents of general registers; cf. Syta 1994; idem 2003; idem 2018 (2).

23 For example, the archive of the Tarnowski family from Dzików, in the light of the information contained in the general summary of this archive prepared in 1767, consisted of about 150 fascicles, containing various numbers of individual documents; cf. ANK: *Archiwum Dzikowskie Tarnowskich*, sig. 187. The archives of the Zamoyski family in the middle of the 18th century contained about 500 fascicles; cf. AGAD: *Archiwum Zamoyskich*, sig. 3.

24 This work is mainly evidenced by archival records, as the final outcome of the work, and by the correspondence of those involved. An example of letters containing a great deal of information on the development of the Czartoryski and Sieniawski archives in the 18th century is the correspondence of Jan Józef Witoszyński; cf. Syta 2002.

25 Idem 2010, pp. 193–194.

content and physical form. However, it sometimes happened that this reflected the recommendations of the owner of the archive.[26]

2. Landowner archives of the 19th–20th century

Archive status

The turn of the 19th century heralded revolutionary changes in the most important areas of social life in Poland – i. e., politics and the economy. The relative stability enjoyed by the magnate families as the political and economic elite of the Republic of Poland in the 18th century was abruptly shaken. The borders dividing the territories of the Polish-Lithuanian state established in the partition treaties were also often divided by extensive magnate latifundia, and their owners had to choose the citizenship of one of the partitioning powers, thus risking the loss of some of their property, and thus also relative pauperisation – both material as well as social. The loss of at least some landed estates, participation in national uprisings, starting from the Napoleonic era, and especially the repression inflicted by the authorities of the partitioning states as a consequence of them – indeed, the day-to-day peripety of a family nature – are just a few factors that had a diametrical impact not only on the lives of the creators and owners of family archives, but also served to destabilise the archives themselves. This usually involved the dispersion of holdings, which often went hand-in-hand with significant losses, often irreversible. The archive of the Radziwiłł family from Nieśwież or that of the Branicki family from Białystok are just two instances of a much wider phenomenon. At the beginning of the 19th century, both of these archives underwent a similar process of dispersal and, in part, destruction. In the case of the Radziwiłł Archive, the misfortune was initiated by the death of Dominik Radziwiłł, the ordinate of Nieśwież and Ołyka in 1813. The Commission and Proxy of the post-Radziwiłł Property (*Komisja i Prokuratoria Poradziwiłłowskiej Masy*) appointed by the tsarist authorities until 1839 to sort out the material and legal affairs of the significantly indebted estates that fell to his underage five-year-old daughter Stefania recommended that the archive be transported to Vilnius. Over the 20 years when the Nieśwież archives were stored there, a large part of it, in rather murky circumstances, ended up in the Czartoryski libraries in Puławy, Działyński in Kórnik and the Raczyński Library in Poznań. It was not until the end of the 1830s that the archives of Nieśwież were

26 This is evidenced by surviving archival instructions from the 18th century; cf. Tyszkowski 1935.

returned to their home with considerable losses.[27] In the case of the Branicki Archives from Białystok, the initial moment of dispersal occurred at the death of Izabela Branicka in 1808, the lifelong heiress of the palace in Białystok.[28] Most of the archives from the *Branicki Białystok Archives* (*Archium Branickich z Białegostoku*) were adopted by the Potocki family from Rosi, while some remained in the form of a deposit in the presbytery of one of the Białystok churches, and others were taken by collectors, including Zygmunt Gloger.[29]

One might venture that the dramatic adventures for the Polish nation and state, which also affected the history of magnate archives at the turn and first decades of the 19th century, had a positive outcome for them. First of all, the period of the partitions aroused a deeper interest in the Polish landed gentry not only in terms of the history of their families and kin – for example, through the necessity to document noble origin and property rights for the new government – but also national history. The effect of this was a greater and far-reaching interest in the remnants of previous generations, what we now call national heritage, as well as in historical sources and, above all, archives. It is no coincidence that at that time a large number of private foundations were established in Poland in all three partitions, whose purpose was to preserve library collections, archives and works of art from destruction and oblivion. One might mention, for example, the libraries of the Czartoryski counts (1876), the Krasiński Library (1844), the Przezdzieckis (1842), the Raczyńskis (1829), the Zamoyski Library (1811). Private collectors were active, though on a slightly smaller scale, sometimes creating large archival collections, mainly derived from noble archives, including, of course, magnate holdings. Among these collectors were Aleksander Czołowski, Zygmunt Gloger, Adam Mieleszko-Maliszkiewicz or Hipolit Skimborowicz.[30]

The owners and heirs of former magnate archives were fortunately infected in the 19th century with a passion for expanding their archives. During this period, for the second time in their history, family archives experienced a heyday, and the following collections positively flourished: the archives of the Branickis in Sucha and Wilanów, the Chodkiewiczs in Młynów, the Lubomirskis in Rzeszów, the Potockis in Krzeszowice, Łańcut, Rosi and Wilanów, the Radziwiłłs in Nieśwież,

27 Barwiński 1909–1913, p. 4. About the fate of the Nieśwież archive of the Radziwiłł family; cf. Jankowski 2000 (2); idem 2001.

28 Łopatecki 2015, pp. 88–91.

29 Smoleńska / Zielińska 1962, pp. 170–171.

30 They are currently stored in the AGAD: *Zbiór Aleksandra Czołowskiego*; ibid.: *Zbiór Adama Mieleszki-Maliszkiewicza*; ibid.: *Archiwum Hipolita Skimborowicza* and in the ANK: *Zbiór Zygmunta Glogera.*

the Rzewuskis in Podhorce, the Sanguszkos in Sławuta and Gumniska, and the Tarnowskis in Dzików.[31]

Landowner archives of the 19th and first half of the 20th centuries differed organisationally from their 18th-century predecessors by separating personal and family documents from historical ones. They were treated with exceptional reverence, stored in safer rooms, fitted with appropriate furniture and other equipment for storing various forms of archives, and they were often combined with library collections at that time. One example may be Jan Feliks Tarnowski who, in the 1830s, secured the historical and family part of the Tarnowski archives in Dzików in vaulted rooms on the first floor of the local castle. The library collections were located in rooms on the first floor.[32] Current records, produced primarily as part of the legal-material and economic-financial affairs of the landed manor and property, was usually stored in the premises of property management offices. Such administrative centres, encompassing all or a part of landed property, were established very often in private estates in the 19th century.[33] To a large extent, their creation was forced not only by the economic pragmatism of the owners, but also by applicable legislation, for example tax law.

Landowner archives during the partitions and the interwar period did not change much in terms of function. Archives were collected, preserved and arranged, and were still to a small extent disposed. However, private archives did adopt a new role during this period by providing access for academic work, mainly in the area of editing archival sources. Roman Sanguszko, the owner of several holdings-rich archives – located, *inter alia*, in Gumniska near Tarnów, Podhorce and Sławuta in Wołyń – was very active in this regard. He financed a dozen or so serious publications in the form of monographs, catalogues and source editions, whose author or co-author was Sławuta archivist Bronisław Gorczak. They all dealt with the Sanguszko family and their archival and library collections.[34]

Certainly, the family archives of the 19th and 20th centuries, compared to the 18th, did indeed open their doors to scientists, mainly historians. That this was not a revolutionary process, however, is evidenced by Eugeniusz Barwiński's refer-

31 All the archives mentioned above are stored in the holdings of the: AGAD: *Zbiór Branickich z Suchej*; *Archiwum Gospodarcze Wilanowskie*; *Archiwum Potockich z Łańcuta*; *Archiwum Publiczne Potockich*; *Archiwum Radziwiłłów z Nieświeża*; ANK: *Archiwum Młynowskie Chodkiewiczów*; *Archiwum Dzikowskie Tarnowskich*; *Archiwum Lubomirskich*; *Archiwum Potockich z Krzeszowic*; *Archiwum Sanguszków* and at the Archiwum Państwowe w Rzeszowie: *Archiwum Lubomirskich*.

32 ANK: *Wstęp do inwentarza Archiwum Dzikowskiego Tarnowskich*, p. 9.

33 As an example one might cite the administration of the Potocki family's Wilanów estate or the Zamoyski estate in the 19th century; cf. Smoleńska 1957, pp. 218–222; eadem 1975, pp. 73–138; Mroczek 2010.

34 Długosz 1992–1993, pp. 507–509.

ence regarding inquiries made in the Radziwiłł archive in Nieśwież for scientific purposes in the second half of the 19th century. According to his knowledge, until 1908 the archives were used by philologist Ioan Bianu, a member of the Romanian Academy, Edward Kotłubaj, Stanisław Krzyżanowski, Antoni Prohaska, Stanisław Ptaszycki, Wacław Sobieski, and Kazimierz Waliszewski.[35]

Finally, it is worth noting that in the 19th and first half of the 20th century, it was quite common for private owners of archives and libraries to hand over archival materials and manuscripts to public institutions housing archival and library collections.[36]

Archivists

Landowner archives in the 19th century, in contrast to the previous epoch, were usually under the long-term, ongoing and often professional care of archival staff employed as archivists (variously called) and librarians. The lists naming the archivists employed in private archives during this period would be very long. In the case of some archives, it is even possible to recreate an uninterrupted sequence of full-time archive keepers from at least the beginning of the 19th century. Even in the first decades of that century, people responsible for family archives performed various functions for their employers, most often of a legal and material nature. Over time, their professional, archival specialisation is clearly noticeable, which was manifested not so much in education as in the duties performed and work methods.[37] Basically, they were pure archivists. Often they were also, if not outstanding, then certainly decent historians, to mention the aforementioned longtime archivist employed by the Sanguszko family, Bronisław Gorczak,[38] Franciszek Kluczycki[39] associated with the Potocki archives in Krzeszowice and Wilanów, or Michał Bohusz-Szyszka[40] long-time archivist of the Radziwiłł family. Unfortunately, the interwar period heralded a marked regression in this respect. Few of the owners of large archives, burdened with family archival traditions, employed full-time archivists or librarians. The examples of Michał Marczak[41] associated with the Tarnowski collections in Dzików or Bo-

35 Barwiński 1909–1913, p. 2.

36 Pijaj 2012, pp. 53–57.

37 Here it is worth mentioning the work of Nieśwież archivists Romuald Symonowicz and Michał Bohusz Szyszko, who, while arranging the holdings of the Radziwiłł archive in the second half of the 19th century, departed from the old Polish fascicle system and generally divided the collection according to formal and factual criteria; cf. Jankowski 2018, p. 194.

38 Hoszowska 2020, pp. 239–270.

39 Birkenmajerówna 1967–1968, pp. 19–20.

40 Turkowski 1936, pp. 232–233.

41 Biography of Michal Marczak by Adam F. Baran; cf. Baran 1994.

lesław Tuhan Taurogiński[42] in the Radziwiłł Archives in Warsaw are among the noble exceptions. It is worth mentioning at this point that sometimes the owners of the archives were personally involved in the process of arranging archival holdings, for example by developing arrangement instructions, and sometimes even involving themselves in archival work. One example is Katarzyna Potocka who, through her historical interests, initiated archival work in the Krzeszowice archive. She herself also processed archival holdings, for example arranging family correspondence, archival acquisitions for the collection department and manuscripts brought to Wilanów.[43]

Finally, it is worth mentioning that in the interwar period, private owners of archives used the help of state archives to secure and arrange their holdings. However, this would happen rarely. The Potocki archives in Jabłonna were arranged over a period of several years, starting in 1933, by Wincenty Łopaciński and Adam Moraczewski, archivists from Public Enlightenment Archive (*Archiwum Oświecenia Publicznego*).[44] These same archivists and the head of the State Archives in Lublin, Leon Białkowski, in 1937 took part in an operation to transport the archives from the Młynów archive of the Chodkiewicz family to the State Archives in Kraków.[45]

Holdings

From the end of the 18th century, the holdings of magnate archives began to undergo significant transformations, both in terms of the volume and the types of archives cumulating therein. The growing quantity of economic and financial documentation was particularly noticeable.[46] It was, of course, already richly represented in the earlier period, but in the 19th century it was treated in a more systematic and detailed manner by the landowner administration, describing various types of expenses and revenue statements.[47] The legal and material archives also began to change, and during the course of the 19th century, old Polish excerpts (extracts) from court books – mainly town, land, tribunal and underchamberlain records – excerpts from mortgage registers and notarial deeds began to appear. This arose from the transformation of the old type of magnate

42 Frankiewicz 1988, p. 216.
43 Palarczykowa 1985, pp. 99–103.
44 Mamczak-Gadkowska 2006, p. 244.
45 *Sprawozdanie za 1937 r.* 1939, p. 16.
46 This phenomenon was pointed out by Halina Stebelska in her article on property records of the feudal era; cf. Stebelska 1956, p. 153.
47 About the characteristics of documentation of this type produced by the administration of the Potocki family's Wilanów estate in the 19th century; cf. Smoleńska 1957, pp. 223–234.

latifundium, based on the manorial system and agri-livestock production, into centrally managed and increasingly industrialised complexes of landed estates. Their administration required efficient organisation, usually based on multi-level structures of control and supervision.[48] The development of modern accounting contributed even more to the increasing production of economic and financial documentation than in the previous century.

It is difficult to compare the size of magnate archives from the 18th century with the landowner archives of the 19th and early 20th centuries. As mentioned above, in the case of the Zamoyski Archives, the proportions between the old Polish holdings and those from the period of the partitions clearly indicate a significant increase in archives featuring the latter type of documentation from the partition period. Of course, one must bear in mind that this comparison refers to all holdings lying in the hands of one creator – i. e., documentation of both a historical and practical nature, mainly economic-financial as well as legal-material, often kept separately from personal, family and historical archives. The present state of preservation of landowner archives clearly shows a prevalence of documentation produced in the 19th and first decades of the 20th century.

Summary

While searching for the similarities and differences between archives created by families belonging to the elite strata of the Polish society in the 18th–20th centuries, several aspects are worthy of attention. In terms of the organisation of landowner archives, in contrast to the 18th-century magnate archives, holdings were noticeably split between two archives – historical-family and legal-economic. The former were usually located in the manor house, while the second were held in the central estate administration. The functions and roles of the archives clearly shifted. The pragmatic nature in which the magnate archives were used – mainly to maintain and administer the magnate property – was enriched with a more cultural function in landowner archives, both in relation to the owner and his family, and also in a broader sense to the Polish nation and state. Contrary to magnate archives, landowner archives tended to be more structured and in a more thoughtful way. This yielded various types of lists created not only for the needs of the owner of the archive, as well as publications. This remark also

48 During the 19th century, landowners, especially the major ones, very often issued economic instructions for their administrators; cf. Baranowski et al. 1958; eidem 1963; Bielecka 1959. The ANK contain instructions of this type: for example: *Archiwum Potockich z Krzeszowic*, sig. 926–934, 2330–2339 and in the *Archiwum Młynowskie Chodkiewiczów*, sig. 1419–1425, 1918–1921.

applies to the scientific function of the landowner archives. In the 19th and early 20th centuries, many documents were subject to source editing. In a sense, the archives of this period became public, opening up to a community of researchers, mainly historians. Moreover, full-time archivists, often with higher education and academic ambitions, became archive-keepers. In terms of holdings, landowner archives, unlike magnate archives, while maintaining a similar typology for the documentation collected there, underwent transformations in terms of the proportions between individual types of archives. While magnate archives contained more legal and material documentation, in landowner archives priority in this respect was given to economic and financial documentation. It seems that a noticeable change also took place in terms of documentation that illustrated the public activity of the archive creators. The archives of the Old Polish period often contain documents of official provenance. In the case of landowner archives this phenomenon was much less common. Finally, it is worth mentioning that the physical form of the files stored in landowner archives also changed compared to their magnate predecessors. Old Polish fascicles were increasingly replaced by books and notebooks, characteristic of a 19th-century office for case files. They also included a new type of documentation, i. e., official correspondence.

[Translated by Steve Jones]

Bibliography

Archival sources

Archiwum Główne Akt Dawnych w Warszawie:
- *Archiwum Gospodarcze Wilanowskie;*
- *Archiwum Hipolita Skimborowicza;*
- *Archiwum Platerów z Antuzowa*, sig. 1;
- *Archiwum Potockich z Łańcuta;*
- *Archiwum Publiczne Potockich;*
- *Archiwum Radziwiłłów z Nieświeża;*
- *Archiwum Roskie / rodzinno-majątkowe*, sig. 29, 32;
- *Archiwum Warszawskie Radziwiłłów*, sig. 14–17, 25–27;
- *Archiwum Zamoyskich*, sig. 1, 3;
- *Zbiór Adama Mieleszki-Maliszewskiego;*
- *Zbiór Aleksandra Czołowskiego;*
- *Zbiór Branickich z Suchej.*

Archiwum Narodowe w Krakowie:
- *Archiwum Młynowskie Chodkiewiczów;*
- *Archiwum Dzikowskie Tarnowskich*, sig. 187–192;

- *Archiwum Lubomirskich;*
- *Archiwum Potockich z Krzeszowic*, sig. 13–18;
- *Archiwum Sanguszków;*
- *Wstęp do inwentarza Archiwum Dzikowskiego Tarnowskich.* 2003 (finding aid available at the headquarters of the Archives);
- *Zbiór Zygmunta Glogera.*

Archiwum Państwowe w Lublinie: *Archiwum Ordynacji Zamoyskich ze Zwierzyńca*, in: *Szukaj w archiwach*, URL: https://www.szukajwarchiwach.gov.pl/zespol/-/zespol/2005 [23.11.2021].

Archiwum Państwowe w Rzeszowie: *Archiwum Lubomirskich.*

Printed sources

Baranowski, Bohdan / Bartyś, Julian / Keckowa, Antonina / Leskiewicz, Janina (eds.): *Instrukcje gospodarcze dla dóbr magnackich i szlacheckich z XVII–XIX.* 1958/1.

Baranowski, Bohdan / Bartyś, Julian / Sobczak, Tadeusz (eds.): *Instrukcje gospodarcze dla dóbr magnackich i szlacheckich z XVII–XIX.* 1963/2.

Bielecka, Janina (ed.): *Instrukcje gospodarcze dla majątków wielkopolskich w pierwszej połowie XIX wieku.* 1959.

Literature

Baran, Adam: *Bibliotekarz z Dzikowa. Dr Michał Marczak (1886–1945).* 1994.

Barwiński, Eugeniusz: *Archiwum ks. Radziwiłłów w Nieświeżu. Rys jego historii i sprawozdanie z poszukiwań*, in: *Archiwum Komisji Historycznej.* 1909–1913/11, pp. 1–10.

Birkenmajerówna, Aleksandra: *Kluczycki Franciszek Ksawery*, in: *Polski słownik biograficzny.* 1967–1968/13/01, pp. 19–20.

Buczek, Karol: *Archiwa polskie*, in: *Nauka Polska. Materjały do spisu instytucyj i towarzystw naukowych w Polsce.* 1927/7, pp. 1–97.

Buczek, Karol: *Archiwa polskie*, in: *Nauka Polska. Materjały do spisu instytucyj i towarzystw naukowych w Polsce. Suplement do t. 7.* 1930/12, pp. 1–85.

Buczek, Karol: *Z dziejów polskiej archiwistyki prywatnej (Archiwa XX Czartoryskich)*, in: *Studia historyczne ku czci Stanisława Kutrzeby.* 1938/2, pp. 41–86.

Chwalewik, Antoni: *Zbiory polskie: archiwa, bibljoteki, gabinety, galerje, muzea i inne zbiory pamiątek przeszłości w ojczyźnie i na obczyźnie w porządku alfabetycznym według miejscowości ułożone.* 1926–1927/1–2.

Długosz, Józef: *Sanguszko Roman Damian*, in: *Polski słownik biograficzny.* 1992–1993/34/04, pp. 507–509.

Frankiewicz, Bogdan: *Tuhan-Taurogiński Bolesław*, in: *Słownik biograficzny archiwistów polskich.* 1988/1, p. 216.

Gorczak, Bronisław: *Katalog rękopisów X.X. Sanguszków w Sławucie.* 1902.

Górski, Robert: *Archiwa osobiste. Problemy gromadzenia, opracowywania i udostępniania*, in: *Problemy archiwistyki.* 2009/2, pp. 22–30.

Horodyski, Bogdan: *Z pogranicza bibliotekarstwa i archiwistyki*, in: *Przegląd Biblioteczny*. 1956/24/3, pp. 201–212.

Hoszowska, Mariola: *Bronisław Gorczak – historyk i wołyński archiwista (1854–1918)*, in. *Archeion*. 2020/121, pp. 239–270.

Jankowski, Rafał: *Archiwiści i instrukcje archiwalne napisane dla nich w Archiwum Głównym Radziwiłłów w Nieświeżu*, in: *Archiwista Polski*. 2000/18, pp. 35–36. (1)

Jankowski, Rafał: *Burzliwe losy Archiwum Radziwiłłów z Nieświeża od XVI w. do 1838 r.*, in: *Miscellanea Historico-Archivistica*. 2000/11, pp. 35–68. (2)

Jankowski, Rafał: *Archiwum Radziwiłłów z Nieświeża od 1838 r. do XX w.*, in: *Miscellanea Historico-Archivistica*. 2001/13, pp. 131–168.

Jankowski, Rafał: *Rękopisy biblioteczne w Warszawskim Archiwum Radziwiłłów*, in: *Miscellanea Historico-Archivistica*. 2018, pp. 191–220.

Kupczewska, Marta / Łopatecki, Karol: *Testament Izabeli z Poniatowskich Branickiej (3 XI 1805 r.)*, in: *Kwartalnik Historii Kultury Materialnej*. 2016/64/1, pp. 103–119.

Łopatecki, Karol: *Sprzedaż dóbr białostockich przez spadkobierców Jana Klemensa Branickiego*, in: *Studia Podlaskie*. 2015/23, pp. 75–99.

Mamczak-Gadkowska, Irena: *Archiwa państwowe w II Rzeczypospolitej*. 2006.

Matwijów, Maciej: *Zbiory materiałów życia publicznego jako typ książki rękopiśmiennej w czasach staropolskich (1660–1760)*. 2000.

Mroczek, Michał: *Administracja gospodarcza dóbr Ordynacji Zamoyskiej w latach 1864–1914. Uwarunkowania – organizacja – ludzie*, in: Górak, Artur / Latawiec, Krzysztof / Magier, Dariusz (eds.): *Dzieje biurokracji na ziemiach polskich*. 2010/3/1, pp. 451–472.

Palarczykowa, Anna: *Dzieje Archiwum Potockich z Krzeszowic*, in: *Archeion*. 1985/79, pp. 93–114.

Pijaj, Stanisław: *Archiwa rodzinno-majątkowe i spuścizny z terytorium dawnej Galicji (ich losy i stan obecny)*, in: *Studia Historyczne*. 2012/55/1, pp. 51–70.

Smoleńska, Barbara: *Administracja dóbr gospodarczych wilanowskich i ich kancelaria rachunkowo-kontrolna (XIX–XX wiek)*, in: *Archeion*. 1957/27, pp. 217–234.

Smoleńska, Barbara / Zielińska, Teresa: *Archiwalia prywatne w Archiwum Głównym Akt Dawnych w Warszawie (Archiwa magnackie)*, in: *Archeion*. 1962/38, pp. 167–197.

Smoleńska, Barbara: *Struktura i funkcjonowanie zarządu dóbr wilanowskich (1800–1864)*. 1975.

Stebelska, Halina: *Typy akt majątkowych epoki feudalnej w archiwach podworskich*, in: *Archeion*. 1956/26, pp. 152–171.

Stebelski, Adam: *Rękopis archiwalny i biblioteczny*, in: *Archeion*. 1951/19–20, pp. 30–40.

Syta, Krzysztof: *Archiwum Jana Tarły, wojewody sandomierskiego w świetle rewizji z roku 1761*, in: *Studia o bibliotekach i zbiorach polskich*. 1994/6, pp. 31–53.

Syta, Krzysztof: *Jan Józef Witoszyński – archiwista Sieniawskich i Czartoryskich z XVIII wieku. Przyczynek do dziejów archiwistyki prywatnej okresu staropolskiego*, in: *Archiwista Polski*. 2002/2, pp. 23–36.

Syta, Krzysztof: *Sumariusze archiwalne Rzewuskich z Podhorzec z XVIII i XIX w. w zasobie Archiwum Państwowego w Krakowie*, in: *Archiwista Polski*. 2003/8/4, pp. 15–31.

Syta, Krzysztof: *Archiwa magnackie w XVIII w. Studium kultury kancelaryjno-archiwalnej*. 2010.

Syta, Krzysztof: *Białostockie archiwum Branickich w II poł. XVIII w. w świetle listów Piotra Piramowicza do Izabeli Branickiej z lat 1773–1785*, in: Jabłońska, Marlena / Degen,

Robert / Roman, Wanda Krystyna (eds): *Zarządzanie dokumentacją, archiwistyka i... koty. Księga jubileuszowa prof. Haliny Robótki.* 2016, pp. 133–144. (1)

Syta, Krzysztof: *Zarządzanie dokumentacją w kancelariach magnackich: kierunki i możliwości badawcze*, in: Degen, Robert / Jabłońska, Marlena (eds.): *Zarządzanie dokumentacją. Badania i dydaktyka.* 2016/7, pp. 95–112. (2)

Syta, Krzysztof: *Dokumentacja gospodarczo-finansowa w administracji latyfundium Branickich h. Gryf w XVIII w. Kilka uwag na marginesie procesu aktotwórczego*, in: *Wschodni Rocznik Humanistyczny.* 2018/15/3, pp. 23–34. (1)

Syta, Krzysztof: *XVII-wieczne rejestry archiwalne w Archiwum Dzikowskim Tarnowskich*, in: Rosowska, Ewa / Wajs, Hubert (eds): *Archiwa, źródła, historia. Prace ofiarowane w siedemdziesiąte urodziny profesora Władysława Stępniaka.* 2018, pp. 274–291. (2)

Szydłowski, Tadeusz: *Ruiny Polski. Opis szkód wyrządzonych przez wojnę w dziedzinie zabytków sztuki na ziemiach Małopolski i Rusi Czerwonej z 227 rycinami i mapką orjentacyjną.* 1919.

Turkowski, Tadeusz: *Bohusz-Szyszko Michał*, in: *Polski słownik biograficzny.* 1936/2/03, pp. 232–233.

Tomczak, Andrzej: *Zarys dziejów archiwów polskich i ich współczesna organizacja*, in: Robótka, Halina / Ryszewski, Bohdan / Tomczak, Andrzej (eds.): *Archiwistyka.* 1989, pp. 238–243, 301–306.

Tyszkowski, Kazimierz: *Z dziejów polskiej archiwistyki prywatnej. Instrukcja archiwalna z XVIII w.*, in: *Archeion.* 1935/13, pp. 71–82.

Zielińska, Teresa: *Archiwalia prywatne (pojęcie, zakres gromadzenia, metody opracowania)*, in: *Archeion.* 1971/56, pp. 71–88.

Zielińska, Teresa: *Archiwa Radziwiłłów i ich twórcy*, in: *Archeion.* 1978/66, pp. 105–129.

Robert Degen

The History of Selection. Polish Attempts to Make a Selection of Archival Materials While Preserving Their Organic Context Before 1939

Abstract
In the years 1918–1939, when performing archival selection, Polish archivists considered the organic ties that bound archival materials to be the reason for permanent preservation of records. With the massive influx of records into archives, relationships within archival fonds began to lose importance in favour of the historical value of the records. In the late 1930s, however, ideas emerged that enabled the preservation of records in selected institutions in their entirety in order to protect the organic relationships that linked the records in exemplary registries.
Keywords: Polish archives; archival selection; archival appraisal and disposal; principle of provenance; Kazimierz Konarski

In the first chapter of *Using functional analysis in archival appraisal*, Marcus C. Robyns stated that the period up to the end of World War II is considered by archivists to be the Custodial Era, "because practitioners during this time believed that the archivist's sole responsibility was to care for the records left to them."[1] Robyns traced the genesis of this approach back to positivist ideology and the findings of Samuel Muller, Johan A. Faith, and Robert Fruin embedded in this ideology and included in the Dutch Manual *Handleiding voor het ordenen en beschrijven van archieven* of 1898.[2] Keeping them in mind, archivists, convinced of the historical value of almost all official records, left it up to the archives creators to destroy documentation that was worthless, and played a passive role in the evaluation process. Due to their passive attitude, organically formed archival fonds, whose official, intact provenance ensured the authenticity and lasting value of the documents that comprised them, ended up in the archives' storage spaces.[3]

Assoc. prof. Robert Degen, Nicolaus Copernicus University, ORCID: https://orcid.org/0000-0003-3467-9341.

1 Robyns 2014, p. 3.
2 Muller / Feith / Fruin 1898.
3 Robyns 2014, pp. 3–6.

The handbook of the Dutch trio also laid foundations for Polish archival theory. It was well known in Poland in translations (primarily German and French).[4] In fact, it was considered the primary methodological study for archivists worldwide, or at least in Europe. The work enjoyed this status among the Polish archivists because the principle of provenance promulgated therein was accepted by the International Congress of Archivists and Librarians held in Brussels in 1910.[5] The Dutch findings were the subject of a lively discussion among Polish archivists, who adapted the notion of archival fonds (Dutch: *archief*) and the aforementioned principle of provenance to the Polish reality.[6] Despite the changes in the political system, in other countries the collection process in the archives ran smoothly, although in Poland in the late 1910s and early 1920s there was no chance for this to happen. Faced with a shortage of storage space, Polish archivists were forced to efficiently secure the records left behind by Russians retreating in 1915, to take over the records of German and Austrian authorities (both those active before 1915 and those under occupation of 1915–1918), and to accept archival materials returned from the Soviet Union.[7] This implied a more active role for archivists, who could not remain mere guardians of the official order of the archival fonds that were taken over. They could not limit their endeavours to preserving the original arrangement of the records; instead, they were forced to reconstruct the order of fonds and undertake actions that for the records creators were unprecedented. These works included archival appraisal and disposal.

While selecting materials that were worthy of permanent preservation, Polish archivists of the interwar period tried to make use of the then current scientific achievements in archival science, adapting them to the local reality. With the rapid and massive influx of documentation, they began to realize that they would have to become more actively involved in the collection of archival materials and develop their own rules, methods, and selection criteria. These included ideas for preserving materials while respecting their organic context. This article is devoted to their presentation.

The historical method used in the study involved establishing facts by analysing information from literature and archival sources. It should be noted that historical evaluations of Polish achievements concerning methods and selection criteria before World War II have so far remained on the margins of archival research.[8] Efforts made by archives to evaluate and dispose of their own records

4 Muller / Feith / Fruin 1905; eidem 1910.
5 Ryszewski 1972, pp. 25–26.
6 Roman 2021, pp. 28–30; cf. the attached list of studies used: ibid., pp. 239–249.
7 Mamczak-Gadkowska 2006, pp. 37–55, 247–270.
8 Cf. Chmielewski 1994, pp. 82–84.

have proved unpopular, although this has recently changed.[9] However, the issue of disposing of documentation by records creators who were active in the years 1918–1939 was much more popular. The first reviews of their activities in this field appeared even before 1939;[10] the research continued after 1945[11] and is still being undertaken today.[12]

The sources for the research undertaken and presented in this article were theoretical studies published before 1939 that dealt with the issues of archival appraisal and disposal.[13] The paper draws on reports on the activities of state archives published in the Polish scientific journal *Archeion.*[14] Archival materials also played an important role among the sources used. Sadly, the records of the central body of state archival network from 1918–1939, i. e., the Department of State Archives (*Wydział Archiwów Państwowych*, hereinafter: WAP), did not survive the war, and only small percentages of the fonds of Warsaw archives did. Luckily, in the case of the latter, we still have materials of the Archives of Modern Records in Warsaw (*Archiwum Akt Nowych w Warszawie*).[15] The fonds of local state archives have survived to the present day in a satisfactory condition. The research made use of the records from pre-war archives in Bydgoszcz, Kielce, Lviv, Radom, and Vilnius.[16] Particularly noteworthy is the correspondence between Witold Suchodolski, Director of the State Archives and Tadeusz Esman, head of the Bydgoszcz branch of the State Archives in Poznań from autumn 1938 (from September 7 to November 4).[17] The subject of the correspondence was the disposal of the records at the Voivodeship Headquarters of the State Police in Toruń in the context of the new regulations concerning the storage of records in the police force, which were just being drafted. Although the draft has not sur-

9 Falkowski 2019, pp. 105–125.

10 Moraczewski 1937–1938, pp. 35–48.

11 Cf. Tarakanowska 1967, pp. 43–55.

12 Cf. Dąbrowski 2012; Degen 2010.

13 Kaleński 1934; Konarski 1927; idem 1929; Pawłowski 1928.

14 *Archiwum Akt Dawnych w Warszawie* 1927; Łopaciński 1930; Rybarski 1935; idem 1936; idem 1937–1938; idem 1938–1939 (1); idem 1938–1939 (2); *Sprawozdanie z działalności Wydziału Archiwów Państwowych w roku 1936* 1937–1938.

15 Archiwum Akt Nowych w Warszawie: *Archiwum Akt Nowych w Warszawie* (hereinafter: AAN).

16 Archiwum Państwowe w Bydgoszczy: *Archiwum Państwowe w Poznaniu Oddział w Bydgoszczy* (hereinafter: APB); Archiwum Państwowe w Kielcach: *Archiwum Państwowe w Kielcach* (hereinafter: APK); Centralnij deržavnij istoričnij arhiv Ukraïni m. L'viv [Централний Державний Іцторичний Архів України м. Львів]: *Deržavnij arhiv u L'vovi* [*Державний архів у Львові*] (hereinafter: CDIAUL); Archiwum Państwowe w Radomiu: *Archiwum Państwowe w Radomiu* (hereinafter: APR); Lietuvos Centrinis Valstybės Archyvas Vilnius: *Archiwum Państwowe w Wilnie. Ministerstwo Wyznań Religijnych i Oświecenia Publicznego RP* (hereinafter: LCVAV).

17 Falkowski 2019, pp. 115–120. Here, extensive summaries of the correspondence excerpts.

vived, it is possible to deduce its main assumptions from the correspondence, together with the suggestions made by the archival administration.[18]

In the 1920s, Polish archivists were convinced that the problem of archival selection was extremely difficult and that the principles and methods of selecting documentation that was worth preserving permanently had not yet been established by science. It was noted that these issues were among the most important matters to be dealt with by the Brussels Congress in 1910, but the volume containing materials from that meeting did not include a single paper devoted to archival appraisal and disposal.[19] It was pointed out that textbooks on archival science published up to that time either tried to omit these issues or treated them very generally. German studies by Franz Löher[20] and Georg Holtzinger[21] were cited as examples. These authors not only saw materials that were worthy of permanent preservation in the archives, but as far as the documentation of negligible value was concerned, they argued that it should be carefully examined before destruction.[22] In addition to German research, the Dutch Manual was regarded as a compendium that could serve as a basis for archival selection,[23] and the concepts of archive fonds and the principle of provenance were the general considerations in selecting records for permanent preservation.

Kazimierz Konarski, considered to be one of the "fathers" of Polish archival science, when formulating the notion of archival fonds directly adopted Dutch findings and stated that each fonds:

- is an organic creation;
- is created as a result of the official activities of an institution over a closed period and within a defined territory;
- consists of all documentation produced by an institution (*registratura*).[24]

When presenting methods of arranging the fonds, he emphasised that only the reconstruction of the original, organic order, in accordance with the principle of provenance, guarantees the preservation of the full informational potential of the documentation.[25] According to Konarski, the use of other methods (such as the one based on the French *principe du respect des fonds*) may lead to the destruction of the links between the records, which in turn poses a threat of

18 APB: sig. 67.
19 Konarski 1927, p. 123.
20 Löher 1890, p. 324.
21 Holtzinger 1908, p. 161.
22 Konarski 1927, p. 123; Pawłowski 1928, p. 23.
23 Pawłowski 1928, p. 24.
24 Konarski 1929, pp. 15–18.
25 Ibid., pp. 55–60.

> [...] depletion to the records themselves. When a document is pulled out of the group to which it originally belonged it often loses all of its meaning and content, all of its archival, or even historical foundation. The correlation between records corresponds closely to the correlation between facts; for the historian this is a phenomenon of unprecedented importance; if the connection between the records that have grown out of a single organisational unit is destroyed, the possibility of reconstructing the causal connection between the records is also destroyed.[26]

This perception of the archival fonds and the principle of provenance led to a very literal treatment of §65 and, above all, §66 of the Dutch handbook.[27] The following were considered not to be part of archival fonds:
- records produced by other institutions, even if they were previously stored with the materials of the creator of the fonds;
- publications purchased by the creator of the fonds and used by the staff of the institution to perform their daily official duties, such as manuscripts or printed collections of laws or clerical manuals;
- letters received and accepted by the creator of the fonds that did not initiate the decision-making procedure, were not registered or processed and, because of that, no replies were sent to the sender; also blank correspondence forms, unfilled forms, tables, etc.

Consequently, it was assumed that the fonds should be stripped of all external records. Records produced by other institutions were to be included in the appropriate archival fonds, or possibly placed in a clearly separated section. All library items were to be placed in archival book collections, while the remaining materials, e.g. those not considered by the archives creator, posters and prints not included in official documentation and blank forms, were to be destroyed.[28] The latter group of documents, Konarski explicitly referred to as "chaff", which should be separated from the "wheat", and this activity was to be performed by state archivists.[29] Among those responsible for the selection was Konarski himself, who, in the years 1921–1944, held the post of director of Warsaw's Archives of Historical Records (*Archiwum Akt Dawnych w Warszawie*, hereinafter: AAD). An interesting example of an attempt to implement the outlined concepts comes from the practice of this archive.

---

26 "[...] wyjałowieniem samych aktów. Dokument wyrwany z grupy, do której pierwotnie należał, traci niejednokrotnie całe swoje znaczenie i treść, całe swe już nie tylko archiwalne, ale wraz z nim dziejowe podłoże. Korelacji akt odpowiada jak najściślej korelacja faktów; dla historyka zjawisko niesłychanej wagi; przez proste mechaniczne choćby tylko zniweczenie związku, jaki łączy z sobą wyrosłe na gruncie jednej organizacyjnej komórki akta, niszczymy możliwość odtworzenia przyczynowego związku między aktami." Ibid., p. 62.

27 Muller / Feith / Fruin 1905, pp. 92–94.

28 Pawłowski 1928, p. 24.

29 Konarski 1927, p. 123.

The AAD was created in 1867 with the aim of collecting the archives of the central bodies of the illusively independent Kingdom of Poland, which was then being liquidated by Tsar Alexander II. The first records submitted to the Archives were the materials of the Administrative Council and the Council of State of the Kingdom of Poland, and its fonds grew gradually until the summer of 1915. After Poland had regained its independence in 1918, the AAD became the central archive which was to receive the records of all institutions that governed the territory of the former Kingdom of Poland, produced by the Russians until their retreat in 1915.[30]

The change in the profile of acquired records and the mass archiving of the documentation by the partitioning authorities led to a significant increase in the AAD's archival holdings. It can be estimated that it was at least fivefold.[31] From the late 1918 to 1921, it received materials transferred directly from the offices of the Chancellery of the General Governor of Warsaw, the Mazovian Voivodeship Commission, the Governor of Warsaw from 1867–1918, and the Governorate operating at the same time. Starting in 1922, records recovered from the Soviet Union began to return to the archives' storage spaces. Most of the fonds, whether they came to this facility from the decommissioned offices or returned from Russia, needed to be fully processed. One of them, partly taken over from the office and partly recovered, was the fonds of the Warsaw Chief of Police Force from 1839–1917.[32]

The arrangement and description of the fonds was initiated back in the early 1920s, so in the second part of the decade only a small part of it remained unarranged.[33] The work on it was completed by 1934, when Adam Próchnik reconstructed the layout of the materials of the so-called Secret Section and Special Department and compiled an index to the political files of the 1880s.[34] In 1935, Próchnik began inventorying and indexing the materials, and these activities in the archives continued until 1938.[35] It is possible that they were not completed until the outbreak of World War II.

Currently, we do not have at our disposal the details on the structure of the fonds that it was given during the arrangement. All that is certain is that it was decided that the original order be recreated in it. In accordance with the principle

30 Idem 1956 (2), pp. 281–290.

31 Idem 1956 (1), pp. 72–73. The increase in the AAD fonds given is an estimate. In 1870, after most of the fonds had been archived and remained in it until 1915, the fonds was calculated to contain 120,000 volumes and books. In 1929, after the fonds had been recovered and the new materials had been acquired, there were about 600,000 units in the AAD.

32 Idem 1956 (2), pp. 290–292.

33 *Archiwum Akt Dawnych w Warszawie* 1927, p. 156.

34 Rybarski 1935, p. 195.

35 Idem 1936, p. 107; idem 1937–1938, p. 160; idem 1938–1939, p. 161; Konarski 1937–1938, p. 353.

of provenance, files on police surveillance, arrests, matters related to the police and politics, documentation of the capital's Secret Section and "Special" Department, and the Department for Combating Emigration Propaganda took their rightful place in the fonds.[36]

The latter department was created to fight against "emigration agents" loitering in the Kingdom of Poland in the early 20th century. The documentation that it left behind consisted of 2 groups. The first, and rather sparse, comprised the files produced within the scope of the clerks' work. The second, much more abundant, is a huge collection of so-called "American letters". This was primarily Russian-seized correspondence from America (from the United States, as well as from South American countries, such as Brazil), sent by Polish economic migrants to their families who remained in the Kingdom of Poland. The collection also included propaganda prints smuggled into Poland by emigration organisations.[37]

At the time the fonds was being arranged, the documentation belonging to the first of the aforementioned groups did not raise the archivists' doubts. They found the right place for it in the fonds, placed it there, and reconstructed the natural ties that emerged between the records produced in the course of the work of the officials of the Department for Combating Emigration Propaganda. The situation was different with the "American letters". The confiscated correspondence, which had been used by Russian officials as a valuable source of information in their daily work, did not merge with the official records, nor did it establish an organic relationship, characteristic of any archival fonds, with the rest of the records. It constituted a separate collection in the office of the chief of the police force and remained a separate series even after its inclusion in the AAD holdings. The letters could be easily separated from the other archived materials, one of the reasons being that they were stored separately in several boxes.[38]

Therefore, for the AAD archivists, the "American letters" did not belong to the fonds. They saw them as appendices to the actual official work of the Russian police authorities. They may also have regarded them as correspondence that did not initiate the procedure for dealing with specific issues. In any case, as early as 1921, the board of the archive decided to destroy the letters which "constituted a formless mass and were not directly linked to the records."[39] This intention never materialised and the fate of the correspondence in the 1920s was saved by the suggestion that it could be used to write a monograph on the life of Polish emigrants overseas. The idea to save the "American letters" did not come from

36 Konarski 1956 (1), pp. 167–168.

37 Ibid., p. 168.

38 Ibid.

39 "[...] stanowiących bezkształtną masę i nie mających żadnego bezpośredniego związku z aktami." Konarski 1927, p. 123.

any of the archivists working at AAD but was "suggested by a third party".[40] It can be assumed that it was expressed by one of the scholars who visited the archive's research room. Perhaps it was one of the historians associated with the University of Warsaw.

The only documentation singled out from the files of the chief of the police and actually destroyed during the interwar period was the so-called "apparent waste paper". It could include, for example, damaged paper, unfilled and no longer useful official forms. Several shipments of this type of documents had already been removed from the files of the chief of the police before 1926 and transferred to the State Printing House for processing.[41] Between 1933 and 1934, almost 13 tons of waste paper of the same origin were sold to the State Securities Printing House.[42]

The fonds of the Warsaw Chief of Police Force was the only certain example for the AAD that conditioned the recognition of some of the materials as worthy of permanent preservation on the existence of an organic relationship between the records. We can surmise with a high degree of probability that the records of other fonds may have been subjected to selection based on the same premise. We know that between 1918 and 1926, as the remains of records from other institutions were being processed, some of the records were singled out and made up a sizeable collection of "miscellaneous, mostly ownerless records".[43] In 1926, it was decided that they should be taken care of: "The work schedule, calculated for the period of several years, provides for the gradual clearance of the entire building via the completion of individual archival fonds and removing everything that does not belong to a given collection."[44] It is also possible that the suggestion made with regard to the files of the chief of the police meant that "If the miscellaneous texts are by no means capable of being included in any of the fonds, they are put in a separate room and in time they will be treated as a separate collection, sorted by subject matter and inventoried."[45]

Just as we do not know whether the conduct described in the case of the records of the chief of the police was common for AAD, we are not sure whether other Polish archives followed similar principles in selecting records for per-

40 Ibid., pp. 123–124.

41 *Archiwum Akt Dawnych w Warszawie* 1927, p. 155.

42 It was exactly 12.750 kg; cf. Rybarski 1935, p. 195.

43 "[…] różnych, mieszanych, przeważnie bezpańskich akt"; *Archiwum Akt Dawnych w Warszawie* 1927, p. 156.

44 "[…] Program prac obliczony na parę lat, przewiduje stopniowe oczyszczenie całego gmachu, przez wykańczanie poszczególnych zespołów archiwalnych i usuwanie z nich wszystkiego tego, co danego zbioru należeć nie może." Ibid.

45 "[…] Varia jeśli żadną miarą nie dadzą się włączyć do któregokolwiek z zespołów, uzyskują osobne pomieszczenie i z czasem zostaną potraktowane jako osobny zbiór, posegregowane wg układu rzeczowego i zinwentaryzowane." Ibid.

manent preservation. This is of course likely, if only because the archival literature with works by Konarski, for example, was widely available and the discussion on the basic principles of the developing Polish archival science took place in public on many occasions and involved researchers from various centres, not only from Warsaw.[46] It is certain that other Polish state archives disposed of "apparent waste paper" before the outbreak of World War II (Vilnius).[47] Clean paper was also removed and given to institutions to be recycled (Radom).[48] We know that the decision to actually destroy the separated records was not always made at once and that some archives kept the materials that they had previously designated for destruction for a long time (Kielce, Radom, Vilnius)[49]. We know of examples where all materials produced by institutions were taken over from offices to the archives without prior disposal, even at the explicit request of the WAP (Kielce, Radom, Kraków, Lviv, Bydgoszcz branch of State Archives in Poznań and Piotrków Trybunalski).[50] However, we do not know if this was done in these cases to preserve the organic context of the materials in the archival fonds. Perhaps the intention of the archival administration was to relieve the burden on the clerks who were transferring the records and to delegate the assessment of value to state archivists who were better equipped to do so. Even then, the belief was increasingly expressed that the creators of the archives were assessing value "without a proper understanding of the historical value of the records."[51]

If even some state archives chose to base the selection of materials on the existence of an organic relationship between records, we do not know how long they used this criterion for. As time passed, more and more often – including in the case of records that had already been accumulated in the storage spaces of state archives – the selection for preservation was determined by the informational value of the records. It became important not to preserve the relationship between the documents, but to select the records that were valuable in official, scientific, and particularly historical terms.[52] This approach began to prevail in Polish archival science in the 1930s, when the first Polish handbook on archival

46 Degen 2009, pp. 76–82 (2); Roman 2021, pp. 28–30.

47 LCVAV: sig. 55, pp. 74–92, 105, 115.

48 APR: sig. 5, p. 8.

49 APK: sig. 18, pp. 16–23; ibid.: sig. 72, pp. 25–27; APR: sig. 25; *Sprawozdanie Archiwum Państwowego w Radomiu za okres pracy od 1.07. do 20.09.1934*; LCVA: sig. 102, pp. 16, 29.

50 AAN: sig. 73, pp. 13, 58; APR: sig. 34; *Odpis pisma nr II S-2383/36 MWRiOP do kuratoriów w Krakowie, Lwowie, Poznaniu i Warszawie w sprawie przekazania akt zlikwidowanych seminariów nauczycielskich do archiwów państwowych*; CDIAU: op. 1, sig. 33, p. 9.

51 "[...] bez należytego zrozumienia historycznej wartości akt;" APB: sig. 67; *Pismo Kazimierza Kaczmarczyka kierownika w AP w Poznaniu nr 636/2/38 w sprawie brakowania dzienników podawczych w policji. 4.06.1938*; cf. Degen 2010, pp. 550–551.

52 CDIAU: op. 1, sig. 26, p. 4.

selection, written by Gustaw Kaleński and titled *Brakowanie akt* (*Disposal of Records*) was published.[53] Published in 1934, the compendium, in addition to outlining the history of selection and general remarks, included a set of specific criteria for selecting archival materials. In the Polish reality, it was universally important, because it could not only facilitate the work of state archivists, but also give the appropriate tools to offices that produced records.

The experience of the first years of independence and the mass archiving of records of Russian, Prussian, and Austrian authorities did not induce Polish archivists to assume full responsibility for the selection of materials created after 1918 in the offices of the reborn Poland. Quite the contrary, they were even more aware that they would not be able to control the influx of new archival materials if these were not selected in advance by the records creators.[54] Even as early as in the autumn of 1920, with the participation of state archivists, regulations were drawn up prohibiting offices from destroying documentation without the consent of the state archives, and these came into force in 1921.[55] At the end of that decade, work was initiated on the concept of a new mechanism for archival selection and disposal,[56] and this resulted in the issuance of the *Regulations on the preservation of records in government administration offices* (*Przepisy o przechowywaniu akt w urzędach administracji rządowej*) in late 1931.[57]

The scope of the new regulations was not limited to assessing the value of records and the mechanism for their disposal. They identified a place in each government office that was to be used to store records not needed for day-to-day running of the office and called it a records repository. Generally, they characterised the principles and duration of records retention, the tools used to describe the holdings, and the relationship between repositories and state archives. They were important for the selection of archival materials because they divided documentation into that which was worthy of permanent preservation (category A records) and that of temporary importance (category B records); they generally defined the characteristics of both groups, and specified the person responsible for making the evaluation. This person was the clerk who was in charge of the records repository and acted in consultation with a representative of the organisational unit the records of which he was reviewing. His decision was to be approved by the head of the entire institution and, ultimately, the relevant state archives. Unfortunately, the 1931 regulations did not clearly define the subject of selection. It was only noted in the commentary to them that the appropriate category should include a class of documentation, i. e., records related by the

53 Kaleński 1934. For English translation see: idem 1976.
54 Konarski 1927, p. 122–123; Pawłowski 1928, p. 26.
55 Degen 2010, p. 247.
56 Robótka 1993, pp. 46–52; Smoczyński 2020, pp. 105–120, 164–165.
57 Enacted by resolution of the Council of Ministers on 21. 12. 1931.

subject matter, which in the repository could be divided into filing units established on an annual basis.[58]

The regulations of 1931 had a framework structure and forced central offices to develop regulations for themselves and subordinate institutions. By the autumn of 1939, ten of them had developed regulations in this area: Ministry of Social Welfare (1935), Ministry of Internal Affairs (for voivodeship offices and starost offices in 1936 and 1938), Ministry of the Treasury (separately for itself in 1932 and separately for tax authorities and offices in 1936), Ministry of Foreign Affairs (for foreign posts in 1937), Ministry of Justice (for courts in 1937), National Police Headquarters (*Komenda Główna Policji Państwowej*, hereinafter: KGPP) (1937), Ministry of Communications (for itself and subordinate offices in 1938), Ministry of Industry and Commerce (1938), Ministry of Military Affairs, and Central Statistical Office (1938).[59]

The idea behind the framework structure of the regulations was to bring common solutions to the entire state administration, something that even the departments mentioned earlier failed to do. While all of the standards developed from 1932 confirmed the division of records into categories A and B and enumerated the groups of records eligible for them, they were not unanimous with regard to identifying the officials who would perform the selection. The 1931 recommendations only reiterated the guidelines of the Ministry of Social Welfare. In the voivodeship and starost offices, the clerks were instructed to become involved in the evaluation process: although in the end it was the archivists at the records repositories that were to make the selection, it was the clerks who were to write their own proposals for archival categories on the documents while the cases were being handled. The solutions designed by the Ministry of Treasury and Ministry of Justice shifted selection onto the shoulders of clerks and judges.[60] Also in the state police, it was the officials who were supposed to assess the value of the records, although they were supposed to do so in the presence of a committee.[61] The object of selection was also defined in different ways, taking advantage of the lack of decisiveness in the framework regulations. As mentioned earlier, the regulations for voivodeship and starost offices required an assessment of the value of individual case files, and the guidelines for courts required an

58 Stosyk 1936, pp. 26–27.

59 Dąbrowski 2012, pp. 229–336; Moraczewski 1937–1938, pp. 36–37; *Przepisy o przechowywaniu akt w Ministerstwie Skarbu* 1932; APB: sig. 67: *Instrukcja o przechowywaniu akt w Ministerstwie Komunikacji i w urzędach podległych. Warszawa 1938*; *Instrukcja szczegółowa Ministra Przemysłu i Handlu z dnia 14 października 1938 r. o przechowywaniu akt. Warszawa 1938*; *Instrukcja [Ministerstwa Spraw Wojskowych] o przechowywaniu, wydzielaniu i niszczeniu akt. Warszawa 1938* oraz *Instrukcja o przechowywaniu akt w Głównym Urzędzie Statystycznym. Warszawa 1938.*

60 Moraczewski 1937–1938, p. 39.

61 APB: sig. 87, pp. 250–251.

assessment of the materials of separate proceedings. This led to a situation where officials qualified only selected cases from a given class or filing unit, or in extreme cases – single documents, for permanent preservation, rather than all of them, which the state archivists tried to combat.[62]

The implementation of the new and universally applicable selection and disposal mechanism in Poland was not complete until the outbreak of World War II. This is not only due to the fact that some records creators did not manage to adapt their solutions to the framework regulations. Some institutions actually attempted at correcting the newly introduced rules. One example is the KGPP, which in the autumn of 1938, in conjunction with the WAP, worked on even newer record preservation regulations for the state police.[63]

The regulations that were being drafted could have introduced a new selection and disposal mechanism in the state police which would be different from what was a norm at the time. Representatives of the police, in cooperation with the archival administration, planned the appraisal to be comprehensive, and that the files of all police administration bodies and their field offices operating at that time would be subjected to this assessment. It was initially assumed that materials worthy of permanent preservation would be identified in the registries of the KGPP, voivodeship headquarters and bureaus of investigation operating in the voivodeships. On the other hand, they were not expected to be found in the records of nearly all district police headquarters, police stations (except for books of orders and descriptions of police stations), and precincts (except for registries selected for preservation in their entirety). This was based on the simple assumption that in police institutions, which had a highly formalised and hierarchical structure, files of the same cases (the so-called duplicate cases) as well as individual documents were preserved in the registries of many institutions. In order to carry out the selection, a decision was made to identify the police facilities that would be most appropriate for preserving the archives and to recommend the destruction of records in all others.[64]

Particularly noteworthy is the solution proposed for police stations. According to WAP officials, their records contained a negligible amount of material suitable for permanent preservation. The documentation produced and preserved there was usually related to trivial matters or those that could only be resolved by the decision of higher police authorities. Therefore, the WAP proposed that the KGPP select only about a dozen or so police stations out of all those operating in Poland and recommend that all the documentation in each of

62 Moraczewski 1937–1938, pp. 45–46; Rybarski 1938–1939, p. 143.

63 APB: sig. 67.

64 APB: sig. 67; *Pismo Dyrektora Archiwów Państwowych Witolda Suchodolskiego nr Arch-711/38 w sprawie brakowania akt policyjnych. 4.11.1938*; cf. Falkowski 2019, pp. 115–120.

them be transferred to the appropriate state archives "as templates for police station registries".[65]

Unfortunately, it is not clear what purpose the preservation of "registry templates" was intended to serve. The use of the term registry (*registratura)*, appropriate for archival terminology, may suggest that archivists were concerned with preserving the entirety of records produced by selected police stations precisely in order to preserve all the characteristic relationships that linked the documents, records of individual cases, filing units and their series. It is possible, however, that the archival administration considered an accurate assessment of the value of the police station documentation to be a waste of time, an activity, the result of which being sparse archival materials, would not be worth the effort invested. Preserving the materials of selected precincts may have allowed future researchers to learn the operation methods of some law enforcement agencies of the 1920s and 1930s, especially as it was recommended that precincts "typical of certain cases" be selected.[66]

The elaboration and implementation of the new regulations for the police was probably hampered by the increasing threat of war and German aggression in September 1939. However, by late autumn of 1938, they were in such an advanced form that the WAP recommended them to be used by Tadeusz Esman, the head of the Bydgoszcz branch of the State Archives in Poznań, when assessing the value of the files of the Voivodeship Headquarters of the State Police in Toruń and when disposing of the police records from Pomorskie Voivodeship. One may form the impression that this was an opportunity for archival headquarters to try out the prepared solutions and verify the design, as it turned out to be successful. In the reports on the actions taken, Esman was more cautious than the proposed regulations provided. He acknowledged the legitimacy of removing "duplicate cases", indicated the appropriate levels of the police hierarchy for preserving certain types of records primarily at the voivodeship level, but proposed keeping some documentation produced by district police headquarters. He did not question the insignificant value of the documentation from the precincts and considered it a good choice of the voivodeship headquarters in Toruń to indicate one of the stations operating in the district of Tczew. According to Esman, the facility that operated there was characteristic of this frontier territory that was diverse in material, economic, political, and nationality terms.[67]

65 "[…] jako wzory registratury posterunku policyjnego"; APB: sig. 67; *Pismo Dyrektora Archiwów Państwowych Witolda Suchodolskiego nr Arch-711/38 w sprawie brakowania akt policyjnych. 7.09.1938.*

66 "[…] typowych dla pewnych spraw i ośrodków"; Ibid.

67 APB: sig. 67; *Sprawozdanie Tadeusza Esmana z wyjazdu do Komendy Wojewódzkiej Policji Państwowej w Toruniu nr 343/8/38.* 28.09.1938; Falkowski 2019, p. 118.

The selection mechanism that currently operates in Poland began to form during the interwar period and took its final form in the mid-1950s. It first assumes the selection of records creators and the identification of a certain group of institutions that produce records of permanent value. The selection of archival materials is in fact made, not very consciously though, by officials who create the documentation by converting letters into cases and classifying them using a list of records provided with symbols of archival qualification. The choices they make may be adjusted by the current archives staff and the state archivists that authorise the disposal, who in some cases must (and in others may) conduct an expert review of the records set aside for destruction. The materials separated in this way comprise the fonds that lack most of the organic ties that are characteristic of complete registries of records creators. Only the documents that were linked with regard to cases, case records within filing units, and filing units within a class retain their full organic context.

It is widely emphasised that this mechanism serves to preserve materials that contain information of historical value and for scholarly use, although scholars have raised concerns about its effectiveness.[68] It can be assumed, however, that on the basis of the archival materials selected in this way, even if imperfect, it is possible to study the past and create its image, albeit probably incompletely.[69]

Could the inclusion in the selection mechanism of solutions leading to the preservation of full organic relationships between documents produce a more satisfactory result? Striving to convert entire registries into archival fonds and removing from them only the non-fonds documentation seems to be misleading. After all, it would not guarantee the preservation of all valuable information, as the initial decision made at the AAD with regard to the "American letters" may have demonstrated. In contrast, an idea that was discarded prematurely, despite attempts to revert to it,[70] was the desire to preserve sample registries. The identification of institutions typical of certain groups of archive creators and the collection of their registries without disposing of them, could make it possible not only to study the functioning of the administration on selected examples and to formulate generalisations in this regard. It would provide an opportunity to fully understand the process of information flow within typical administrative structures, enable the discovery of algorithms for data processing and preservation, and, consequently, enable a more complete criticism of historical sources that are created today, and improve archival selection.

[Translated by Tomasz Leszczuk]

68 Górak / Magier 2011, pp. 131–143; Kwiatkowska 2011, pp. 191–204.
69 Degen 2009 (1), pp. 142–143.
70 Bielińska 1954, p. 56.

Bibliography

Archival sources

Archiwum Akt Nowych w Warszawie: *Archiwum Akt Nowych w Warszawie*, sig. 73.
Archiwum Państwowe w Bydgoszczy: *Archiwum Państwowe w Poznaniu Oddział w Bydgoszczy*, sig. 67, 87.
Archiwum Państwowe w Kielcach: *Archiwum Państwowe w Kielcach*, sig. 18, 72.
Archiwum Państwowe w Radomiu: *Archiwum Państwowe w Radomiu*, sig. 5, 25, 34.
Centralnij deržavnij istoričnij arhiv Ukraïni m. L'viv [Централний Державний Іцторичний Архів України м. Львів]: *Deržavnij arhiv u L'vovi* [*Державний архів у Львові*], sig. op.1, 26; op. 1, 33.
Lietuvos Centrinis Valstybės Archyvas Vilnius: *Archiwum Państwowe w Wilnie. Ministerstwo Wyznań Religijnych i Oświecenia Publicznego RP*, sig. 55, 102.

Printed sources

Archiwum Akt Dawnych w Warszawie w latach 1918–1926, in: *Archeion.* 1927/2, pp. 151–166.
Łopaciński, Wincenty: *Dział Urzędowy. Sprawozdanie z działalności archiwów państwowych. Rok 1928*, in: *Archeion.* 1930/6–7, pp. 11–69.
Przepisy o przechowywaniu akt w Ministerstwie Skarbu, in: *Dziennik Urzędowy Ministerstwa Skarbu.* 1932/22/341, pp. 299–305.
Przepisy o przechowywaniu akt w urzędach administracji rządowej, in: *Monitor Polski.* 1932/2/3, pp. 1–2.
Rybarski, Antoni: *Sprawozdanie z działalności archiwów państwowych. Lata 1933 i 1934: na podstawie materiałów dostarczonych przez poszczególne archiwa państwowe*, in: *Archeion.* 1935/13, pp. 187–265.
Rybarski Antoni: *Sprawozdanie z działalności archiwów państwowych. Rok 1935: na podstawie materiałów dostarczonych przez poszczególne archiwa państwowe*, in: *Archeion.* 1936/14, pp. 101–170.
Rybarski Antoni: *Sprawozdanie z działalności archiwów państwowych. Rok 1936: na podstawie materiałów dostarczonych przez poszczególne archiwa państwowe*, in: *Archeion.* 1937–1938/15, pp. 154–208.
Rybarski Antoni: *Sprawozdanie z działalności archiwów państwowych. Rok 1937: na podstawie materiałów dostarczonych przez poszczególne archiwa państwowe*, in: *Archeion.* 1938–1939/16, pp. 155–216. (1)
Rybarski Antoni: *Sprawozdanie z działalności Wydziału Archiwów Państwowych w roku 1937*, in: *Archeion.* 1938–1939/16, pp. 133–54. (2)
Sprawozdanie z działalności Wydziału Archiwów Państwowych w roku 1936, in: *Archeion.* 1937–1938/15, pp. 141–53.

Literature

Bielińska, Maria: *Pozaarchiwalne brakowanie akt w świetle obowiązujących przepisów*, in: *Archeion*. 1954/22, pp. 48–58.

Chmielewski, Zdzisław: *Polska myśl archiwalna w XIX i XX wieku*. 1994.

Dąbrowski, Adam Grzegorz: *Wartościowanie i selekcja akt w Ministerstwie Spraw Wewnętrznych i podległych mu urzędach administracji ogólnej oraz Policji Państwowej w świetle przepisów o przechowywaniu akt z lat 1931–1939*, in: Mamczak-Gadkowska, Irena / Stryjkowski, Krzysztof (eds.): *Dokumentacja masowa. Z problematyki kształtowania zasobu archiwalnego*. 2012, pp. 209–242.

Degen, Robert: *Garść uwag na temat selekcji w Polsce*, in: Chorążyczewski, Waldemar / Rosa, Agnieszka (eds.): *Archiwistyka na uniwersytetach, archiwistyka w archiwach*. 2009, pp. 133–143. (1)

Degen, Robert: *Myśl archiwalna Ryszarda Mienickiego*, in: Chorążyczewski, Waldemar / Degen, Robert (eds.): *Ryszard Mienicki (1886–1956): archiwista i historyk*. 2009, pp. 67–88. (2)

Degen, Robert: *Urzędnicy, selekcja i brakowanie dokumentacji w Polsce w XX wieku*, in: Górak, Artur / Latawiec, Krzysztof / Magier, Dariusz (eds.): *Dzieje biurokracji na ziemiach polskich*. 2010/3/2, pp. 545–555.

Falkowski, Piotr: *Brakowanie akt w okresie międzywojennym w Archiwum Państwowym w Poznaniu Oddział w Bydgoszczy*, in: Czyż, Piotr A. / Magier, Dariusz (eds.): *Oblicza archiwów i współczesne wyzwania archiwistyki: studia archiwistyczne*. 2019, pp. 105–125.

Górak, Artur / Magier, Dariusz: *Selekcja archiwalna jako konstruowanie zasobu źródeł historycznych*, in: *Archiwa - Kancelarie - Zbiory*. 2011/2 (4), pp. 131–143.

Handelsman, Marceli: *Metoda poszukiwań archiwalnych*, in: *Archeion*. 1927/2, pp. 31–48.

Holtzinger, Georg: *Handbuch der Registratur und Archivwissenschaft, Leitfaden für das Registratur- und Archivwesen bei den Reichs, Staats, Hof-Kirchen-, Schul-, und Gemeindebehörden, den Rechtsanwälten u.s.w. sowie bei den Staatsarchiven*. 1908.

Kaleński, Gustaw: *Brakowanie akt*. 1934.

Kaleński, Gustaw: *Record Selection*, in: *The American Archivist*. 1976/39/1, pp. 25–43.

Konarski, Kazimierz: *Archiwalia Powstania Styczniowego w Archiwum Akt Dawnych*, in: *Przegląd Historyczny*. 1937–1938/34/2, pp. 347–358.

Konarski, Kazimierz: *Archiwum Akt Dawnych w Warszawie*, in: *Straty archiwów i bibliotek warszawskich w zakresie rękopiśmiennych źródeł kultury*. 1956/2, pp. 71–209. (1)

Konarski, Kazimierz: *Archiwum Akt Dawnych w Warszawie. Jego dzieje, zawartość i zagłada*, in: *Archeion*. 1956/25, pp. 282–308. (2)

Konarski, Kazimierz: *Nowożytna archiwistyka polska i jej zadania*. 1929.

Konarski, Kazimierz: *Z zagadnień nowożytnej archiwistyki polskiej*, in: *Archeion*. 1927/1, pp. 106–124.

Kwiatkowska, Wiesława: *Co mogą, a co powinny wiedzieć o naszych czasach przyszłe pokolenia? Kulturowe aspekty selekcji dokumentacji*, in: *Archeion*. 2011/112, pp. 191–204.

Löher, Franz von: *Archivlehre. Grundzüge der Geschichte, Aufgaben und Einrichtung unserer Archive*. 1890.

Mamczak-Gadkowska, Irena: *Archiwa państwowe w II Rzeczypospolitej*. 2006.

Moraczewski, Adam: *Sprawa przekazywania akt administracji rządowej do archiwów państwowych w świetle obowiązujących przepisów*, in: *Archeion*. 1937–1938/15, pp. 35–48.

Muller, Samuel / Feith, Johan Adriaan / Fruin, Robert: *Anleitung zum Ordnen und Beschreiben von Archiven*. 1905.

Muller, Samuel / Feith, Johan Adriaan / Fruin, Robert: *Handleiding voor het ordenen en beschrijven van archieven*. 1898.

Muller, Samuel / Feith, Johan Adriaan / Fruin, Robert: *Manuel pour le classement et la description des archives*. 1910.

Pawłowski, Bronisław: *Nieco o brakowaniu akt*, in: *Archeion*. 1928/3, pp. 23–29.

Robótka, Halina: *Kancelaria urzędów administracji państwowej II Rzeczypospolitej. Procesy aktotwórcze*. 1993.

Roman, Wanda Krystyna: *Wkład powszechnych zjazdów historyków i archiwistów polskich do dorobku archiwistyki*. 2021.

Robyns, Marcus C.: *Using Functional Analysis in Archival Appraisal. A Practical and Effective Alternative to Traditional Appraisal Methodologies*. 2014.

Ryszewski, Bohdan: *Archiwistyka: przedmiot, zakres, podział (studia nad problemem)*. 1972.

Smoczyński, Marcin: *Walczmy o usprawnienie administracji! Komisje usprawnienia administracji publicznej i ich rola w racjonalizacji polskiej biurowości do roku 1956*. 2020 (Doctoral dissertation, Biblioteka Uniwersytecka w Toruniu: Oddział Zbiorów Specjalnych, sig. Dr 3927).

Stosyk, Stefan: *Przepisy o przechowywaniu akt w urzędach administracji publicznej (komentarz)*. 1936.

Tarakanowska, Maria: *Problem brakowania akt w Polsce w świetle przepisów i literatury archiwalnej w latach 1918–1965*, in: *Archeion*. 1967/46, pp. 43–55.

Marcin Smoczyński

Polnische und deutsche Büroreformen in der Zwischenkriegszeit[1]

Abstract
Polish and German Office Reforms in the Interwar Period
One feature shared by Polish and German administration is their rich history of reforms. Both administrative apparatuses were involved in office reorganisation during the mid-interwar period. This chapter presents the history, assumptions, instigators and effects of rationalisation aimed at improving the handling of documentation in public offices. The research clearly demonstrates that solutions adopted in Germany were fully and consciously modelled in Poland.
Keywords: office reform; office reform in Poland; office reform in Germany; documentation management

Einleitung

Die uns umgebende Wirklichkeit interpretieren wir durch Kontexte. Erst ein breiterer, über den engen Rahmen der oberflächlichen Erkenntnis hinausgehender Horizont erlaubt es uns, die Umgebung und die darin verlaufenden Prozesse richtig zu verstehen. Ein Apfel ist ja nicht nur eine Frucht, sondern auch ein reichhaltiges Symbol, das seine Bedeutung erst in bestimmten Kontexten entfaltet. Nur auf Evas Hand bedeutet der Apfel die verbotene Erkenntnis, im Hesperidengarten verweist er demgegenüber auf die göttliche Unsterblichkeit und über Newtons Kopf auf die Gravitation. In einem bestimmten Kontext werden auch historische Quellen, darunter archivalische Informationsquellen interpretiert. Informationen zum Archivbildner, zu seiner Geschichte und den Faktoren, die die von ihm erstellten Dokumente und den speziellen Charakter

Dr. Marcin Smoczyński, Nikolaus-Kopernikus-Universität Toruń, ORCID: https://orcid.org/0000-0002-4111-0201.

1 Im vorliegenden Beitrag wurden Materialien benutzt, die dank dem von Seiner Magnifizenz, dem Rektor der Nikolaus-Kopernikus-Universität in Toruń, Prof. Dr. Andrzej Tretyn gestifteten Stipendium der Polnischen Historischen Mission an der Universität Würzburg gesammelt wurden.

der infolge der Amtstätigkeit angewachsenen Akten geprägt haben, spielen nämlich für die Quellenkritik eine Schlüsselrolle. Nichts beeinflusste im 20. Jahrhundert die polnischen und deutschen Archivalien öffentlicher Provenienz so stark wie die Büroreformen, die in beiden Ländern in den zwanziger Jahren durchgeführt wurden. Die damals entworfenen und in Kraft gesetzten Lösungen veränderten irreversibel die Weise, wie in öffentlichen Verwaltungsämtern Dokumente erstellt, benutzt und aufbewahrt wurden.

Das übergeordnete Ziel des vorliegenden Beitrags ist, zwei große Reformen des Bürowesens, die fast gleichzeitig in den benachbarten Ländern Deutschland und Polen implementiert wurden, zu besprechen und zu vergleichen. Das auf diese Weise formulierte übergeordnete Ziel muss von Nebenzielen begleitet werden. Dazu gehören das Kennenlernen der wichtigsten Reformarchitekten, die Bestimmung der in beiden Ländern in Kraft gesetzten Lösungen und die Beschreibung der Effekte der Rationalisierungs- und Organisationsarbeiten.

Die oben skizzierten Ziele wurden grundsätzlich mit zwei unkomplizierten Forschungsmethoden erreicht. Die erste beruhte auf der Kritik der diesbezüglichen Schriften – der Analyse von Texten, rechtlichen Richtlinien und der Forschungsliteratur. Als zweite Methode wurde hier die vergleichende Analyse verwendet, die es erlaubt, Ähnlichkeiten und Unterschiede zwischen polnischen und deutschen Büroreformen in den zwanziger Jahren des 20. Jahrhunderts zu erfassen.

Büroreformen

Ein wesentliches Merkmal der öffentlichen preußischen Verwaltung ist seit dem 18. Jahrhundert ihre schnelle Anpassung an die sich im Laufe der Jahre verändernde politische Situation des Staates. Die Identität und darüber hinaus die Stabilität des deutschen Staatswesens stützten sich in großem Maße auf die Verwaltung und ihr organisatorisches Prinzip des öffentlichen Rechts. Sogar in Krisenmomenten, als politische Regimes völlig zusammenbrachen, was 1918 und – abermals – 1945 passierte, hörte die öffentliche Verwaltung nicht auf, die Aufgaben zu erfüllen, die ihr auferlegt wurden.

Der deutsche Verwaltungsapparat hat eine reichhaltige Reformgeschichte. Als Beispiele dafür kann man die Reorganisation und partielle Demokratisierung der Stadtverwaltung nach der Niederlage Preußens im Jahre 1806, regionale Umwandlungen, die mit dem deutschen Einigungsprozess im 19. Jahrhundert verbunden waren, und die flexible Anpassung an die neuen politischen Regimes im 20. Jahrhundert nennen. Die Prozesse wurden meistens von oben herab von

Beamten höchsten Ranges initiiert.[2] Die deutsche Verwaltungsgeschichte verzeichnet viele geplante und organisierte Bestrebungen, die Effizienz der Arbeit zu erhöhen, und ein Teil davon fand im Rahmen von Kommissionen statt, die zur Optimierung der Verwaltung berufen wurden, die also spezielle kollegiale Körperschaften darstellten, die mit der Aufgabe betraut wurden, Reformen zu entwerfen, die die Rationalisierung der Tätigkeit des Verwaltungsapparates zum Ziel hatten.

Die Ausformung der preußischen Sachakten-Kanzlei begann relativ früh, zu Beginn des 17. Jahrhunderts. 1652 existierten bereits etliche Regelungen, die die Art und Weise, wie man Kanzleitätigkeiten erledigte, bestimmten. Der Prinzipienbestand, nach dem das Bürowesen funktionierte, war im 18. Jahrhundert schon gefestigt und wurde allgemein angewendet, obwohl man weiterhin Modifikationen einführte, die die Organisation der Kanzlei geringfügig modernisierten.[3] Nicht überall wurden jedoch vollkommen einheitliche Lösungen angewendet.[4] Die Folge der drei Teilungen Polens war, dass das für das preußische Bürowesen charakteristische Modell auch in den für die Verwaltung der ehemaligen polnischen Gebiete zuständigen Ämtern eingeführt wurde.[5]

Das Modell der preußischen Sachakten-Kanzlei zeichnete sich grundsätzlich durch Kompliziertheit aus, die von solchen Faktoren beeinflusst war wie der auf dem Aktenplan basierenden Funktionsweise sowie dem detaillierten Registrierungssystem im Geschäftstagebuch und in solchen Hilfsdokumenten wie Index, Rotulus und Verweiszettel, die es *de facto* ermöglichten, an die gesuchte Akte und die darin enthaltenen Informationen zu gelangen, obwohl diese Aufgabe weiterhin sehr schwierig war.[6] Der interne Umlauf der Schriftstücke in den Ämtern war verzweigt, die Aktenbildung geriet in zahlreichen, sich oft wiederholenden Instanzen ins Stocken und der Usus des Fadenheftens der Akten machte die Situation noch komplizierter.[7] Infolge der sich wandelnden Erwartungen der

2 Seibel 1966, S. 74.

3 Bockhorst 2004, S. 269; Zu erwähnen sind auch viele spätere Initiativen, die die Bearbeitung und Verbreitung von den das Bürowesen regulierenden Vorschriften betreffen, wie z.B. die Anweisungen für Magistrate von 1835, die den Umfang der Beamtenkontrolle in geringem Maße einschränkten. In den folgenden Jahren bereitete auch das Justizressort neue Regelungen für das gesamte Gerichtswesen vor und 1894 legte das Bahnwesen eine umfangreiche und neue Anleitung in Bezug auf die Ausübung von amtlichen Tätigkeiten vor. Damals wurde der Umfang der Registrierung im Tagebuch in großem Maße beschränkt. Zu den erwähnungswürdigen Initiativen gehörte auch z.B. der vom Vorstand der Dresdener Städte-Ausstellung im Jahre 1903 ausgeschriebene Wettbewerb, dessen Teilnehmer zahlreiche und interessante, auf das Bürowesen der Städte bezogene Arbeiten verfassten; vgl. Haussmann 1926, S. 13.

4 Brenneke 1953, S. 79.

5 Radtke 1984, S. 165–166.

6 Meisner 1935, S. 160–164.

7 Radtke 1984, S. 192.

Gesellschaft, des Ausbaus der Verwaltung, der durch verschiedene Faktoren wie bewaffnete Konflikte oder den Eingriff des Staates in immer zahlreichere Lebensbereiche der Bürger bedingt war, und schließlich des Phänomens der steigenden Massenhaftigkeit der Dokumentation, erkannte man das Bedürfnis, die Tätigkeit der Kanzlei bzw. Registratur in den Ämtern der staatlichen Verwaltung zu modernisieren.

Die ersten Initiativen zur Reform des preußischen Bürowesens wurden schon gegen Ende des 19. Jahrhunderts ergriffen, vor allem in den staatlichen Unternehmen, unter anderem in der Preußischen Eisenbahnverwaltung, wo seit 1885 etliche Veränderungen eingeführt wurden, die die Arbeit der Kanzlei im Bereich der Registrierung der ein- und ausgehenden Dokumente vereinfachten. Diese Maßnahmen hatten Lösungen, die im Privatsektor angewendet wurden, zum Vorbild.[8] Die Fortsetzung dieser Bestrebungen stellten auch die (anfangs nicht sehr effektiven) Maßnahmen der Regierung dar, die 1897 eingeführt wurden. Im Jahr 1909 wurde die Immediatkommission zur Vorbereitung der Verwaltungsreform ins Leben gerufen. Von ihren sechs Unterkommissionen vollendete allerdings nur eine ihre Arbeit. Es war der Ausschuß für die Vereinfachung des Geschäftsbetriebes, der sich laut seinem Programm mit dem Bürowesen in der öffentlichen Verwaltung beschäftigen sollte. Einen dauerhaften Effekt der Tätigkeit des Ausschusses stellte die Bearbeitung der *Grundzüge für eine (vereinfachte) Geschäftsführung der Regierungen* dar, die mit dem Erlass vom 17. Juni 1910 ratifiziert wurden. Die vorgeschlagenen Lösungen konzentrierten sich auf die Vereinfachung und Beschleunigung des Verwaltungsverfahrens und die Beschränkung der Verwendung des Tagebuches auf das notwendige Minimum, die Dezentralisierung der Aufbewahrung der Tagesdokumentation und die Mechanisierung der Arbeit. Obwohl die Aktivitäten des Kollegiums aus den Jahren 1909–1910 keinen Wendepunkt im deutschen Bürowesen mit sich brachten und ihr realer Einfluss auf praktische Tätigkeiten gering war, setzten sie unzweifelhaft einen Diskurs über eine Veränderung des *status quo* in Gang und bestimmten die Richtung der späteren Reorganisationsarbeiten.[9]

Die nächsten Rationalisierungsansätze fielen auf den Beginn des Jahres 1917 und waren mit der Berufung eines Kommissars verbunden, dem die Aufgabe oblag, Verwaltungsreformen zu entwerfen. Für diese Stelle wurde Bill Drews, der Unterstaatssekretär (später Ressortchef) im Innenministerium bestimmt, der die Denkschrift *Grundzüge einer Verwaltungsreform* verfasste.[10] In der 200 Seiten umfassenden Schrift konzentrierte sich Drews auf die Vorbereitung eines Vorschlags der Verwaltungsreform, insbesondere der Veränderungen in der Struktur

8 Brachmann 1959, S. 6.
9 Enders 1962, S. 48–51; Miller 2003, S. 52–53; Schäfer 1982, S. 94.
10 Drews 1918.

der Zentralbehörden, obwohl er dort auch die Bürotechnik thematisierte.[11] Zu den wichtigsten Postulaten des Kommissars gehörten die Dezentralisierung der Kanzlei und die Abschaffung der Registrierung der eingehenden Schriftstücke im Tagebuch. Drews konstatierte außerdem, dass die Ausweitung der Befugnisse der Beamten ihre Arbeitshaltung positiv beeinflussen werde.[12] Die Denkschrift rief starke Kontroversen hervor und enthielt grundsätzlich keine Vorschläge alternativer Lösungen, sie stellte aber eine weitere Stimme in der Diskussion über die Büroreform in Deutschland dar.[13] Auf die nächste musste man nicht lange warten, denn schon im Frühling 1922 wurde Arnold Brecht (Reichsministerium des Innern) zum Spezialkommissar für Vereinfachungsfragen ernannt. Anhand der von den Ministerien (in denen auch Ressortkommissare berufen wurden) zugesandten Materialien bereitete er eine Studie über die angewandten praktischen Lösungen und erste Vorschläge für die Modernisierung vor. Die Abhandlung war in den Jahren 1924–1925 Gegenstand von weiteren Diskussionen (auch auf der Ministerialebene) und ihre endgültige Fassung wurde erst im Mai 1926 erstellt.[14] Das Projekt bildete die Grundlage für die spätere Büroreform. Zu den Leitthesen der geplanten Reorganisierungen gehörten: Ökonomisierung der Arbeit, Verminderung der Verwaltungskosten, höchstmögliche Arbeitseffizienz, Beschränkung der Innenkontrolle sowie Mechanisierung und Automatisierung der Kanzlei- und Bürotätigkeiten in Einklang mit den Verordnungsprinzipien, die von Frederic Winslow Taylor erarbeitet wurden.[15]

1926 wurde die für die Kanzleien bestimmte Anleitung *Gemeinsame Geschäftsordnung der Reichministerien* veröffentlicht, die ab 1. Januar 1927 gelten sollte.[16] Die Abhandlung setzte den Standard für die Erledigung und Dokumentierung von Amtsangelegenheiten in den Ministerien auf Reichsebene. Es wurden zwei Organisationsvorschläge für das neukonzipierte deutsche Bürowesen vorgelegt: Der erste, das heißt die vereinfachte Registratur (die in der Praxis auch als Expedientenregistratur oder Fachaktei bezeichnet wurde), stellte gewissermaßen eine Übergangsphase dar, der zweite führte das registraturlose Arbeiten ein. Zu den grundlegenden Prinzipien des ersten Modells gehörten: die Abschaffung der Überwachung und Eintragung von einzelnen Etappen des in-

11 Haussmann 1926, S. 14–15.

12 Menne-Haritz 1999, S. 164–167.

13 Miller 2003, S. 55.

14 Ibid., S. 56–58.

15 Haussmann 1926, S. 18; Erwähnenswert ist, dass die auf der Basis von amerikanischen Arbeiten entwickelte Theorie der Arbeitsorganisation (worin auch Büroarbeit inbegriffen war) seit Anfang der Zwischenkriegszeit in Polen immer populärer wurde. Man übersetzte und druckte die Arbeiten von Frederic Winslow Taylor, die Autoren veröffentlichten auch eigene Studien, z. B. Krzymuski 1927; Punicki 1929.

16 Bundesarchiv Koblenz (in Folgenden: BArch): *Gemeinsame Geschäftsordnung der Reichsministerien*, Sign. R 29/50433, S. 30–85.

neren Dokumentenganges (es sollten ausschließlich Abweichungen vom festgelegten, normalen Lauf der Eingänge vermerkt werden), die Eintragung bestimmter Angelegenheiten (auch in Form von Sammeleinträgen) in eine spezielle alphabetische Kartei unter Benutzung der sogenannten Einsenderkarten und die Registrierung der Schriftstücke nach der sachlichen Einteilung der Angelegenheiten in einem Aktenplan, das auf der Dewey-Dezimalklassifkation basierte.[17] Das Geschäftszeichen bestand aus der Angabe der Organisationseinheit, dem Kennzeichen aus dem Aktenplan und dem Datum des ersten Eingangs in einer bestimmten Angelegenheit (das letzte Element galt manchmal als überflüssig). Auf Ministerialebene legte man individuelle Aktenpläne mit vierstufiger Dezimalklassifikation für jedes Referat an, in kleineren Ämtern verwendete man ein dreistufiges System und ein einheitliches Sachregister für die ganze Organisationseinheit. Es stellte sich heraus, dass die Bearbeitung eines Aktenplans auf geeignetem Niveau zu den schwierigsten Herausforderungen bei der Einführung der Reform gehörte. Bereits in den Verordnungen, mit denen die neue Organisation eingeführt wurde, unterstrich man, dass „[d]ie Güte dieses Verzeichnisses […] Voraussetzung sowohl für einen guten Bürobetrieb wie für den sachlichen Nutzen der Akten" sei.[18] In den Schriften, die die Reform thematisierten, empfahl man, die Aktenpläne mit der Einteilung von Tätigkeiten in einem Amt zu verbinden.[19] Die Registrierung des Schriftsguts fiel den Registraturen der einzelnen Referate zu, in denen durchschnittlich bis zu drei Registratoren beschäftigt wurden. Die eingehenden Schreiben wurden an der Eingangsstelle grob eingeteilt. Die Registratoren versahen die Dokumente mit dem Geschäftszeichen und überwiesen die Angelegenheiten an einzelne Referenten. Das zweite Organisationsmodell – die registraturlose Arbeit – bildete einen weiteren Schritt zur Vereinfachung der Büroarbeit, löste die Registraturen der einzelnen Referate ganz auf und wies alle Tätigkeiten, die mit der Kennzeichnung der Schriftstücke verbunden waren, den Referenten zu.[20]

Die Reform brachte eine Wende im Bereich der Aufbewahrung der Dokumente, die seitdem völlig dezentralisiert wurde. In Verbindung mit der Vereinfachung des Entscheidungsprozesses beschleunigte das wesentlich den Schriftenlauf. Die Verwaltung des Schriftguts oblag von nun an den Referenten, und die Akten wurden in den immer populärer werdenden mechanischen Ordnern aufbewahrt, das heißt in Ordnern, die über eine mechanische Vorrichtung für das Heften und Anordnen der Schriftstücke verfügte. Man benutzte auch Aktenhefter (Mappen) und Halbhefter (Schutzumschläge). Man verzichtete also auf

17 Für ein Anwendungsbeispiel von 1940 vgl. Hochedlinger 2009, S. 109.

18 BArch: *Gemeinsame Geschäftsordnung der Reichsministerien*, Sign. R 29/50433, S. 71.

19 Haussmann 1926, S. 29.

20 Ibid.

das kraft- und mittelaufreibende Fadenheften der Dokumente, das hatte allerdings zur Folge, dass archivalische Schriftstücke ungeordnet, in schlechterem technischen Zustand und mit Metallelementen, die man entfernen musste, in die Staatsarchive gelangten.[21]

Im Laufe der Reorganisation wurde die Bedeutung der Mechanisierung der Arbeit unterstrichen, die man als automatische und geordnete Ausübung von Tätigkeiten verstand. Es wurde empfohlen, die Arbeit in Einklang mit einem Tagesplan zu verrichten (zum Beispiel im Bereich des internen Umlaufs der Akten), bei regelmäßig wiederkehrenden Arbeiten von Stempeln und Formularen ausgiebig Gebrauch zu machen sowie Karteien und Tabellen zu benutzen.[22]

Die Reform wurde von einer breiten Informationsaktion begleitet, die in der Tages- und Fachliteratur ausgetragen wurde. Es wurden viele Arbeiten veröffentlicht, deren Gegenstand die neuen Grundsätze und ihre praktische Realisierung bildeten. Diese Schriften hatten einen Bildungswert, stellten Schulungsmaterial dar und wurden im Beamtenmilieu kolportiert.[23] Das Ende der zwanziger Jahre war eine Zeit, in der die reorganisatorischen Aktivitäten fortgesetzt wurden und Kanzleinormative für bestimmte Fachgruppen wie Eisenbahn, Polizei, Post, Justiz und Kommunalverwaltung erarbeitet wurden.[24] Die neuen Lösungen wurden nicht überall ohne Verzögerung eingeführt. Laut Informationen von 1929 gab es reformierte Kanzleien nur in 20 % der öffentlichen Ämter, in den meisten Fällen wurde die Implementierung der neuen Lösungen auf das zweite Jahrzehnt der Zwischenkriegszeit verschoben.[25]

Reform des polnischen Bürowesens

Die polnische öffentliche Verwaltung entwickelte sich anders, als es in den meisten westeuropäischen Ländern der Fall war. Die von den Teilungsmächten Österreich, Russland und vor allem Preußen geführte Politik verhinderte im 19. Jahrhundert den Aufbau einer Verwaltungskultur und -tradition und die Entstehung einer qualifizierten und sozial etablierten, genuin polnischen Beamtenschicht. Der Staatsapparat, der seit 1919 unter außergewöhnlichen Nach-

21 Hochedlinger 2009, S. 111.

22 Haussmann 1926, S. 34.

23 U.a. die oben angeführte und ins Polnische übersetzte Arbeit des Regierungspräsidenten Hermann Haussmann sowie: Brecht 1927; Steeg 1927; Gaertner 1931; Kaisenberg 1932; *Wirtschaftliche Arbeit in der öffentlichen Verwaltung: ein Beitrag zur Verwaltungs- und Büroreform* 1929; *Büroreformen in einzelnen Verwaltungen* 1927.

24 Hochedlinger 2009, S. 108.

25 Stosyk 1929, S. 2; Die Reform verzeichnete man auch in Kirchenkanzleien auf Lokalebene, u.a. 1928 in Breslau (Wrocław). Dem Artikel wurde der Gesamtregistraturplan beigefügt. Vgl. Plonka 1928, S. 81–84.

kriegsumständen aufgebaut wurde, bedurfte nahezu von Anfang an rationalisierender Maßnahmen. Die Organisatoren und Rationalisatoren der Verwaltung (darunter des Bürowesens) in der Zweiten Polnischen Republik standen vor einer besonders schwierigen Herausforderung.

Zu den wichtigsten Merkmalen des polnischen Bürowesens auf allen Verwaltungsebenen sollte man das Funktionieren der Kanzleien in Anlehnung an das Tagebuchsystem, die Unterscheidung von Hauptkanzleien, die zentrale Tätigkeiten erfüllten, und der Bearbeitung und Ablage bei den einzelnen Organisationseinheiten zählen. Die Benutzung von zahlreichen und komplizierten Hilfsmitteln für die Datenerfassung wie Tagebücher mit übermäßiger (und in der Praxis zum Teil überflüssiger) Spaltenanzahl, die Führung von zahlreichen Verzeichnissen, ein komplizierter Dokumentenlauf sowie die etliche Phasen umfassende Registrierung von Schriftstücken und Angelegenheiten waren allgemein üblich. Es fehlten auch qualifizierte, auf die Arbeit gut vorbereitete Beamte. Das starke Bedürfnis nach Vereinheitlichung der Vorschriften und Behebung älterer, von den Besatzern geerbter Lösungen konnte in den ersten Monaten nach der Erlangung der Unabhängigkeit durch Polen nicht realisiert werden. Kanzleien, die in zentralisierter, auf dem Geschäftstagebuch basierender Weise funktionierten, waren von einer rationalen und modernen Organisation der Büroarbeit weit entfernt.[26]

Die Notwendigkeit, die Kanzleitätigkeiten zu modernisieren, ihre Effizienz zu optimieren und an die Bedürfnisse der Verwaltung eines Staates anzupassen, der nach der Teilungszeit und den Kriegsverlusten im Wiederaufbau begriffen war, wurde von den Entscheidungsträgern, im Prinzip gleich nachdem Polen die Unabhängigkeit wiedererlangt hatte, wahrgenommen. Die Reform der polnischen Verwaltung der Zwischenkriegszeit, darunter auch des Bürowesens, wurde in großem Maße den speziell zu diesem Zweck berufenen, kollegialen Körperschaften anvertraut, die als Ausschüsse für Optimierung der Verwaltung bezeichnet wurden.[27] Aus verschiedenen Gründen brachten diese Aktivitäten bis

26 Robótka 1993, S. 19–25.

27 Bereits 1917 bildete man den Beamtenausschuss des Polnischen Staates (*Komisja Urzędnicza Państwa Polskiego*). In der Zwischenkriegszeit wirkten nacheinander: Interministerieller Qualifikationsausschuss (*Międzyministerialna Komisja Kwalifikacyjna*), Ausschuss für Staatliche Sparmaßnahmen betreffende Angelegenheiten (*Komisja dla Spraw Oszczędności Państwowych*), Ausschuss für Verwaltungsreform (*Komisja dla Reformy Administracji*) von 1923, Außergewöhnlicher Kommissar für Sparmaßnahmen (*Nadzwyczajny Komisarz Oszczędnościowy*; gleichzeitig Vorsitzender im Kollegium des Staatlichen Rates für Sparmaßnahmen (*Państwowa Rada Oszczędnościowa*)), Ausschuss für Verwaltungsreform (*Komisja dla Reformy Administracji*) von 1926, Ausschuss für Reorganisierung des Bürowesens (*Komisja dla Reorganizacji Biurowości*), Ausschuss für Reorganisierung der Verwaltung (*Komisja dla Reorganizacji Administracji*) und Ausschuss für Optimierung der Öffentlichen Verwaltung (*Komisja dla Usprawnienia Administracji Publicznej*); Smoczyński 2019, S. 143–158.

Ende der zwanziger Jahre keine brauchbaren Lösungen hervor. Am 27. November 1928 wurde vom Ministerrat der Ausschuss für Optimierung der Öffentlichen Verwaltung (*Komisja dla Usprawnienia Administracji Publicznej*) berufen. Bereits in der ersten offiziellen Bekanntmachung legte man seine allgemeinen Aufgaben fest. Dazu gehörte der Entwurf eines Optimierungsplans für die Verwaltung im Bereich der Organisation, der Tätigkeiten, der Arbeitsmethoden und der Ausbildung des Beamtenpersonals.[28] Das Gremium nahm die Arbeit mit Energie und großem Elan auf. Man griff auf das Potenzial einheimischer Wissenschaftler, Theoretiker und Praktiker zurück und berief viele (über hundert) Sachverständige.[29] Es wurden über fünftausend Werke, darunter amerikanische, belgische, französische und deutsche Arbeiten, zu Rate gezogen.[30] Man stützte sich auch auf frühere polnische und ausländische Erfahrungen. Man machte sich auch mit Materialien vertraut, die in dem Zeitraum von zehn Jahren von den seit 1918 bestehenden, zu dem Zweck der Verwaltungsoptimierung eingesetzten Kollegien gesammelt und bearbeitet worden waren. Man entsandte ferner Mitglieder verschiedener Sektionen, um sich vor Ort über die Ergebnisse ausländischer Reformen zu informieren.[31] Man reiste in die Tschechoslowakei (um die Rechnungs- und Kassenprozedur, die Verwaltung von Sachmitteln und die Tätigkeit der Regierungskommission für Verwaltungsreform und des Nationalen Komitees für Vereinfachung der Öffentlichen Verwaltung kennenzulernen, die dort zur gleichen Zeit aktiv waren), nach Großbritannien (wo man sich besonders für das System der kommunalen Selbstverwaltung interessierte), nach Deutschland (mit dem Ziel, Kontakte zu Institutionen aufzunehmen, die an der Frage der Verwaltungsoptimierung und Untersuchung des Bürowesens arbeiteten), nach Frankreich, Belgien und Holland (um die in den Kanzleien implementierten Lösungen zu beobachten). Vertreter der Kommission nahmen auch an Sitzungen des Internationalen Instituts für Verwaltungswissenschaften in Madrid im Jahre 1930 und drei Jahre später in Wien teil.[32]

Im Rahmen des Ausschusses für Optimierung der Öffentlichen Verwaltung wurden einige Sektionen gebildet, darunter eine Sektion für die mit dem Arbeitssystem in den Ämtern verbundenen Angelegenheiten. Sie hatte drei übergeordnete Ziele: die Ausarbeitung von weitgefassten Prinzipien der Amtsausübung, die Erstellung eines neuen Systems für die Verrichtung von Kanzleitä-

28 *Z Prezydjum Rady Ministrów* 1928, S. 2.

29 *Z Komisji dla Usprawnienia Administracji Publicznej* 1930/3, S. 13.

30 Robótka 1993, S. 37.

31 Das geht u.a. aus einem Bericht von 1928 hervor, der die Leistungen aller früheren Kommissionen für Optimierung der Verwaltung und des Außergewöhnlichen Kommissars für Sparmaßnahmen erfasste; Archiwum Akt Nowych w Warszawie: *Prezydium Rady Ministrów w Warszawie 1917–1939*, Sign. rkt. 14/3.

32 Hausner 1935, S. 217.

tigkeiten und die Anpassung der Bürogeräte an die neuen Verfahrensweisen.[33] Die Arbeiten, die die Grundsätze für die künftige Büroreform vorbereiten sollten, setzten sofort ein, nachdem sich die personale Zusammensetzung der Abteilung konstituiert hatte.[34] Das Jahr 1929 verstrich mit der Analyse von einheimischen Lösungen und von Ergebnissen der Auslandsreisen. Die Mitglieder des Gremiums besuchten Deutschland, Frankreich, Belgien, Holland, Dänemark und die Tschechoslowakei.[35] Besonders fruchtbar wurde die Reise der Mitglieder der Arbeitsgruppe von Stefan Stosyk (den man für den Hauptautor der Reform hält) und Ewaryst Czarnecki nach Deutschland. In dem nach der Rückkehr verfassten Bericht postulierte Stosyk geradezu die Übernahme der Prinzipien des deutschen Systems als Grundlage für die damals im Entwurf begriffenen polnischen Lösungen.[36]

Nach einer Vorbereitungszeit ging man dazu über, die Grundsätze der Büroreform festzulegen und Regelungen zu erarbeiten, die die Einführung der Neuerungen ermöglichen sollten. Parallel zum Abschluss der Arbeiten an den Rahmenvorschriften veröffentlichte man eine kurze Erklärung des Projekts. Man bezog sich darin auf die Tätigkeit der früheren Kommissionen, die für die Verwaltungsoptimierung seit 1918 eingesetzt worden waren, auf die Budgetsituation des Staates (die Sparmaßnahmen erforderte) und legte die wichtigsten Grundsätze der Reform dar: die Dezentralisierung der Registratur, die Übertragung der meisten Kanzleitätigkeiten an die Referenten, die Beschränkung der Aufgaben des Kanzleipersonals und die Abschaffung übermäßiger formaler Kontrolle.[37] Stosyk nannte – noch bevor das Projekt offiziell zur Realisierung zugelassen worden war – unter den Hauptprinzipien, von denen sich die die neuen Vorschriften erstellende Arbeitsgemeinschaft leiten ließ, die Büroführung in Anlehnung an das Prinzip des gegenseitigen Vertrauens, die Einschränkung der formalen und den Ausbau der tatsächlichen Kontrolle und die klare Bestimmung der Dienstverantwortung für die ausgeübten Tätigkeiten.[38]

Die größte Reform in der Geschichte des polnischen Bürowesens wurde durch eine lediglich 16 Paragraphen umfassende Vorschriftensammlung *Przepisy kancelaryjne dla administracji rządowej* (*Kanzleivorschriften für die Re-*

33 Brzozowski 1929, S. 3.

34 Das konnte nicht eindeutig ermittelt werden. Die Zusammensetzung des Gremiums könnte ganz oder teilweise der Arbeitsgruppe entsprechen, die für die Erarbeitung der Vorschriften von 1931 zuständig war: Ewaryst Czarnecki, W. Karasiński, Bolesław Mikiewicz, Antoni Robaczewski, Tomasz Serafin, Stefan Stosyk, R. Średnicki, J. Zieleniewski; *Z Komisji dla Usprawnienia Administracji Publicznej* 1931/12, S. 20.

35 *Z Komisji dla Usprawnienia Administracji Publicznej* 1929/13, S. 15 und 1929/15, S. 15; *Z Prezydjum Rady Ministrów* 1929, S. 3.

36 Stosyk 1929, S. 1.

37 *Z Komisji dla Usprawnienia Administracji Publicznej* 1931/12, S. 19.

38 Stosyk 1930, S. 9–10.

gierungsverwaltung) eingeleitet, die man zusammen mit dem Beschluss des Ministerrates vom 24. August 1931 veröffentlichte.[39] Die Vorschriften, die auf Initiative des Ausschusses für Optimierung der Öffentlichen Verwaltung ausgearbeitet wurden, veränderten die Organisation der Kanzlei. Die Tätigkeiten der Hauptkanzlei (der man nun die Funktion eines allgemeinen Sekretariats zuwies) wurden auf den Empfang und die Verteilung der Eingänge, Absendung der Post, Aufbewahrung von Akten, die für aktuelle Amtsverfahren nicht notwendig waren, und das Abschreiben von Konzepten beschränkt. Die Aufrechterhaltung des *Status quo* in Bezug auf die Anfertigung von Reinschriften ergab sich einerseits aus dem beschränkten Zugang zu Schreibmaschinen, andererseits aus den aufkommenden Vorwürfen, dass das teurere und besser qualifizierte Referendarpersonal übermäßig mit Tätigkeiten belastet werde, die bislang von schlechter bezahlten Kanzleiangestellten ausgeübt worden seien.[40] Die Veränderung im Bereich der Aufgabenverteilung unter den Referenten war geradezu revolutionär. Man betraute sie mit Bildung, Kennzeichnung, Registrierung und Aufbewahrung von Akten. Es wurde also eine völlige Dezentralisierung der Kanzleitätigkeiten geplant.

Die Reform setzte damit einen Umbruch im Bereich der Registrierung voraus. Statt wie früher alle Schriften zu verbuchen, vermerkte man nunmehr Sachbetreffe. Der Aktenplan wurde zur Grundlage für die Kennzeichnung, Registrierung und Aufbewahrung der Dokumente. In den Rahmenvorschriften wurde der Aktenplan mit Verteilung von sachbezogenen Zuständigkeiten verbunden, die sich aus der Organisationsstruktur einer Abteilung ergaben. Aus dieser Regelung leitet sich die spätere Verbreitung von Aktenplänen her, die auf der Organisationsstruktur basierten, die also nicht konstant waren und bei jeder Veränderung der internen Institutionsorganisation einer Korrektur bedurften.[41] Die Aktenpläne hatten jedoch den Vorteil, dass ihre Bearbeitung einfacher war und auf angemessenes Umredigieren (um eine unkomplizierte Formulierung von Aktenzeichen zu ermöglichen) von existierenden und von den Ämtern allgemein benutzten detaillierten Verteilungen der Zuständigkeiten zurückgeführt werden konnte. Der Vorschlag eines struktur- und sachbezogenen Aktenplans, der mit wenig Aufwand zu erstellen war, konnte eine gute Idee sein, um die Beamten für das für den Erfolg der Reform wesentliche Instrument und die neuen Methoden der Büroarbeit zu gewinnen. Einer der Architekten der Veränderungen, Stefan

39 *Uchwała Rady Ministrów z dnia 24 sierpnia 1931 r. o przepisach kancelaryjnych w administracji publicznej* 1931.

40 Auf solche Vorwürfe wies man in einem der Berichte über die Arbeiten des Ausschusses für Optimierung der Öffentlichen Verwaltung hin. *Z Komisji dla Usprawnienia Administracji Publicznej* 1931/12, S. 20.

41 Manteuffel 1935, S. 13–14; Zur Geschichte von Aktenplänen mit einem auf der Dezimalklassifikation beruhenden Signatursystem vgl. Smoczyński 2020, S. 27–44.

Stosyk, der sich der fragilen Aktualität der auf die Organisationsstruktur bezogenen Aktenpläne bewusst war, sprach sich für Benutzung eines von der internen Organisation einer Einheit getrennten Sachmodells aus, was, wie er unterstrich, nicht unmittelbar nach der Einführung der Vorschriften implementiert werden konnte.[42]

Der interne Dokumentenumlauf sollte ab 1931 vereinfacht und – was die Beobachtung von Regelwidrigkeiten und das Entwerfen von Modifikationen erleichtern sollte – in jeder Organisationseinheit individuell grafisch veranschaulicht werden. Die Rahmenvorschriften enthielten sechs Regelungen für den internen Schriftenumlauf. Großen Wert legte man auf die Schnelligkeit bei der Erledigung der Angelegenheiten (die Zeit sollte genauso wichtig wie die korrekte Erledigung sein), Vermeidung von Stockungen im Geschäftsgang (die Akten sollten in einer bestimmten Abteilung nur einmal bearbeitet werden, und zwar zu festgelegten Tageszeiten, um das an verschiedenen Stellen stattfindende Verfahren zu harmonisieren), die Vereinfachung des Dokumentenumlaufs (es wurde gänzlich auf das interne Quittieren verzichtet) und die Systematisierung des Dokumentenumlaufs (man forderte seitdem, dass die Arbeit in Einklang mit der grafischen Darstellung des Aktenumlaufs in der jeweiligen Institution verrichtet wurde). Nach Erledigung einer Angelegenheit sollten die Akten unverzüglich in den zuständigen Kanzleieinheiten abgelegt werden.

Die Rahmenvorschriften vom August 1931 waren unter mehreren Aspekten revolutionär. Erstens war es nie zuvor gelungen, die Büroarbeit der Ämter auf allen Verwaltungsebenen rechtlich zu vereinheitlichen. Wie bereits erwähnt, wurden Versuche dieser Art zwar unternommen, aber die Pläne waren bislang nicht verwirklicht worden. Erst nach 1931 sollten Kanzleien aller drei Verwaltungsebenen nach denselben Regeln funktionieren. Eine Neuerung stellte auch der Umfang der Registratur dar, die nicht mehr alle Schriftstücke, sondern von nun an ganze Vorgänge Sachen umfasste. Es wurde ferner das Kanzleisystem modifiziert – an die Stelle früherer Geschäftstagebücher sollten Akten- und Sachverzeichnisse treten. Besondere Aufmerksamkeit verdienen das Prinzip der schnellstmöglichen (doch weiterhin korrekten) Erledigung von Angelegenheiten, die Optimierung des internen Dokumentenumlaufs, unter anderem durch grafische Darstellung der Aktenbewegungen, und die Abschaffung der schriftlichen Bestätigung des zwischen den Einheiten einer Institution stattfindenden Dokumentenaustausches.

Die Vorschriften wurden sehr allgemein formuliert und sollten den Bearbeitern von detaillierten, an die Bedürfnisse konkreter Ämter angepassten Richtlinien als Wegweiser dienen. Ohne Zweifel war es ein Versuch, einen gewissen

42 Stosyk 1934, S. 32; Die Diskussion über ein für das Bürowesen günstigeres Modell des Aktenplans wurde auch nach dem Zweiten Weltkrieg fortgesetzt, Ostaszewicz 1948, S. 230.

Kompromiss zwischen vielen für den Prozess der Vorschriftenvorbereitung engagierten Institutionen auszuarbeiten, und – zu einem bestimmten Grad – die radikalen Veränderungen, die dem polnischen Bürowesen bevorstanden, zu mildern und zeitlich zu strecken.[43]

Die Kanzleivorschriften von 1931 entsprachen den Auslandstrends und platzierten Polen ohne Zweifel unter die Länder mit einem modernen Bürosystem, aber die Vorbereitung von theoretischen, rechtlichen Reformgrundlagen bildete nur die erste Etappe. Die zweite, weitaus schwierigere Phase stellte die Einführung von Vorschriften dar, die in der Praxis angewendet werden konnten. Die Implementierung der Vorschriften wurde von speziellen, die neuen Lösungen erläuternden Kommentaren und Beiträgen in der Fachliteratur begleitet.[44]

Die nächste Herausforderung war die Ausarbeitung von detaillierten Richtlinien für Ämter der einzelnen Verwaltungsebenen und ihre Durchsetzung. Letztendlich gelang es, die Reformgrundsätze in den Ämtern der untersten Verwaltungsebene – den Landratsämtern (*starostwa powiatowe*), also in den Einheiten mit relativ geringer „Aktenproduktion“ und einer kleinen Anzahl von Angestellten, was die Schulung des Personals begünstigte – vollständig zu verwirklichen. Die 1931 entworfenen Regelungen konnte man teilweise in Woiwodschaftsämtern einführen (wo jedoch die Absicht, die Tätigkeiten der Kanzleien völlig zu dezentralisieren, misslang). Auf der Zentralebene, in den Ministerien, arbeitete die Verwaltung ohne größere Veränderungen weiter.[45] Die Diskussion über die Rationalisierung der Büroarbeit wurde gegen Ende der Zwischenkriegszeit wiederaufgenommen, alle Aktivitäten in diesem Bereich wurden jedoch durch den Ausbruch des Zweiten Weltkrieges abgebrochen.

Fazit

Obwohl die polnische und die deutsche Verwaltung im 19. und in den ersten Jahrzehnten des 20. Jahrhunderts einen ganz anderen Entwicklungsweg durchschritten, standen sie am Anfang der Zwischenkriegszeit vor ähnlichen Herausforderungen: der Vereinfachung von Strukturen und Verfahrensweisen, der Ökonomisierung der Arbeit und Rationalisierung der Bürotätigkeiten. In beiden Ländern unternahm man zahlreiche Versuche, die jedoch erst 1926/1927 in Deutschland und 1931 in Polen gelangen.

Die vergleichende Analyse der in beiden Ländern angewandten Neuerungen zeigt viele Ähnlichkeiten. Die Reformgrundsätze und konkreten Lösungen waren

43 Degen 2018, S. 69–76.
44 Stosyk 1934.
45 Robótka 1993, S. 180–185.

gleich: die Delegierung der Verantwortung für das anwachsende Schriftgut und seiner Verwaltung an die Referenten, die Abschaffung des Quittierens des internen Schriftenumlaufs, die auf meistens struktur- und sachbezogenen Aktenplänen beruhende Registratur (obwohl in den beiden Ländern auch die homogene Variante auftrat), die Ordnung der Akten nach Dewey-Dezimalklassifikation, das Prinzip der schnellen, aber weiterhin korrekten Erledigung einer Angelegenheit und der Rahmencharakter der Vorschriften an sich (mit dem ausdrücklichen Vorbehalt, dass die einzelnen Verwaltungsabteilungen sie nach eigenen Bedürfnissen ergänzen sollten) – damit sind die Analogien genannt, die die reformierten Registraturen in Deutschland und Polen verbanden.

Ohne Zweifel kann man behaupten, dass sich die polnische Büroreform aus dem Jahre 1931 prononciert und bewusst an den fünf Jahre zuvor in Deutschland entworfenen Lösungen orientierte. Die westlichen Erfahrungen waren in Polen bekannt und verbreitet, sie wurden auch während des Aufenthalts des Ausschusses für Optimierung der Öffentlichen Verwaltung in Deutschland vor Ort untersucht.[46] Die Implementierung der Reformen wurde in beiden Ländern von einer Informations- und Bildungsinitiative begleitet, die in der wissenschaftlichen Literatur sowie der Fach- und Tagespresse ausgetragen wurde.

In Polen verzichtete man ganz auf die Übergangsphase der vereinfachten Registratur, die den revolutionären Charakter der Veränderungen abmilderte und die Reform zeitlich streckte. Man traf die Entscheidung, die Kanzleien sofort zu dezentralisieren, was den Prinzipien der deutschen registraturlosen Arbeit entsprach und Abneigung der Beamten erwecken konnte. Auch die Effekte der Reorganisation waren anders. In Deutschland verzeichnete man einen größeren Erfolg, die Modernisierung (die zwar nicht ohne Schwierigkeiten verlief) umfasste öffentliche Ämter aller Ebenen, in Polen demgegenüber nur einen Teil der Organisationseinheiten, vor allem auf der untersten Verwaltungsebene, und gelang dort in vollem Umfang erst nach dem Zweiten Weltkrieg. Der Grund für den polnischen Misserfolg lag bestimmt in der schlechteren Sachvorbereitung der polnischen Beamten und in einer starken konservativen Lobby, die sich für die Erhaltung früherer Arbeitsmethoden aussprach. In der deutschen Büroreform spielten das Deutsche Institut für Wirtschaftliche Arbeit in der Öffentlichen Verwaltung und das zentrale Rationalisierungsorgan – das Reichskuratorium für Wirtschaftlichkeit – eine große Rolle, während es in Polen keine Institution gab, die das ganze Unternehmen koordiniert hätte.[47] Man setzte zwar am Präsidium des Ministerrates ein Büro für Optimierung der Verwaltung (*Biuro Usprawnienia Administracji*) ein, dieses Organ unternahm aber höchstwahrscheinlich keine

46 Die oben zitierte Arbeit von Hausmann wurde bereits 1926 übersetzt und in Polen herausgegeben; Stosyk 1929; Hausner 1929; Tomaszewicz 1928; Robaczewski 1930; Stosyk 1936.
47 Brachmann 1959, S. 11.

weiter angelegten Arbeiten im Bereich der Bürorationalisierung.[48] Auf das Ergebnis wirkte sich auch die Zeit, in der die Einführung der polnischen Modernisierungen erfolgte, unvorteilhaft aus. In Deutschland begann die Reorganisation fünf Jahre früher, sie hatte damit für ihre Durchführung mehr Zeit zur Verfügung. Alle Bestrebungen wurden leider durch die tragischen Ereignisse von 1939 abgebrochen. Zuallerletzt waren die Grundsätze der Reform wohl nicht an die Möglichkeiten und die spezifischen Bedürfnisse der polnischen Ämter angepasst, da sie in Anlehnung an ausländische Lösungen entworfen wurden.

Zu den Hauptarchitekten des deutschen Reformunternehmens gehören Arnold Brecht und Hermann Haussmann. Unter den polnischen Rationalisatoren sollte man an erster Stelle Stefan Stosyk nennen, obwohl mit der Vorbereitung der neuen Vorschriften, wie schon erwähnt, eine Arbeitsgemeinschaft betraut wurde.

Die in der Zwischenkriegszeit ausgearbeiteten und in der polnischen und deutschen Verwaltung letztendlich implementierten Lösungen veränderten zweifellos die Funktionsweise der Ämter. Sie prägten die Form, die Anordnung und den Informationsgehalt der angefallenen Akten. Auf diese Weise erhielt das Schrift- und Archivgut öffentlicher Provenienz eine neue Gestalt und einen neuen Interpretationskontext. Die Organisationsmuster, die zu Beginn der zwanziger Jahre in Deutschland ausgearbeitet und später in Polen übernommen wurden, blieben auch nach 1945 aktuell. Bis zu einem gewissen Grad behalten sie ihre Gültigkeit noch heute.

[Übersetzung: Katarzyna Szczerbowska-Prusevicius]

Bibliografie

Archivalische Quellen

Archiwum Akt Nowych w Warszawie: *Prezydium Rady Ministrów w Warszawie 1917–1939*, Sign. rkt. 14/3.

Bundesarchiv Koblenz: *Gemeinsame Geschäftsordnung der Reichsministerien*, Sign. R 29/50433, S. 30–85.

Gedruckte Quellen

Uchwała Rady Ministrów z dnia 24 sierpnia 1931 r. o przepisach kancelaryjnych w administracji publicznej, in: *Monitor Polski.* 1931/196/213.

48 Hausner 1935, S. 239–241.

Z Komisji dla Usprawnienia Administracji Publicznej, in: *Gazeta Administracji i Policji Państwowej.* 1929/13, S. 15; 1929/15, S. 15; 1930/3, S. 13; 1931/12, S. 19–20.
Z Prezydjum Rady Ministrów, in: *Monitor Polski.* 1928/224, S. 2; 1929/64, S. 3.

Literatur

Bockhorst, Wolfgang: *Quellenkunde*, in: Nimz, Brigitta / Bockhorst, Wolfgang (Hg.): *Praktische Archivkunde. Ein Leitfaden für Fachangestellte für Medien- und Informationsdienste. Fachrichtung Archiv.* 2004, S. 263–272.
Brachmann, Botho: *Zur Geschichte der Büroreform*, in: *Archivmitteilungen.* 1959/9, S. 6–14.
Brecht, Arnold: *Die Geschäftsordnung der Reichsministerien: ihre staatsrechtliche und geschäftstechnische Bedeutung. Zugleich ein Lehrbuch der Büroreform.* 1927.
Brenneke, Adolf: *Archivkunde. Ein Beitrag zur Theorie und Geschichte des europäischen Archivwesens.* 1953.
Brzozowski, Jerzy: *Sprawozdanie z działalności Komisji dla Usprawnienia Administracji Publicznej*, in: *Gazeta Administracji i Policji Państwowej.* 1929/7, S. 2–3.
Büroreformen in einzelnen Verwaltungen. 1927.
Degen, Robert: *Ramowe przepisy kancelaryjne. Co jest ich istotą i czy współcześnie warto z nich korzystać w administracji?*, in: Mamczak-Gadkowska, Irena / Stryjkowski, Krzysztof (Hg.): *Współczesna dokumentacja – współczesne archiwa.* 2018, S. 69–76.
Drews, Bill: *Grundzüge einer Verwaltungsreform.* 1918.
Enders, Gerhart: *Archivverwaltungslehre.* 1962.
Gaertner, Walter: *Die Aufgaben des Diwiv bei der behördlichen Büroreform.* 1931.
Hausner, Roman: *Poczynania organizacyjno-oszczędnościowe w Polsce w latach 1918–1934.* 1935.
Haussmann, Hermann: *Reforma biurowości jako część reformy administracji.* 1926.
Hochedlinger, Michael: *Aktenkunde. Urkunden- und Aktenlehre der Neuzeit.* 2009.
Kaisenberg, Georg: *Öffentliche Verwaltung und Büroreform.* 1932.
Krzymuski, L.: *Obecne poglądy na rolę i organizację biurowości w przedsiębiorstwie*, in: *Przegląd Organizacji.* 1927/3, S. 92–102.
Manteuffel, Tadeusz: *Wykaz akt. Wskazówki praktyczne.* 1935.
Meisner, Heinrich Otto: *Aktenkunde. Ein Handbuch für Archivbenutzer mit besonderer Berücksichtigung Brandenburg-Preußens.* 1935.
Menne-Haritz, Angelika: *Geschäftsprozesse der öffentlichen Verwaltung. Grundlagen für ein Referenzmodell für elektronische Bürosysteme.* 1999.
Miller, Thea: *The German Registry. The Evolution of a Recordkeeping Model*, in: *Archival Science.* 2003/3/1, S. 43–63.
Ostaszewicz, N.: *Funkcjonalny czy oderwany podział akt?*, in: *Przegląd Organizacji.* 1948/7–8, S. 230.
Plonka, R.: *Registraturreform*, in: *Schlesisches Pastoralblatt.* 1928/5, S. 81–84.
Punicki, Stanisław: *Zasady racjonalizacji pracy biurowej*, in: *Gazeta Administracji i Policji Państwowej.* 1929/1, S. 11–12.
Radtke, Irena: *Akta spraw w systemie kancelarii pruskiej*, in: *Archeion.* 1984/78, S. 163–192.
Robótka, Halina: *Kancelaria urzędów administracji państwowej II Rzeczypospolitej.* 1993.

Schäfer, Peter: *Zentralisation und Dezentralisation: eine verwaltungswissenschaftliche Studie zur Kompetenzverteilung im politisch-administrativen System der Bundesrepublik Deutschland, empirisch illustriert am Beispiel der Funktionalreform in Nordrhein-Westfalen.* 1982.

Seibel, Wolfgang: *Administrative Science as Reform. German Public Administration*, in: *Public Administration Review.* 1996/56/1, S. 74–81.

Smoczyński, Marcin: *Racjonalizacja biurowości w działaniach komisji dla usprawnienia administracji publicznej w II Rzeczypospolitej*, in: Górak, Artur / Kukarina, Julia / Magier, Dariusz (Hg.): *Dzieje Biurokracji.* 2019/10, S. 143–158.

Smoczyński, Marcin: *Wykaz akt jako narzędzie sprawnego zarządzania dokumentacją*, in: Degen, Robert / Jabłońska, Marlena (Hg.): *Zarządzanie dokumentacją w instytucji. Czynniki sprzyjające i ograniczenia.* 2020, S. 27–44.

Steeg, Ludwig: *Neue Wege zur Büroreform in der öffentlichen Verwaltung.* 1929.

Stosyk, Stefan: *Przepisy kancelaryjne dla urzędów administracji publicznej w teorii i praktyce.* 1934.

Stosyk, Stefan: *Przepisy o przechowywaniu akt w urzędach administracji publicznej (komentarz).* 1936.

Stosyk, Stefan: *Racjonalna organizacja biurowości*, in: *Gazeta Administracji i Policji Państwowej.* 1930/6, S. 8–12; 1930/7, S. 5–11; 1930/8, S. 7–11.

Stosyk, Stefan: *Współczesny system biurowy w niemieckiej administracji publicznej*, in: *Gazeta Administracji i Policji Państwowej.* 1929/12, S. 1–9.

Tomaszewicz, Stanisław: *Biurowość w administracji na tle naukowej organizacji pracy*, in: *Gazeta Administracji i Policji Państwowej.* 1928/11, S. 33–36.

Wirtschaftliche Arbeit in der öffentlichen Verwaltung. Ein Beitrag zur Verwaltungs- und Büroreform. 1929.

Bogdan-Florin Popovici

Considerations About the Soviet Influence on Archival Operations in Romania

Abstract
Radical changes that affected Romania after World War II, with the introduction of the communist system and the influence of the Union of Soviet Socialist Republics, also affected State Archives. By using three marks of control (status before communism, Soviet practice and new Romanian developments), the author identifies the changes, the actors involved and their reasoning. Comparative examination of various pieces of legislation and professional standards demonstrates that the impact of Soviet recordkeeping practice was significant, but not necessarily negative.
Keywords: archival theory; archival methodology; archives in Romania; history of archival ideas

Introduction

Based on a personal research project on the history of archival ideas in Romania,[1] in the present report I shall focus on the influence that the Sovietization of Romania exerted on archival thinking. Direct references are rather hard to find. In this respect, the fact that the first decade of communism in Romania (1950s) was followed by a "national" flavour of relative independence from the Soviet Union, the references of the Romanian actors involved about cooperation with the Union of Soviet Socialist Republics (hereinafter: USSR) in the initial years were not necessarily abundant. Furthermore, the participation of the inter-war professionals in the process of "communisation" during the inter-war period can be also seen as a sort of complicity with the new political regime-again, not very commendable. Last but not least, the fact that some concepts, ideas and practices that are still alive and even cherished in Romanian archival practice were adopted during that time and under Soviet influence may be embarrassing for some. As a

Dr Bogdan-Florin Popovici, National Archives of Romania, Brasov County Division, ORCID: https://orcid.org/0000-0002-7644-0446.

1 Popovici 2008; idem 2013 (1); idem 2013 (2); idem 2014.

result, while developing the topic, I used pieces of legislation and professional standards adopted from the beginning of 1950s until the beginning of the 1960s, comparing them with the situation before 1950 and with professional handbooks / procedures of Soviet archival science.

High level organisation

Before the 1950s, the activity of the State Archives in Romania was directed by the Law on Archives, adopted in 1925.[2] According to this law, the institution was organised as a General Directorate under the authority of the Ministry of Public Education. Its territorial organisation revealed a trend towards the geographical centralisation of archives,[3] sometimes branded as regional "concentration".[4] The opposition to concentration posed by local authorities with a long tradition in preserving old archives, the complexity of tasks and the number of archives led to the creation of more regional archives: in 1950, the number of regional directorates had increased to nine.

In 1948, Romania adopted a new constitution, enshrining the political regime of a "people's republic". Step by step, new rules and regulations were adopted, to align the legal, administrative, economic and social organisation to the new status quo modelled on the Soviet Union. Following this approach, in September 1950 the administrative system was changed to a Soviet model: regions and rayons with new administrative institutions (people's councils). Their number varied from 28 in 1950 to 16 in 1960.

A short time after the Communists seized power in Russia, the State Archives of the USSR came under the subordination of the Ministry of Education, but were transferred to the authority of the Ministry of Interior, starting from 1938. "After that, the Main Archival Administrations in Moscow and the republics were headed by ranking officers of the infamous ministry, with Captain of State Security I. Nikitinsky the first to head the federal administration."[5]

In January 1951, several months after the administrative reforms in Romania, Aurelian Sacerdoţeanu, the general director of the State Archives was asked by the Ministry of Interior, Teohari Georgescu, to gather some thoughts about the reorganisation of the State Archives, envisaging the imminent change of the ministerial authority over Archives, from Education to Internal Affairs.[6] This transfer occurred several days later.[7]

2 *Lege pentru organizarea Arhivelor Statului* 1925.
3 Ibid., Art. 5.
4 Saceroţeanu 1948, p. 14.
5 Iechelcik 2002, p. 86.
6 Diaconu 2016, pp. 185–189.

The fact that USSR was the model is incontestable. In his report mentioned above, Sacerdoţeanu referenced and praised several times the professional solutions offered by Soviet Archives. Moreover, when pleading for a new archival law, he wrote: "The Stalinist Law from 1929 can be fully adapted to our specificities."[8] In a letter sent to the Romanian Academy in 1957, the deputy of the Ministry of Interior wrote:

> This transition was made, on the one hand, because the State Archives belonged to the Ministry of Interior in the USSR, the Czechoslovak Republic, the Poland P.R., the Bulgaria P.R. etc., and, on the other hand, because the Ministry of Education was unable to meet the tasks imposed on the State Archives in order to clear the backlog in this sector.[9]

It worth mentioning one aspect which was remarked by Olga Leontieva for Soviet Archives.

> For a long time, Russian archivists and researchers thought that the centralization of archival affairs was a reflection of the Bolsheviks' policy of the centralization of the management of Russia. However [...] in 1918 the Soviet Government enacted ideas originating from Russian archivists, not from the Bolsheviks. In my opinion, the idea of centralizing Russian archival affairs is a reflection of public traditions in Russia. It is independent of political regimes.[10]

In the same way, one can notice a certain inclination to centralise Romanian archival administration, prior to the communist regime. In this regard, I consider Leontieva's remarks can be valid for Romanian archives too: a centralised network of state archives was implemented by the communist government, but this does not mean at all that it was not consistent with (some) prior professional or administrative preferences or traditions. However, it is also true that local traditions are created, not naturally born. For instance, if in USSR the Committee for State Security relinquished authority over the Archives in 1961 whereas in Romania the National Archives remained under the authority of the Ministry of Internal Affairs.

The effects of this transfer of authority are yet to be evaluated in full. On the one hand, the rationale of wielding control over the past is certain in that it could

7 *Decretul nr 17 privind trecerea Arhivelor Statului de la Ministrul Învăţământului Public la Ministerul Afacerilor Interne* 1951; *Hotărârea 472 privitoare la atribuţiile şi normele de funcţionare ale Direcţiei Arhivelor* 1951.

8 "[...] Legea stalinistă din 1929 poate fi complet adaptată specificului nostrum" [this and all subsequent quotations in this chapter translated by the author]. Diaconu 2016, p. 186.

9 "[...] Această trecere a fost făcută, pe de o parte, deoarece Arhivele Statului aparţin Ministerului de Interne în URSS, RP Cehoslovacă, RP Polonă, RP Bulgară etc, şi, pe de altă parte, deoarece ministerul Instrucţiunii nu putea îndeplini sarcinile cerute Arhivelor Statului de a elimina întârzierile în acest sector." Lungu / Diaconu / Tineghe 2006, p. 364.

10 Leontieva 2002, p. 45.

be better enforced through the Ministry of Internal Affairs; otherwise, it is hard to explain the presence of the State Archives in the same department as units of law and political police enforcement, like the Militia and State Security.[11] This control began with the archivists, and in this regard, it may be eloquent to quote one of Sacerdoţeanu's reports, where he was satisfied that, despite still existing "reactionary" attitudes, the "clarifications" and "leads" brought by the Ministry of Internal Affairs were consistent.[12] On the other hand, the administrative network and the staff enjoyed unprecedented growth: from ten divisions with 125 employees in 1951, the State Archives reached 70 divisions with 518 employees in 1957, covering all administrative divisions of the country; additionally, new repositories were built.[13] It was also claimed that the authority of the Ministry of Internal Affairs in society led to the expansion of the "authority and the reputation" of the State Archives, as the "only authorized agency in solving problems associated with recordkeeping."[14]

According to the law from 1925,[15] the State Archives were entrusted with the preservation of historical archives of the State older than 30 years, and, in certain circumstances, those of private provenance. While actions to regulate the takeover of some ethnic minority archives were attempted, the influence of politicians[16] and the protection of private property rights prevailed.

In the USSR, on 1 June 1918, the *State Archival Fonds* (*Gosudarstvennyi arkhivnyi fond*, hereinafter: SAF) were introduced,[17] which included all archival material with historical relevance. According to a later definition, the SAF represented "all the documentary material belonging to the Soviet State, bearing scientific, political and practical importance, regardless of the time of their issue, technique of execution and it is created for a centralized control, for preservation, scientific and practical use of these materials."[18] This concept was adopted later

11 Iechelcik 2002, p. 86. About the clear intent to secure records of the past political regimes in controlled access environments, see how archival materials designated as "secrets", including ones created by the Royal House or Romanian Parliament, and all those produced after 23.08. 1944; cf. Diaconu 2016, pp. 261–262.

12 Lungu / Diaconu / Tineghe 2006, p. 356.

13 Ibid., pp. 350, 364.

14 *Raport de activitate* 1957, pp. 3–4.

15 *Lege pentru organizarea Arhivelor Statului* 1925.

16 Cf.: *Iorga dankt den sächsichen Archivaren* 1932, p. 3.

17 The term "fonds" is misleading. While translated and promoted as such even in international professional literature, its meaning is rather "holdings" or "heritage"; cf.: Popovici 2008, pp. 39–40.

18 "[…] Totalitatea materialelor documentare aparţinând Statului sovietic, având importanţă ştiinţifică, politică şi practică, indiferent de timpul apariţiei lor, de tehnica şi modul de executare şi este create în scopul asigurării evidenţei centralizate, a păstrării, folosirii ştiinţifice şi practice a acestor materiale." *Direcţia Generală a Arhivelor. Norme de bază pentru activitatea în Arhivele Statului* 1962 (hereinafter: Direcţia 1962), p. 9.

by many other communist European countries (Hungary, Czechoslovakia, Poland), and China.[19]

In Romania, the SAF was officially adopted by Decree No. 353 from 1957.[20] It emulated Soviet definitions, indicating types of records and type of content within the records, as well as the categories of creators that produce or have produced them.[21] These creators were divided between public institutions or private establishments before communism (including personalities from science, culture, art etc.) and current (public) state institutions, voluntary organisations and personalities. The State Archives were appointed as the administrator of SAF in order to organise, direct, and inspect the recordkeeping activities over the records that were part of the SAF (controlling, preservation, acquisition, processing and use); to compile the rules for transfer, arrangement, preservation, technical and scientific processing and use of documentary material of SAF; and to decide exclusively on the scientific and practical activity of SAF archival material. The State Archives were supposed to transfer all documentary materials from libraries, museums or other institutions to their repositories, with the sole exception of those held by the Romanian Academy, three university libraries and the Central State Library.

In fact, the drafting of the decree started earlier. According to the manuscripts preserved in Sacerdoţeanu's personal fonds,[22] at the beginning of April 1953 a working group was assigned with the task of preparing the text of a decree concerning the introduction of State Archival Fonds in Romania. The tasks were assigned to Pavel Ştefan, Minister of Interior, Gheorghe Stan, Deputy Minister of Interior, Aurelian Sacerdoţeanu, director of the State Archives. Sacerdoţeanu's files contain three editions of the draft, the first belonging "to himself", the second to "the deputy minister". Although the two texts are different from each other, and also from the version adopted in 1957, it can be said, with certainty, that at least one initial version of the State Archival Fonds Decree was drafted by Sacerdoţeanu himself. As far as motivation for the decree goes, he wrote that the SAF was necessary, because measures taken in 1951 were still insufficient and the destruction of records continued. He referred to Lenin's decree from 1918, highlighting the source of inspiration for the concept.

The first remark is the surprisingly high level of participation to this working group: a minister and his deputy, the latter playing an active role by sending a version of the text. This very likely reflects the importance granted to the sit-

19 Lian 2017, p. 110.

20 *Decretul 353* 1957, pp. 1–3.

21 The latter aspect, though very important in my opinion, was ignored in the subsequent legal acts defining National Archival Fonds of Romania (1971, 1996).

22 Arhivele Naţionale Istorice Centrale Bucureşti (hereinafter: ANICB): *Fond A. Sacerdoţeanu*, file No. 50, sig. BU–F–01189–50.

uation of the archives by the communist state. The working group acted rather fast, and between April and June at least three versions were edited, but then a radical change occurred. So far, I have not identified any information to clarify the circumstances, but in 26 June 1953 Sacerdoţeanu is known to have been relieved of his position as director of the State Archives. In a note about his farewell meeting, "in the presence of the deputy minister Gheorghe Stan", he was outraged by an officer's comment "check your library"[23] – maybe hinting at his activity as a historian before the communists came to power. The fact is after Sacerdoţeanu's dismissal, the adoption of the decree was delayed for almost four years. A coincidence or not, but the decree was adopted only two months after Pavel Ştefan himself was removed from the position of the Ministry of Interior.[24]

A second remark regards the differences between the content of the official decree and the initiator's draft. Without going into many details, it ought to be noted that, in his first version, Sacerdoţeanu emphasised the fact that SAF encompasses "the entirety of documentary materials and is the property of all the people", while the adopted version excluded any reference to propriety, indicating only that the State Archives was the "administrator" of SAF. Also, while the initial draft only indicated the creators based on their function (State power institutions, local institutions etc.), the adopted version, based on the Soviet model, divided the SAF into historical periods: before and after the communists' accession to power (23 August 1944, in the Romanian case). Finally, while Sacerdoţeanu stated in his initial draft that the State Archives are a "scientific research institution", this designation disappeared from both the ministry version and the published decree.

Examining the adoption of the concept of SAF in Romania, similar to other communist states (and only to them!), it should be considered that this may reflect a societal utility. The implementation of communist doctrine implied a severe break with the past. Public institutions ceased to exist, or their competences were declared irrelevant to the new administration. Nationalisation and expropriations led to many economic or financial archives with no master. The State Archives dealt with this by declaring them to be of "state interest" and implement a centralised policy of management.[25] A consideration from a Soviet archival handbook is relevant: "The decree from 1 June 1918 ended the decentralized archival activity and documentary materials could not be destroyed any longer without the approval of the General Direction of the Archives."[26]

23 Lungu / Diaconu / Tineghe 2006, p. 357.

24 The State Archives mentioned the "un-justifiable delay in adopting the Decree", ibid, p. 358.

25 Popovici 2008, pp. 33–34.

26 "[…] Decretul de la 1 iunie 1918 punea capăt descentralizării activităţii arhivistice, iar materialele documentare nu mai puteau fi distruse fără aprobarea Direcţiei generale a Arhivelor." Belov et al. 1958, p. 6.

By designating almost all the running institution as creators of archival material belonging to SAF, the decree confirmed the expansion of the authority of the State Archives over what may be called the "records management" of public institutions. And this was the crowning of a trend started during the Interwar period, and definitely a goal of a recordkeeping professional, to control the production of records, to stop selling archives as waste and protect documentary historical sources.[27]

On the other hand, the introduction of a centralised administration of "archival materials" – as they were designated-posed several side effects. One has already been mentioned – centralisation allows for better control over access and information. Also, it creates a unique centre of thinking in recordkeeping matters – State Archives. This monopoly, understandable under the political regime, had an inherent impact on the shaping of memory.[28] This would be visible in the regulations in the following years.

In terminology, the ubiquitous use of the expression "archival materials", and ignoring any references to record grouping or of the creator's relevance, reflect a position whereby the archival value is intrinsic only to the records, to the information contained by them, while the context is irrelevant. The draft of the *Instructions for Organization and Work of the Commissions of Examination and Control*[29] from 1954 highlights this approach, stating that permanent records – no matter from which creator – are those that mirror essential parts of the institutional activity for building socialism, reflecting the basic conditions of work and workers in the framework of the national economy, those with scientific and historical relevance, and those with practical relevance for the needs of people working in other organisations.

Records management

The Interwar archival legislation did not grant the State Archives power to regulate records management for creating bodies. According to the law from 1925 and further amendments, the only obligation was the transfer of archival material older than 30 years to the State Archives. The public administration was guided by some field-specific regulations,[30] like those from 1933 and 1943 that regulated the registration of records, the implementation of classification schemes and a

27 It needs nevertheless to notice the main purpose was to preserve the historical sources not to increase the efficiency of the administration of the creating bodies.
28 Popovici 2008, pp. 35–36.
29 Diaconu 2016, pp. 250–260.
30 Sacerdoţeanu 1970, p. 87.

system of disposition/destruction, upon the approval of the State Archives (though, legally, not mandated!).[31]

Though various concerns existed about how creating bodies should preserve their archives,[32] it was Aurelian Sacerdoţeanu who actively promoted the idea of archives as a whole and the need for record management regulations. Acting most likely under the influence of Italian archival literature,[33] Sacerdoţeanu asserted this in various moments of his carrier.[34] As such, his plan was to prepare regulations for each stage in the life of records,[35] but this did not materialise until 1950. In this context, the Soviet model was examined.

Maybe political opportunism, maybe just professional curiosity, but the USSR recordkeeping system was familiar to Sacerdoţeanu, as proved by the references[36] and by his report to the Ministry of Interior, in January 1951.[37] Referential texts were published as translations in the next years by the State Archives.[38]

At that time, the USSR had a far more complex and articulated system for managing records in organisations than Romania. The handbook about recordkeeping theory and practice presented many theoretical aspects, defining various divisions and classifications for the typology of documentation, workflows and methods to process the records, from creation to filing, including various pieces of advice for optimisation and savings. The registration system was based on book registers or cards, detailing standard and specific workflows.[39] A consistent chapter was devoted to classification (or "scientific grouping") of records, both physical (aggregation into folders) and intellectual (into logical groupings). The tools used were "nomenclator" (list of titles), "indicator" (list of retention periods) and classification. *Nomenclator* was a list containing the titles of files which was compiled every year, and served as a filing plan.[40] The *classification tool* was a list of headings, either by structure of organisation or by

31 Popovici 2013 (2), p. 270.

32 Lungu / Diaconu / Tineghe 2006, pp. 66–67.

33 Though, at least to my knowledge, no study has been performed on his source of his archival knowledge, the continuous references to Italian archivists, like Taddei, Casanova or Angarano (Sacerdoţeanu 1946), or references to current archives – repository archives – historical archives, as presented by Casanova; Diaconu 2016, p. 185 may lead to this conclusion.

34 Diaconu 2016, pp. 81, 85–186; Sacerdoţeanu 1946, p. 7.

35 Diaconu 2016, p. 81.

36 Sacerdoţeanu 1948, p. 8.

37 Diaconu 2016, pp. 185–186.

38 We did not manage to trace all the texts available to the State Archives in Romania at that time. Our analysis, further on, will be based on three works presenting the Soviet system: *Norme de sistematizare a materialelor arhivistice la Arhivele Statului din URSS (1938)*, Belov et al. 1958; Direcţia 1962. Though later than the date of the events, these texts did not indicate that a sharp change in practice occurred between 1950–1960.

39 Belov et al. 1958, pp. 40–44.

40 Ibid., pp. 44–48.

function; it was emphasised that the latter was more useful, since it was more stable. In this context, an implementation of decimal classification was presented.[41] The last tool was *indicator*, whose main purpose was to list the retention periods, in a structured manner, based on functions.[42] For the yearly transfer to the records repository, folders should be listed in inventories, in three copies (files with temporary retention periods) or four copies (permanent ones), for each division of the organisation. For disposition of records, the Soviet system used a network of Expertising Commissions (at the creators and in the State Archives), which were mandated to assess the preservation value of archival material.[43] These "values" were "permanent preservation" – i.e., "long time practical or scientific" and "temporary" – practical value.[44]

Since 1951, the Romanian legislation mandated the State Archives with the release of standards for the management of records within the creating bodies.[45] In this regard, Sacerdoţeanu intended for the State Archives to draft *Instructions for the Organisation of Registries and Records Repositories for all Creators.*[46] This task was postponed many times, since in 1958–1959 there were still discussions about the best direction to follow.[47] In the end, except for the mandatory registration of records, no instructions for registry offices were issued by the State Archives until the present day.

The regulation of the filing and management in the records repository met a different fate. Even before his dismissal, Sacerdoţeanu managed to draft a *General Instructions for the Organisation and Activity of the Archives of Ministries, Central and Local Institutions* (*Instrucţiuni generale pentru orgniazarea şi activitatea arhivelor ministerelor şi instituţiilor centrale şi locale,* hereinafter: *General Instructions*).[48] It was the task of his successors to finalise and issue this document for application, after a year.[49] A similar version, slightly changed, was issued after the publication of the above-mentioned SAF decree, in 1957.[50]

The document outlines a system that, with some modification, is still in force today. After registration, the records were organised in folders, according

41 Ibid., pp. 49–51.
42 Ibid., pp. 51–53.
43 Ibid., pp. 108–110.
44 Ibid., p. 110.
45 *Hotărârea 472 privitoare la atribuţiile şi normele de funcţionare ale Direcţiei Arhivelor Statului* 1951, Art. 4.a.
46 Lungu / Diaconu / Tineghe 2006, p. 349.
47 ANICB: *Fond Direcţia Generală a Arhivelor Statului,* sig. 21/1958; 53/1959; 54/1959.
48 Ibid.: *Fond A. Sacerdoţeanu,* file No. 50, sig. BU–F–01189–50, fols. 294–337. Of course, it is difficult to state how much of this document was created by Sacerdoţeanu himself. It is very likely that, due to his inclination towards recordkeeping theory and methodology, he was the main actor in its drafting, but this does not exclude co-authoring.
49 *Instrucţiuni generale* 1955, pp. 3–37.
50 Diaconu 2016, pp. 334–357.

to the *nomenclator*, i.e., a list of titles of folders (which later on included the book-registers too), grouped based on the organisational structure of the creator. The retention periods were taken from another tool, called the *indicator*, where groupings of records were divided based on topics. Once created, folders were transferred annually to the records repository, based on lists called *inventories*, compiled in four copies,[51] a separate one each folder planned for permanent or temporary preservation (based on their value, historical or practical). For the ease of disposition, it was recommended that temporary folders to be grouped on inventory based on their retention periods. For control purposes, the repository had to have a table of fonds[52] and the Current Control Register (listing each accession).

Though the Soviet influence is clearly visible, some remarks are required. Firstly, *nomenclator* resembled Soviet regulations in name rather than content. In the Romanian version, it was not drawn up annually, but was permanent, until organisational changes required its update. Also, the structure of the *nomenclator* (called *folder's title list* in an annotation)[53] is a mixture between – and a simplification of – the Soviet *nomenclator* and a classification tool, and a continuation of the classification plan announced by Sacerdoţeanu's presentation based on Italian tradition,[54] and described in the first draft and the first publication of the *General Instructions.*[55]

One fine nuance involves how the titles are arranged. The Soviet handbook discussed deeply, pertinently and convincingly about the difference between organisational structure and functional structure. Nevertheless, Romanian archivists paid attention to this matter neither at the time nor afterwards. Of course, practice showed (mainly after the fall of communism) that organisations are subject to frequent changes and that groupings based on organisation structure are short-lived. This has had a serious impact over the organisation of records and implied a lot of effort for all the parties involved, due to frequent updates of the *nomenclator.*

Another specificity was introduced in the Romanian regulations in terms of the folder titles grouping on retention periods. While the argument (easy for the disposition process) is pertinent, breaking the connection between records resulting from the same activity creates a major obstacle when it comes to the

51 Three, in Sacerdoţeanu's version.

52 In Sacerdoţeanu s version, "list of fonds", then handwritten "table of fonds".

53 ANICB: *Fond A. Sacerdoţeanu*, file No. 50, sig. BU–F–01189–50, fol. 339.

54 Sacerdoţeanu 1946, p. 11.

55 In time, it was noted that, in the form adopted in Romania, categories of records are repeated in *indicator*, so with the legislation in 1996 the two instruments, *nomenclator* and *indicator*, were merged. However, practice seems to indicate that the filing plan and retention periods list should be separated.

creator retrieving information – this effort is hampered by an imposition to procure finding aids suitable for the disposition process.

All along with the *General Instructions*, another field regulation concerned the so-called Expertising Commissions. Initially, this regulation was part of the draft for the SAF decree,[56] but after dismissing Sacerdoţeanu, a separate instruction was developed. According to the newly appointed director Vasile Maciu, this fresh regulation, significantly expanded, was developed under the coordination of "comrade adviser Nikolai Romanovici Prokopenko."[57] While the Soviet influence needs no further explanation, it should be highlighted that the rules for the *indicator* structure (presented here as a fixed, rationalised line of headings) contradicted the looser structure of the *indicator* as presented in the *General Instructions*. Another point of contradiction was on the flow of inventories for appraisal. While the *General Instructions* required one inventory, with groupings based on the retention periods, the *Instructions for Expertizing Commissions* (*Instrucţiuni pentru comisiile de expertizare*) required a list of materials with expired retentions periods, without asking for special groupings in inventories (avoiding the issue mentioned above). In the end, the Romanian version prevailed even though, in my opinion, it did not have the best approach.

Archives management

Despite the State Archives of Romania having a strong cultural stance in the Interwar period, concerns about the standardisation of processing historical archives were rather few and far between. This situation was subject to change since Aurelian Sacerdoţeanu was appointed general director of the State Archives. Starting in 1939, he issued a series of normative orders – the first in the history of the Romanian State Archives, as far as we know – that were developed and reissued in 1948. They mostly concerned the creation of various types finding aids,[58] but to Sacerdoţeanu's merit, he also attempted to add a coherent theoretical background to its methodologies. The understanding of historical archives as a continuous phase in the life of records after current and repository archives (as influenced by Eugenio Casanova), the attempt to enforce the concept of *archival fonds* as professional usage or other options were not mere personal semantic options, but intentional actions to modernise archival thinking in Romania.

56 ANICB: *Fond A. Sacerdoţeanu*, file No. 50, sig. BU-F-01189-50, fols. 193–195.
57 Diaconu 2016, pp. 249–261.
58 Sacerdoţeanu 1948.

In terms of arrangement, intellectual debates among archivists reflected the fight between provenance and pertinence. Director of State Archives Directorates from Braşov, Chişinău or Iaşi aimed to preserve the creator's arrangements; those from Bucharest, Cluj and Cernăuţi considered records should be organised on other criteria, mostly practical: if they were transferred, based on dates or topics, it would be easier for the users etc.

As General Director, Sacerdoţeanu denounced the practice of grouping documents on language or form criteria, disrespecting provenance. He cited the principles of provenance and pertinence, giving priority to the former, clarifying where the chronological arrangement had a place and insisting on the need to respect the integrity of fonds.[59]

Sacerdoţeanu attempted to create consistency in methods to produce finding aids. Before him, the terminology used varied from one Directorate to another, much like the purpose and methodology of this activity. Coming from the perspective of a historian-user of archives, he pleaded for the compilation of many types of finding aids for archival description and control, in order to facilitate as wide as possible access to the documents. The creation of finding aids was, in his view, the ultimate goal for archivists, who must be aware that "we [archivists] do not work for what we know now or our contemporaries, but for the future, and this is why we have to assume that a moment will come when the interest [of researchers] will cover any topic".[60] He also called for an accelerated campaign for inventorying fonds with no finding aid, stating that "the archivist ought not to endlessly postpone the fulfilment of his tasks; such delays damaging his prestige and the interest of the community [of users]."[61]

The Soviet standards on processing historical archives presents once again a coherent corpus in itself, with various solutions for various cases. For any objective reader, from the point of view of methodology, the archival handbooks and working standards from USSR were more sophisticated than any of those edited in Romania before 1950. The work methodology,[62] principles for arrangement[63] (that explicitly rejected provenance as "bourgeoise")[64] and methods of execution[65] (even a universal and rationalised scheme of arrangement for

59 Popovici 2013 (2), p. 275.

60 "[...] Noi [arhiviştii] u lucrăm pentru ceea ce ştim noi sau contemporanii noştri, ci pentru viitor, şi de aceea trebuie să presupunem că va veni un moment în care interesul [cercetătorilor] va acoperi orice subiect." Ibid, p. 275.

61 "[...] Arhivistul nu trebuie să amâne la nesfârşit îndeplinirea sarcinilor sale; asemenea întârzieri afectează prestigiul său şi interesul comunităţii [de utilizatori]." Ibid, p. 275.

62 Belov at al.1958, pp. 77–80; Direcţia 1962, pp. 39, 57–58, 68.

63 Belov et al. 1958, p. 58.

64 Ibid., pp. 58, 61.

65 Ibid., pp. 81–89; Direcţia 1962, p. 60; *Norme de sistematizare a materialelor arhivistice la Arhivele Statului din URSS (1938)* 1953, p. 153.

personal fonds),[66] a complex system of finding aids for control and information,[67] rules or repositories management and records retrieval,[68] were all areas that had no – or scarce – equivalence to Romanian methodology. In his report to the ministry from January 1951, Sacerdoţeanu referred to the Soviet standards for arrangement from 1938 as a model.[69] But influences from Soviet methodology went further than these standards.

One initial area of influence was in terminology. Sacerdoţeanu himself, based on Italian archivists, used the terms *ordonare* (arrangement), *inventariere* (inventorying), *selecţionare* (appraisal), *fişare* (card creating). To these terms, Soviet literature added "fonding", "systematization", "expertizing", "description". In the first regulations after 1950, there was an attempt to use the Soviet terms, then the previous terms prevailed. In some cases, an interesting evolution occurred. For "arrangement", the Soviet term "fonding", and sometimes also "systematizing", was used.[70] In Romanian, there was only one term – *ordonare*. All editions of the standard for archival processing released by State Archives of Romania (1962, 1973, 1984) used the latter for all activities associated with arrangement of records based on a criterium, no matter the level (fonds, subfonds / series, folder). However, in the latest edition, from 1996, a new term appeared: "fonding", meaning arrangement at fonds level.[71] Also, for "systematizing" was a Romanian equivalent *ordonare*. In practice, and in some official rules for managing and describing activities, "systematizing" is used to define the physical arrangement of records in a repository.

Another line of change brought by Soviet practices concerned the perception of archival work itself. Sacerdoţeanu, as stated above, considered the compilation of finding aids for the public to be an essential part of the job. This view is obvious even later, from his notes for a practical handbook for archivists: he wrote two pages about repositories, registration, the library of the archives but only three pages for the inventory. Reading through the Soviet handbooks, one is surprised to see almost no reference to the user, as if the entirety of archival work was a purpose unto itself. And this perspective was reflected then in the Romanian *Instructions for Compiling Documents Descriptive Cards for the Administrative Control of Archival Fonds* (13 January 1953), where it was written: "[...] the final

66 Belov et al. 1958, pp. 90–92.
67 Ibid., p. 148; Direcţia 1962, pp. 100–101.
68 Belov et al. 1958, pp. 97, 100.
69 Diaconu 2016, p. 186.
70 Belov et al. 1958, p. 83. "Fonding" meant classification of records into fonds or collections and consisted of determining the materials belonging to a fonds, while "systematizing" refers to the arrangement within a fonds and within folders.
71 The term was not new per se but as an activity, M. Ciucă indicated explicitly that "fonding" means arrangement of fonds level; cf.: Ciucă 1979, p. 286.

goal of the archival science: compiling the control lists of archival materials."[72] Maybe it is a speculation of words, but this change reflects a certain perspective on the role of archivists and their work in society, which was, moreover, specific to the new position of the State Archives within the new institutional framework.

On 14 May 1954, the State Archives issued the *Instructions for the Control of Documentary Material Belonging to the State Archival Fonds of PRR*,[73] where the finding aids system for archival material was almost completely copied from the Soviet ones. The exception is the *General Register of the Archive (Registrul general de arhivă*, hereinafter: GRA).[74] In Romania, the problem of a tool listing accessions had been raised years ago. In 1941, Sacerdoţeanu asked for implementation of a special register for transfers.[75] Then, in 1953, the GRA was regulated.[76] It is beyond doubt that Sacerdoţeanu knew about the Soviet practice; on the other hand, this GRA had a slightly different content than the possible model, so, considering the precedent too, it may be concluded the Soviet influence was minimal in this case. Also, a proposition for a statistical card and a file for the administrative documentation about a fonds was made from 1951,[77] but very likely it was the Soviet model that prevailed.

Because historical archives processing had methodological tradition in Romania (as indicated above, mainly due to Sacerdoţeanu's efforts), the methods from Soviet practices were adopted in part. Those concerning work methodology and planning were adopted in a simplified manner,[78] but this simplification was not obviously beneficial. In the workflow of archival processing, Sacerdoţeanu's approach has prevailed until today, despite the fact the complexity of archival processing would have required a different architecture.[79] The Soviet principles for arrangement were rejected in silence, although no other principles were endorsed (except in some theoretical studies).[80] In arrangement and inventorying, some useful nuances of the Soviet literature were ignored and a simplified version was used.[81] In time, some of these rules were updated, but other provisions were stubbornly maintained, like the one that requires reviewing records

72 "[…] Scopul final al arhivisticii: întocmirea de liste de evidenţă pentru materialul arhivistic." Diaconu 2016, p. 233.

73 Ibid., pp. 266–272.

74 Ironically, the Soviet handbook put a clearer name for it – "the accession register".

75 Diaconu 2016, p. 79.

76 Ibid., p. 243.

77 Ibid., p. 199.

78 *Instrucţiuni pentru ordonarea* 1962, p. 6.

79 Ibid.

80 The most notable Ciuca 1979, p. 286. Lacking a methodological rule for respecting original order, re-arrangement based on "better" archivist order is a common practice, recording though the former reference code in description.

81 *Instrucţiuni pentru ordonarea* 1962, pp. 19–20; Ciuca 1979, p. 285.

(like yearly reports) to be arranged according to the date of the content, not the date of the record.[82]

Conclusions

The change of political regime in Romania after World War II had a significant impact on professional archival activity. After this – albeit brief – passage through the regulations and professional rules produced in 1950s, some conclusions become apparent.

From a political point of view, the transfer of the State Archives from the Ministry of Education to the Ministry of the Interior was an act of political interest for the architecture of the Communist state, and of real impact for institutional goals. At that very moment, it may be appreciated as a positive step for the protection of records. It is scarcely believable that subordination to the Ministry of Education would have helped halt the destruction of archives or institutional development as effectively as the authority of the Ministry of Interior. In terms of access to archives, as it is perceived today, this action was instead aimed at establishing control over historical sources and, therefore, over the writing of history.

Centralisation, the spirit of order and discipline, obsession for standardisation and consistency managed to impose a uniformity of archival practice onto the whole country. While this had its downside, in sometimes promoting the uniformity of a bad practice, it nevertheless helped to create a network of local archives and a consistent professional practice, which the next generation could inherit and develop.

Methodological changes were performed professionally by Romanian archivists, many of them with longstanding positions in the previous "capitalist regime". While a sense of opportunism and subservience cannot be excluded, it cannot be asserted that the decisions taken and models adopted would have led to less professionalism at the State Archives on the whole. Frankly, at that moment, Soviet records and archival management was superior, at least methodologically, to the Romanian version. Some of the solutions borrowed were previously discussed in Romania, but never implemented, and they were rather isolated solutions, without any goal of standardisation on a national scale. An authoritarian regime was required to impose centralisation, which brought the possibility to push for methodologies and their implementations, securing a major win for the institution, a leap towards professional modernisation.

82 *Instrucţiuni pentru ordonarea* 1962, p. 20.

Of course, this accelerated adoption of solutions was not perfect. Sometimes it meant a paradigm shift – for example, from being an open scientific and cultural institution to an instrument of administration and control of historical information; it was the political context that left no other option. The detailed description of records right down to the last folder privileged control over information, despite the huge amount of work involved and, therefore, the blocking of access because of the unprocessed archives – gives an indication about what was relevant.

Anyway, it cannot be argued that this was a question of complete professional subordination to Soviet models. It is easy provable that ideas and procedures were taken "creatively", sometimes oversimplified because records production in Romania was less complex or the models were not completely understood. Sometimes it seems that this was only a label stuck onto a different reality, just to mimic a sort of a compliance. No matter the reasons, what is clear is that Soviet recordkeeping practice had a huge influence over Romanian theory, methodologies and practice in archival science. This is not necessary a bad thing, as long as those solutions engendered modernity. Perhaps the saddest part is the immutability of some rules and practices, more than 70 years afterwards, that are questionable in terms of social or professional use.

Bibliography

Archival sources

Arhivele Naţionale Istorice Centrale Bucureşti:
- *Fond A. Sacerdoţeanu*, file No. 50, sig. BU-F-01189-50;
- *Fond Direcţia Generală a Arhivelor Statului*, sig. 21/1958; 53/1959; 54/1959.

Printed sources

Decretul 353 / 16. 07. 1957 privind înfiinţarea FAS al RPR, in: *Buletinul Oficial.* 1957, No. 19, 07.26.1957.

Decretul nr 17 privind trecerea Arhivelor Statului de la Ministrul Învăţământului Public la Ministerul Afacerilor Interne, in: *Buletinul Oficial.* 1951, No. 14, 1.02.1951.

Diaconu, Ana-Felicia: *Crestomaţie de acte normative şi documente privind teoria şi practica arhivistică (1862–1974).* 2016.

Direcţia Generală a Arhivelor. Norme de bază pentru activitatea în Arhivele Statului. 1962 (typescript for internal use within the Archives).

Hotărârea 472 privitoare la atribuţiile şi normele de funcţionare ale Direcţiei Arhivelor Statului, in: *Buletinul Oficial.* 1951, No. 67, 16.06.1951.

Instrucţiuni generale, in: *Buletin de informare.* 1955.
Instrucţiuni pentru ordonarea, inventarierea şi expertiza materialelor documentare din depozitele Arhivelor Statului. 1962.
Lege pentru organizarea Arhivelor Statului, in: *Monitorul Oficial.* 1925, No. 153, 25.06. 1925.
Norme de sistematizare a materialelor arhivitice la Arhivele Statului din URSS (1938), in: *Buletin de informare.* 1953.
Raport de activitate pe anul 1956, in: *Buletin de informare.* 1957.

Literature

Belov, G. A. / Loghinova, A. I. / Mitraev K. C. / Prokopenko N. R. (eds.): *Teoria şi practica muncii arhivistice în URSS.* 1958.
Ciuca, Marcel-Dumitru: *Ordonarea şi inventarierea documentelor aflate în depozitele Arhivelor Statului*, in: *Revista Arhivelor.* 1979/3, pp. 284–302.
Desalle, Paul: *A History of Archival Practice.* 2018.
Iechelcik, Serghei: *The Archives of Stalin's Time. Political Use, Symbolic Value, and the Missing Resolutions*, in: *Comma.* 2002/3–4, pp. 83–91.
Iorga dankt den sächsichen Archivaren, in: *Kronstädter Zeitung.* 1932, p. 3.
Leontieva, Olga: *Two Aspects of the Russian Archival System*, in: *Comma.* 2002/3–4, pp. 41–48.
Lian, Zhiying: *A History of Archival Ideas and Practice in China*, in: Gilliland, Anne / McKemmish, Sue / Lau, Andrew (eds.): *Research in the Archival Multiverse.* 2017, pp. 96–121.
Lungu, Corneliu-Mihail / Diaconu, Ana-Felicia / Tineghe, Cristina: *Arhivele înfruntând veacurile. Mărturii documentare.* 2006.
Popovici, Bogdan-Florin: *"Arhiva totală": o experienţă românească. Incursiune în istoria conceptului de Fond Arhivistic Naţional*, in: *Revista Arhivelor.* 2008/1, pp. 24–50.
Popovici, Bogdan-Florin: *Archival Thoughts in the Historical Archives of a Transylvanian Town*, in: *Atlanti. Review for Modern Archival Theory and Practice. Special edition. In honorem Charles Kecskemeti.* 2013, pp. 163–174. (1)
Popovici, Bogdan-Florin: *Private Historical Archives: Between Public Interests and Private Property in Communist Romania*, in: *Atlanti. Review for Modern Archival Theory and Practice.* 2014/24/1, pp. 219–228.
Popovici, Bogdan-Florin: *Snapshots of Romanian Archival Ideas In The Second Half Of 20th Century. Part 1: Preliminaries*, in: *Atlanti. Review for Modern Archival Theory and Practice.* 2013/23/1, pp. 269–278. (2)
Sacerdoţeanu, Aurelian: *Arhivistica.* 1970.
Sacerdoţeanu, Aurelian: *Instrucţiuni arhivistice.* 1948.
Sacerdoţeanu, Aurelian: *Organizarea arhivelor armatei.* 1946.

Robert Rybak

National Defence of the People's Republic of Poland in the Light of Doctrinal Documents – Discussion Illustrated by an Example from the Navy

Abstract
Government and military documents kept in archives constitute the basic source of information on the defence of the People's Republic of Poland. This article describes the nature, content and mutual relations of the essential documents that regulate the matters of defence in the discussed period, which are commonly referred to as doctrinal documents. On account of their diversity, the study describes their types, the context in which they were created, and their mutual relations. Due to the complexity of the studied issue, the paper uses a selected example.
Keywords: doctrine; national security; Warsaw Pact; Polish Navy

Introduction

The purpose of this study is to present matters that concern the defence of the People's Republic of Poland (*Polska Rzeczypospolita Ludowa*, hereinafter: PRL) when it was part of the Warsaw Treaty Organization, commonly known as the Warsaw Pact, based on selected key doctrinal documents. The documents constitute the rules that define the views and the *modus operandi* with regard to the defence and the operations of the armed forces. In the period of the PRL, governmental and military doctrinal documents formed one system and were of a specific nature and character. Governmental documents were very general and referred mainly to the ideas of the defence doctrine in the PRL. They were characterised by a rigid structure that covered three main issues: the diagnosis of the state of national security, the expected threat of war and the countermeasures envisaged in connection with them. Despite the identical nature of the tone of such documents, its structure was not the same. It evolved under the influence of political factors and military considerations that resulted from the Cold War relationship between the United States of America and the Union of Soviet

Dr Robert Rybak, Nicolaus Copernicus University in Toruń, ORCID: https://orcid.org/0000-0003-2935-1982.

Socialist Republics (hereinafter: USSR). In the case of military doctrinal documents, the structure of their content was generally fixed, as a result of the military manner in which the documentation was prepared. However, greater flexibility occurred in the assumptions about how the threat of war would be countered and how the troops would act. This was mainly due to the technical and economic possibilities of the army. Importantly, both types of documents were similar. They constituted a whole within a single system that separately described the political idea and the operational activities of the troops. These documents complemented each other, presenting on the one hand the idea, and on the other the *modus operandi.* At the same time, military doctrinal documents, which were a practical supplement to the assumptions described in the governmental doctrinal documents, were closely connected with military executive documents used to implement binding assumptions and to regulate military cooperation within the Warsaw Pact. Both were among the most important in their respective fields within the defence system in operation at that time and constituted the basis for the entire national security system. The defence of the PRL was based on The Warsaw Treaty Organization, but, unfortunately, this dependence meant that all aspects were dependent on the leadership of the organization and commanding bodies, which were autonomously led by the USSR.[1] This allowed the USSR to impose a real influence on the assumptions described in all kinds of doctrinal regulations and ways of organising and operating the Polish Army. This situation resulted in the fact that for the subsequent 35 years, all the Polish defence assumptions were developed in accordance with the recommendations of the Pact command, i.e., *de facto* the Soviet General Staff, whose primary goal was to secure the defence of the USSR.[2] Therefore, it ensured itself complete control over the national armies of the **lesser allies.** This was facilitated by the organisation that was in force in the Pact, which specified that the national armies of each party would field a component of operational forces participating in frontline strategic operations, as part of a joint force – the Unified Armed Forces of the Warsaw Pact.[3] According to the assumptions:

> the Polish Army was to field a strategic-operational component in the form of a Front composed of three general armies, an air army and support units. The task of the Front was to carry out a strategic offensive operation in the northern coast and Jutland operational direction in order to capture the Baltic straits and the North Sea coast up to

1 Instytut Pamięci Narodowej Biuro Udostępniania (hereinafter: IPN BU): sig. 1420/1, fols. 153, 158; sig. 02958/79/80; 02958/79/81; 02958/79/82; 02958/79/83; 02958/79/425; 02958/86; 02958/105; 02958/106; 02958/107. This involved building a joint automated command control system for allied troops "PASUW"; IPN BU: sig. 02958/123.

2 Burnetko / Onyszkiewicz / Bereś 1999; Pechantov 2017, p. 113; Gaddis 1997, pp. 129–130; Holloway 2017, p. 360; Engerman 2017, pp. 48–49; Nowak 2011.

3 Rybak 2021.

the English Channel, as part of the Unified Armed Forces of the Warsaw Pact. This was to enable the USSR Baltic Fleet and the Navy of the PRL to operate freely in the waters of the North Atlantic.[4]

During the war, the warships of the Navy of the PRL were to operate within the framework of the Warsaw Pact Baltic Fleet of the Unified Armed Forces of the Warsaw Pact (*Zjednoczona Flota Bałtycka Zjednoczonych Sił Zbrojnych Układu Warszawskiego*) created by the Russians in 1956.[5]

The described didactic documents were created in response to the needs that resulted from the unification of the security system of Warsaw Treaty Organization member states, which was carried out mainly for the purpose of its effective management and functioning in accordance with the assumptions of the Soviet security policy of building frontal armour for the USSR with the use of neighbouring countries.[6]

The essential doctrinal documents binding in the PRL during the Warsaw Pact period

Initial work on the documents that describe the defence of the PRL was undertaken in 1957 in the Study Office of the Ministry of Defence and laid the foundations for future doctrinal documents. The efforts made at that time resulted in the preparation of a document entitled *Envisioning the Conditions of Future Warfare.*[7] The document provided a general description of matters concerning Polish security and the rules of engaging the army in a period of war threat. The assumptions contained therein were based primarily on the key role of the Pact for the security of Poland and its leading role in decision-making related to

4 "[...] Wojsko Polskie miało wystawić związek strategiczno-operacyjny w postaci Frontu złożonego z trzech armii ogólnowojskowych, armii lotniczej i jednostek zabezpieczenia. Zadaniem Frontu było przeprowadzenie w ramach ZSZ UW strategicznej operacji zaczepnej na północnonadmorskim i jutlandzkim kierunku operacyjnym w celu opanowania cieśnin Bałtyckich oraz wybrzeża Morza Północnego po kanał La Manche. Miało to umożliwić swobodne operowanie Floty Bałtyckiej ZSRR i Marynarki Wojennej PRL na wodach północnego Atlantyku." Kajetanowicz 2013, p. 29. From the early 1960s it was referred to as the Coastal Front. According to the Offensive Operation Plan for the Coastal Front, it consisted of: 1, 2, 3, 4 Army; 3 Air Army; 36 Operational-Tactical Missile Brigade; 1 Gun Artillery Brigade; 7 Pontoon Brigade; 2, 8 Independent Sapper Brigade; 80 Anti-Aircraft Artillery Regiment; 91 Anti-Tank Artillery Regiment, and detached forces of the Navy of the PRL and its allies. It was to operate in the northern coast and Jutland operational direction as part of a strategic offensive operation by the Unified Armed Forces of the Warsaw Pact participant states; cf. IPN BU: sig. 02958/164; 02958/143.

5 Warsaw Pact Baltic Fleet was also named Unified Baltic Fleet.

6 Gibianskij 2003.

7 Pl. *Przewidywania dotyczące warunków przyszłych działań wojennych.*

military operations and the geopolitical location of Poland as a transit route between the East and the West. It also draws attention to the key role of the Soviet Army stationed in the German Democratic Republic (hereinafter: GDR) as a buffer between Poland and the Federal Republic of Germany, which was a member of NATO. According to the adopted assumptions, in a period of war threat, the armed forces were to be fully prepared for action and regroup in accordance with the operational plans drawn up by the Polish General Staff specially for that purpose.[8] Moreover, in 1958 the Ministry of National Defence developed the concept of dividing the armed forces of the PRL into operational units that would repel external attacks, and national defence units, whose task was to conduct defensive manoeuvres within the country. The suggested solution translated into a new organisation of troops operating from that time according to both external and internal arrangements.[9] The sheer magnitude of defence operations conducted in the second half of the 1950s meant that they needed good coordination. For this purpose, in February 1959, a specialised body was established to direct the defence system – the National Defence Committee. The newly established body issued a resolution in that same year, which, in the event of war, divided the Polish Armed Forces into three parts: operational forces composed of three general military armies, an airforce and a navy, which during the war would be part of the Unified Armed Forces of the Warsaw Pact; forces for the defence of the country's territory composed of the national air defence forces, internal troops and territorial defence units; security and draft units, including military training, depots and warehouses.[10]

The first government doctrinal document which comprehensively described the defence issues of the PRL was the *Basic Assumptions for People's Defence*,[11] prepared in 1961. The assumptions contained therein were a compilation of the ideas contained in the previously existing documents concerning defence, and their practical dimension was accounted for in the *Operational Plan for the Defence of the National Territory*[12] from 1962. The document in question outlined basic strategic assumptions in its general part that took into account the coalition nature of a future war and the circumstances in which it might occur, as well as the size and military capabilities of NATO member states and their allies. It also referred to the European theatre of war operations and the associated projected options for the course of a possible armed conflict. The considered options differed in terms of the scale of operations, depending on their size, whether they would be local or global, and the type of conventional and nuclear

8 Kajetanowicz 2013, pp. 26–27.
9 Ibid., p. 37.
10 Ibid.
11 Pl. *Podstawowe założenia Ludowej Obronności.*
12 Pl. *Plan operacyjny obrony terytorium kraju.*

weapons used in combat. According to the operational plan, the units of the Front were to conduct a land-air-sea operation using airborne forces supported by the navy.[13] The guidelines contained in the document coincided with the assumptions contained in the war doctrine of the USSR.[14]

In February 1965, four years after the *Basic Assumptions for People's Defence* were prepared, a military executive document that supplemented the adopted government doctrine, entitled *Offensive Operation Plan for the Coastal-Front*,[15] came into force. The document comprehensively defined the operational use of Polish troops within the framework of the Pact and constituted a supplemented version of the previously functioning set of documents entitled *OP-61 Operational Plan of Front Forces*,[16] which included the *OP-61 Offensive Operation Plan*.[17] The exchange of documents was prompted by the need to clarify issues concerning preparations for conducting an offensive operation in accordance with the operational task received from the headquarters of the Unified Armed Forces of the Warsaw Pact, for the Armed Forces of the PRL, which were under organisation at that time. From then on, they became part of the so-called Polish Front intended for operations in the northern coast operational direction of the western theatre of war.[18]

13 Kajetanowicz 2013, p. 29; IPN BU: sig. 02958/79.

14 Kajetanowicz 2013, pp. 27–28.

15 Pl. *Plan operacji zaczepnej Frontu Nadmorskiego.*

16 Pl. *Plan operacyjny wojsk Frontu OP-61.*

17 Pl. *Plan operacji zaczepnej OP-61.*

18 The task of the Polish Front was to: "1. Przegrupowanie wojsk Frontu w ciągu dwóch dób z terytorium Polski do północnej części Niemieckiej Republiki Demokratycznej; 2. Przejście do działań zaczepnych z rana trzeciego dnia; 3. Prowadzenie działań zaczepnych w szybkim tempie na dwóch kierunkach: a) Schwerin, Flensburg, Półwysep Jutlandzki z zadaniem opanowania Schleswiga-Holsztynu i Półwyspu Jutlandzkiego oraz wysp i cieśnin duńskich w celu wytrącenia Danii z wojny oraz stworzenia warunków wyjścia sojuszniczych sił morskich z Bałtyku w akwen morza Północengo; b) płn. Wittenberga, Bremen, Haga z zadaniem rozbicia nadmorskiego skrzydła sił NATO oraz opanownaia Dolnej Saksonii i Holandii w celu wytrącenia z wojny Holandii i pozbawienia sił NATO możliwości korzystania z północnoniemieckich i holenderskich baz morskich" [1. Regroup the Front troops within two days from the Polish territory to the northern part of the German Democratic Republic; 2. Transition to offensive operations on the morning of the third day; 3. Conduct offensive operations at a rapid pace in two directions: a) Schwerin, Flensburg, Jutland Peninsula with the task of capturing Schleswig-Holstein and Jutland Peninsula as well as the Danish islands and straits in order to eliminate Denmark from the war and create conditions for the exit of allied naval forces from the Baltic into the North Sea; b) North Wittenberg, Bremen, The Hague with the task of breaking the coastal wing of NATO forces and capturing Lower Saxony and the Netherlands in order to eliminate the Netherlands from the war and deprive NATO forces of the possibility to use the North German and Dutch naval bases]. Kajetanowicz 2013, pp. 27–28; IPN BU: sig. 02958/163, *Plan matriałowo-technicznego i medycznego zabezpieczenia operacji Frontu*; IPN BU: sig. 02958/165, *Dokumenty planowania operacyjnego 1961 roku*; IPN BU: sig. 02958/167, *Plan przegrupowania wojsk Frontu cz. I i II.* The main objective of the Coastal Front operation was to eliminate, in cooperation with the 2nd Tank Army of the

The successor to the *Basic Assumptions for People's Defence* was the *Nodal Defence Assumptions of the People's Republic of Poland,*[19] implemented in 1973. The newly drafted document upheld the existing assumptions and, like its predecessor, contained guidelines which stated that the future conflict would be a global clash with the use of nuclear weapons. The paper pointed out that due to the considerable size of the battles fought and the weapons used, great human and material losses, as well as war damage were to be expected.[20] It is noteworthy that, unlike its predecessor, the introduced document clarified the concept of the national defence system for the first time ever. For the first time it isolated the exterior and interior organisation, known from the military documents of the late 1950s.[21]

In 1978, another version of the *Nodal Defence Assumptions of the People's Republic of Poland* was published. The document contained doctrinal assumptions known from earlier documents; however, the difference was that it took into account the possibility of NATO member states attempting to detach one or several Warsaw Pact member states from the USSR. It was predicted that this could take place as a result of local conflict, provoked by long-standing political and economic tensions and deliberately incited internal social unrest. The next version of the *Nodal Defence Assumptions of the People's Republic of Poland* as published in June 1985 and was the last document of its kind in the PRL. The nature of the document was similar to the previous ones. But this time, however, it was supplemented with conclusions from an analysis of Poland's political-economic relations with Western countries as a result of martial law introduced in 1981, which had a negative impact on the country's economy. It was stated that the reports created by the West are aimed at weakening Poland economically. The document also refers to the threat to the PRL posed by new types of missile weapons deployed in the Western Europe in the first half of the 1980s, such as tactical medium-range ballistic missiles and cruise missiles.[22]

The doctrinal documents described above constituted basic regulations on the defence of the PRL, directly influenced by the political circumstances of the Warsaw Pact. They were prepared in the National Defence Committee and

Northern Front of the Soviet Army, the coastal wing of NATO troops and destroy the 1st Army Corps of the Bundeswehr, part of the Dutch armed forces, a German-Danish army grouping in the Schlęswig-Holstein region and in the territory of Denmark. It was assumed that as a result of the undertaken actions Denmark and the Netherlands would be excluded from the war, and the conditions would be created for making way for the forces of the Unified Baltic Fleet of the Unified Armed Forces of the Warsaw Treaty Organization to enter the North Sea; IPN BU: sig. 02958/164; 02958/165.

19 Pl. *Węzłowe założenia obronne Polskiej Rzeczpospolitej Ludowej.*

20 Kajetanowicz 2013, p. 30.

21 Ibid., p. 41.

22 Ibid., p. 32.

the Polish General Staff, which made it possible to preserve their character and content layout. They formed an essential element of the system of doctrinal documents concerning the defence of the PRL and were complementary, constant in views and cyclical. The works undertaken to prepare them were a logical complement to the actions taken by the USSR in consolidating the national armed forces for its own political-military intentions implemented through the Warsaw Pact. Importantly, apart from the aspect of national security, they determined how the Polish armed forces would be organised, mainly for the needs of the binding coalition agreement.[23]

Selected military documents used to implement doctrinal assumptions. Discussion based on the Navy of the PRL

The essential military executive documents drafted in order to implement the doctrinal assumptions were prepared in the Ministry of National Defence of the PRL by the Polish General Staff. The basic source of the produced materials were the guidelines provided by the command of the Warsaw Pact in accordance with the assumptions of its doctrine.[24] The completed documents were then forwarded for implementation to the commands of those types of armed forces, which were responsible for their implementation. This *modus operandi* has been described using the example of the Navy.

In mid 1950s, the Polish General Staff, which was the central body for planning, directing and commanding the armed forces of the PRL, work was undertaken to study the role and character of the Polish Front in the strategic plans of the Warsaw Pact. The above-mentioned research was carried out between 1957 and 1961 and resulted in the drafting of the *Basic Assumptions for People's Defence.*[25]At the same time extensive work was being carried out on the development of the armed forces of the PRL and the preparation of an operational plan for the defence of the country's territory. In the course of the undertaken activities, a briefing was held on 3 January 1961, during which the duties and composition of the navy were tentatively defined.[26] The conclusions were then consulted with representatives of the USSR Ministry of Defence and the Warsaw Pact Command. As a result of the action undertaken, in March of the same year, basic arrangements concerning tasks for the Polish Navy were adopted. The decisions in question were included in the operational plan drawn up by the

23 IPN BU: sig. 2603/1154.
24 Przybylski 1989, p. 75; Burnetko / Onyszkiewicz / Bereś 1999, p. 93.
25 Puchała 2010, pp. 67–69.
26 Zalewski 2009, p. 419.

Polish General Staff, which pertained to the defence of Polish territory and was approved by the National Defence Committee in 1962. The above document described the defence system of the PRL, in which the Warsaw Pact played a key role. The adopted solution was reflected in the organisation of the state defence system based on two types of organisation: external and internal (territorial). The external organisation consisted of operational-force, to which naval strike forces intended for operations within the Unified Armed Forces of the Warsaw Pact were assigned as the Unified Baltic Fleet.[27] Naval forces, which operated within the framework of operational forces, were subordinate to the Minister of National Defence of the People's Republic of Poland in peacetime, while during a time of war they were to be at the disposal of the Supreme Commander of the Unified Armed Forces of the Warsaw Treaty Organization and, together with the USSR Baltic Fleet and the People's Navy of the GDR, were to perform tasks aimed at destroying enemy naval forces on the Baltic Sea and support land forces operating in coastal directions as well as defend their own sea transport routes.[28] The forces that operated within the internal (territorial) organisation were intended for operations in the internal system of state defence in cooperation with the troops of territorial defence and national air defence.[29] They would be used to defend the coast, shipping routes and naval bases of the PRL.[30]

The adopted division of naval forces was conventional, as there was a great deal of interdependence between the groups. They were expected to have the ability to be mutually combined or reinforced to perform specific tasks.[31]

---

27 "[...]Wojska operacyjne przeznaczone były do prowadzenia dynamicznych działań bojowych o charakterze zaczepnym, jak i obronnym, w każdych warunkach terenowych i atmosferycznych, zarówno w dzień, jak i w nocy. Zgodnie z decyzją władz PRL wojska te na wypadek wojny miały wchodzić w skład ZSZ UW, a ich zasadniczym zadaniem była walka z lądowymi, powietrznymi i morskimi siłami ewentualnego agresora zarówno na terytorium kraju, jak i poza jego granicami" [Operational troops were designed to conduct dynamic offensive and defensive combat operations in all terrain and weather conditions, both day and night. In accordance with the decision of the authorities of the People's Republic of Poland, these troops were to be a part of the Unified Armed Forces of the Warsaw Pact in the event of war, and their main task was to fight with land, air and sea forces of an aggressor both in the territory of the country and beyond its borders]. Kajetanowicz 2008, pp. 290–291. The Unified Baltic Fleet was the basic organisational unit of the fleets of the GDR, the PRL and the USSR, and was established on the initiative of the Russians in 1956, without a specific plan. It was designed to conduct naval operations as part of a frontline offensive operation; Zakatov 2016, p. 286; Veitch [2021]; Przybylski 1989, pp. 75–83.

28 Jaruzelski 1992, p. 113; Jurek / Skrzypkowski 1975, pp. 114, 322; Archiwum Wojskowe w Toruniu Oddział Zamiejscowy w Gdyni (hereinafter: AWTOZG): sig. 3533/75/192, fols. 27–44.

29 Nowak 2011, pp. 283–284.

30 Ibid.; Matczak 1976; *Tyły marynarki wojennej* 1974; *Zasady obrony wybrzeża* 1978; Przybylski 1989, p. 76; Rybak 2015. The National Defence Committee was a body of the Council of Ministers responsible for coordinating and supervising the implementation of defence tasks performed by other state bodies.

31 AWTOZG: sig. 3533/75/192, fol. 28; Przybylski 1989, p. 79.

On the basis of the assumptions included in the operational plan for the defence of the national territory, and in the course of the works conducted in the scope of developing the Navy of the PRL in the years 1961–1963, the Minister of National Defence issued the *Directive No. 0041/Oper. of 22 June 1964 Concerning the Tasks of the Polish Navy in Warfare.*[32] The directive specified that:

> The Navy of the PRL is an operational unit and is a part of operational forces assigned by the Armed Forces of the PRL to the Unified Armed Forces of the Warsaw Pact [...]. The essential task of the Navy in wartime will be:
> - participation in combating NATO naval forces and preventing them from operating in the central part of the Baltic Sea;
> - participation in the defence of the Polish coast together with the Territorial Defence Forces;
> - securing shipment of supplies by sea for the coastal front;
> - carrying out airborne operations together with the troops of the coastal front;
> - participation in organising the system of deploying own forces and allied forces.[33]

Moreover, in accordance with the assumptions of the operational plan, the Navy forces were divided into:

1. Operational forces – dedicated to action on the Baltic Sea, protection of their own shores and conducting airborne operations;
2. Territorial forces – designed to defend their coasts, coastal transport routes and bases and to secure shipments.[34]

The above solutions were included in the *Combat Regulations of the Armed Forces of the People's Republic of Poland*[35] introduced in 1964. It was a military document that described the duties of the Navy of the PRL operating within the framework of operational troops and in the internal organisation of national territory defence, as follows:

32 Pl. *Dyrektywa nr 0041/Oper. z 22.06.1964 r. w sprawie zadań Marynarki Wojennej PRL w działaniach wojennych*; Przybylski 1989, p. 80.

33 "Marynarka Wojenna PRL stanowi związek operacyjny wchodzący w skład wojsk operacyjnych wydzielonych przez Siły Zbrojne PRL do Zjednoczonych Sił Zbrojnych Układu Warszawskiego [...]. Zasadniczym zadaniem Marynarki Wojennej w czasie wojny będzie: uczestnictwo w zwalczaniu sił morskich NATO i niedopuszczenie ich do działań w środkowej części Bałtyku; udział w obronie polskiego wybrzeża wspólnie z wojskami OTK; zabezpieczenie przewozów drogą morską zaopatrzenia dla frontu nadmorskiego; przeprowadzenie operacji desantowych wspólnie z wojskami frontu nadmorskiego; udział w organizowaniu systemu bazowania sił własnych i sojuszniczych." Quoted after Zalewski 2009, p. 421.

34 AWTOZG: sig. 3533/75/192, fol. 28.

35 Pl. *Regulamin Walki Sił Zbrojnych PRL.*

1. Combating enemy naval forces at sea and in base areas;
2. Securing the activities of land forces in the coastal operational direction (participation in airborne operations, anti-airborne operations, supply and delivery of troops, protection of troops from strikes from the sea, fire support of land forces);
3. Defending their own coastal lines of transport;
4. Defending the operational zone of the Navy (participation in coastal defence).[36]

The above regulations constituted the first comprehensive study on the duties of the Navy of the PRL and were the result of work initiated shortly after the establishment of the Warsaw Pact. It is also worth noting that until their implementation, naval duties were governed by day-to-day operational activities. This situation resulted from ongoing conceptual work on the defence of the PRL, i. e., the basic assumptions of the people's defence and plans for the development of the Armed Forces of the People's Republic of Poland, including: the composition, development and principles of using naval forces in the coalition system of naval operational activities within the framework of the Warsaw Pact. Only after the fundamental issues had been settled could the entire duties of the navy within the alliance be defined. Moreover, it should be emphasised that this was a period of work on the overall organisation of the Warsaw Pact forces and the development of uniform procedures for the cooperation of national troops within the framework of a single strategy binding in the Pact, as well as related operational training and unification of military equipment in its member states.

The basic duties of the Navy of the PRL defined in the early 1960s functioned until the late 1980s. However, in spite of great effort and positive results in operational training, limitations that resulted from deficiencies in military equipment posed a significant problem in fulfilling the set tasks.[37]

In tandem with the work conducted on the role of the Polish Navy in the security system of the PRL and the Warsaw Pact, organisational changes were introduced to the Navy which eventually caused it to function within the system of flotillas that were specially created in the Warsaw Pact. Additionally, naval aviation was organised. The adopted organisation was made on the basis of national doctrinal documents prepared in accordance with the needs that arose from the organisation of the Unified Armed Forces of the Warsaw Treaty Organization. On their basis, three flotillas were formed within the Navy of the PRL – two for coastal defence and one flotilla of ships. Coastal defence flotillas were

36 Centralne Archiwum Wojskowe (hereinafter: CAW): sig. 1596/29, fol. 533; Linka 1969, pp. 71–83; Łuczak 1984, pp. 145–153.

37 Zalewski 2009, p. 430.

established in 1965, not long after the first doctrinal guidelines were drafted, as well as a ship flotilla in 1971. The establishment of the latter was aimed at consolidating the strike forces that acted mainly for the Warsaw Pact Baltic Fleet operating within the Unified Armed Forces of the Warsaw Treaty Organization. The adopted organisational solution survived until the beginning of the 21st century. The flotillas were given specific numbers in accordance with the system of organisation of allied fleets adopted in the Warsaw Pact.

Coastal defence flotillas were created around the Hel Peninsula and in Świnoujście. On the Hel Peninsula, the 9th Coastal Defense Flotilla was formed on the basis of the former Brigade of the Main Base Water Area Defence, while in Świnoujście the 8th Coastal Defence Flotilla was established to replace the existing Naval Base. The above-mentioned flotillas formed operational-tactical compounds intended for securing the deployment and development of the basic naval forces, searching and fighting enemy submarines in coastal areas, ensuring the regime of the movement of ships and vessels in their area of responsibility, organising the anti-airborne defence in their own area in cooperation with the land forces, creating a comprehensive defence of the coast and conducting security operations for the main forces of the Navy of the PRL, which were part of the flotilla.[38] Established in the early 1970s, the 3rd Ship Flotilla in Gdynia was a naval operational and tactical unit intended for missile, torpedo and artillery strikes against sea and coastal enemy targets, independently and in cooperation with naval aviation, as part of the allied naval forces of the Warsaw Pact in a designated operational direction. The formed flotilla was based on the former strike units, which included: the 1st Submarine Brigade, the 3rd Motor Torpedo Boat Brigade and the commands of the 7th Destroyer Squadron. The newly formed flotilla was designed to perform the following tasks: destroying enemy ships and vessels; destroying and overpowering the forces and measures of the anti-airborne defence system as part of airborne operations; destroying and overpowering the forces and measures of the enemy's anti-airborne defence system as part of airborne operations; eliminating and overpowering firing positions, groupings of troops and their facilities on land as part of fire support for the operations of the land forces' coastal wing; participation in the defence of their own coast and deployment areas; performing surveillance support and reconnaissance at sea; searching and combating enemy submarines; tracking and combating enemy vessels; tracking NATO warships in peacetime and wartime; placing active and defensive mine barriers; landing reconnaissance and sabotage groups on an enemy coast; rescuing crews of their own and allied aircraft and

38 Mandat / Serafin 1976, pp. 26–27; Miecznikowski 1977, pp. 41–43; Toczek 1985, pp. 102–106; CAW: sig. 1596/29, fol. 537, 538; Tobiasz 1984, pp. 101–109; *Sztuka operacyjna marynarki wojennej* 1974; AWTOZG: sig. 4109/99/3, fols. 6–7.

vessels which had suffered damage during combat operations at sea, independently and in cooperation with aviation and allied fleet ship teams.[39] The duties performed by the naval forces of the flotilla were carried out jointly with the aviation of the Navy of the PRL which initially operated as part of the 33rd Naval Aviation Division. Then, in the course of organisational changes connected with the development of the Navy, it was subordinated to the Naval Aviation and Air Defence Command and to the Naval Aviation Headquarters. Air forces worked within the allied cooperation during offensive naval operations and as part of the defence.[40] All of them consisted in combating enemy naval forces and shore facilities, protection and combating enemy defences during airborne operations, and conducting sea rescues.

The ships of the Navy of the PRL were classified in accordance with the regulations of the Warsaw Pact, i. e., *Recommendations on the Classification of Ships and Auxiliary Naval Units.*[41] They defined the division of naval forces into four warship groups and auxiliary units.[42]

The tasks assigned to the Navy of the PRL resulted from the binding assumptions described in military and government doctrinal documents and were performed in accordance with the role assigned to them within the functioning of the Warsaw Pact Baltic Fleet. These actions were a component of the main task performed by the Unified Armed Forces of the Warsaw Treaty Organization in the form of Fronts in the northern, central and southern operational direction of the western theatre of war. The Polish Navy was responsible for destroying enemy fleet and its forces at coast.[43] However, it should be noted that in the light of the prevailing views and doctrinal assumptions as well as the order adopted in the system and the actual capabilities of the Navy of the PRL, it did not play a leading role in the allied operational activity in the maritime theatre of war.[44] It was mainly designed to carry out tactical airborne and amphibious operations in the straits and bays of the Baltic Sea, and to enable the ships of the Unified Baltic Fleet to exit the Baltic Sea.

39 AWTOZG: sig. 4109/99/3, fol. 2.
40 Chojnacki 2005, pp. 56–64.
41 Pl. *Zalecenia w sprawie klasyfikacji okrętów i pomocniczych jednostek pływających marynarki wojennej*; IPN BU: sig. 1420/18, fol. 60.
42 Ibid., fols. 63–88.
43 Przybylski 1988, p. 72.
44 Lider 1966, p. 184.

Military documents that regulated operational cooperation between the naval forces of the Warsaw Pact. Discussion based on the Unified Baltic Fleet

Polish Navy operations were conducted within the framework of the Warsaw Pact Baltic Fleet of the Unified Armed Forces of the Warsaw Treaty Organization on the basis of a number of regulations included in normative documents (military executive documents). They referred to methods of cooperation between the Polish, East German and Soviet navies, in particular their allied training and the execution of naval operations, including in cooperation with land and air forces. These regulations set out the principles for the preparation of military documentation in force in the Pact.

The first documents that defined the principles of operation of the naval forces of allied fleets concerned the narrow scope of cooperation between national navies. They also formed the basis for the development of a set of documents under the name BALTIKA and referred exclusively to naval forces that operate within the operational armies.[45] The first organisational work on the set began in the early 1970s and was completed nearly a decade later.[46] Eventually, this formed the basis for the operation of the Unitfied Ship Squadron, established in the early 1980s as part of Warsaw Pact Baltic Fleet.

The presented documents are mainly instructions and guidelines and do not constitute a set of all regulations produced during the Warsaw Pact period. This is due to the fact that no list of such documents has yet been found. It is not known if such a list was ever created. Instead, the author's intention is to present their diversity and character.[47] The described documents were executed by orders of the Chief of the Polish General Staff, the commander of the Navy of the PRL and the Chief of the Naval Headquarters. Depending on the period, the described documents were prepared in Polish and Russian, with the latter being the dominant language.

One of the key documents that define the basic principles of cooperation between the USSR Baltic Fleet, the Navy of the PRL, and the People's Navy of the GDR was signed in 1963 and titled *Osnovnye princypy vzaimodejstviâ Krasnoznamennogo Baltijskogo Flota c voenno – morskij flotom PNR i narodnym flotom GDR* [*Основные принцыпы взаимодействия Краснознаменного Балтийского Флота с военно – морский флотом ПНР и народным флотом ГДР*].[48] The document in question regulated the scope of operational cooperation between

45 The name referred to the Baltic Sea.
46 IPN BU: sig. 1420/5, fol. 1.
47 All the discussed documents are in the author's possession in the form of photographs.
48 Photographs of the original documents discussed are in the author's possession.

the three navies within the framework of cooperation in the Baltic theatre of war, mutual technical support and the use of port infrastructure. The rules were a development of the agreement on cooperation concluded on 4 April 1958 between the commanders of the USSR Baltic Fleet and the Navy of the PRL, which was in force in the Polish Navy on the basis of the *Navy Commander's Order No. 06/Oper. of 12 July 1958 on the Organisation of the Navy's Cooperation with the USSR Baltic Fleet.*[49] Additionally, the *Order* implemented sets of regulations including: *Instructions for Mutual Notification of the Staffs of the Baltic Fleet of the USSR and the Polish Navy; The Regime of the Movement of Ships and Vessels of the Baltic Fleet of the USSR and the Navy of the People's Republic of Poland; Rules of Communications in Cooperation and Radar Surveillance with the Baltic Fleet of the USSR; Instructions for the Organisation of a Secret Command in Cooperation Between the Navy and the Baltic Fleet of the USSR.*[50]

In March 1959, the Chief of Staff of the Baltic Fleet of the USSR counter admiral Vladimir Nikolaevich Alekseev sent ready instructions on the exchange of information, movement of ships at sea and reconnaissance to the Chiefs of Staff of the Navy of the PRL and the People's Navy of GDR. Then, in the course of further works on improving the organisation of cooperation between naval forces, another instruction was introduced, which referred to rescue operations: *Instrukciâ po soviestnym dejstviâm VMF PNR i KBF pri okazanil pomoŝi podvodnoj lodke VMF PNR, poterpevšej avariû* [*Инструкция по совиестным действиям ВМФ ПНР и КБФ при оказанил помощи подводной лодке ВМФ ПНР, потерпевшей аварию*].[51] At the same time, the Navy's common principles of communication were put into use.[52] This kind of documents were in force throughout the existence of Warsaw Pact.

Shortly afterwards, in 1963, the existing instructions were replaced by new ones. They were put into service by *Order of the Commander of the Navy of the People's Republic of Poland No. 017/Oper. Dated 11 July.*[53] Separate documents by

49 Pl. *Rozkaz Dowódcy Marynarki Wojennej Nr 06/Oper. z dnia 12 lipca 1958 roku, o organizacji współdziałania Marynarki Wojennej z Flotą Bałtycką ZSRR*; IPN BU: sig. 1420/5, fols. 64–111; AWTOZG: sig. 3982/91/13, fol. 1.

50 Pl. *Instrukcja wzajemnego powiadamiania Sztabów Floty Bałtyckiej ZSRR i Marynarki Wojennej PRL; Reżim pływania okrętów i statków Floty Bałtyckiej ZSRR i Marynarki Wojennej PRL; Zarządzenie łączności współdziałania i rozpoznania radiolokacyjnego z Flotą Bałtycką ZSRR; Instrukcja organizacji tajnego dowodzenia przy współdziałaniu Marynarki Wojennej z Flotą Bałtycką ZSRR*; AWTOZG: sig. 3982/91/13, fol. 1; IPN BU: sig 1420/1, fol. 72. Photographs of original instructions in Russian in the possession of the author.

51 IPN BU: sig. 1420/1, fols. 166–167.

52 Ibid., fols. 1, 49–53, 59, 61, 63–128.

53 Pl. *Zarządzenie dowódcy Marynarki Wojennej PRL nr 017/Oper. z 11 lipca.*

secret command were an exception.[54] Among the documents introduced at the time mentioned were:

- *Instructions for Mutual Notification of the Staffs of the Baltic Fleet of the USSR, the Navy of the People's Republic of Poland and the People's Navy of the GDR;*[55]
- *Instructions for the Regime of the Movement of Ships and Vessels of the Baltic Fleet of the USSR, the Navy of the People's Republic of Poland and the People's Navy of the GDR;*[56]
- *Instructions for Ships of the Baltic Fleet of the USSR, the Navy of the People's Republic of Poland and the People's Navy of the GDR Performing Surveillance;*[57]
- *Instructions on the Reconnaissance Between Ships (Vessels) of the Baltic Fleet of the USSR, the Navy of the People's Republic of Poland and the People's Navy of the GDR with Annexes: Rules of the Use of Tables of Visual Reconnaissance Signals in the Baltic Theatre of Operations (ZOS BMT); Schedule IO - 21 (Individual Reconnaissance) for the 1st Quarter of 1963; Schedule No. 1 (model); ZOS BMT Board - "A" (Example);*[58]
- *Guidelines on Uniform Regimes for the Work of Radioelectronic Warfare of the Baltic Fleet of the USSR, the Navy of the People's Republic of Poland and the People's Navy of the GDR.*[59]

At the same time, the *Instruction on Cooperation of Search and Rescue Forces of Allied Fleets of Warsaw Pact Member States*[60] was implemented.[61] Other documents on the cooperation of allied naval forces were also introduced. They included reconnaissance instructions that described a uniform system for the reconnaissance of ships, aircraft and helicopters of the Warsaw Pact armed forces on the Baltic Sea, as well as regulations on the organisation and use of technical

54 AWTOZG: sig. 3982/91/10, fol. 68.

55 Pl. *Instrukcja o wzajemnym powiadamianiu Sztabów Floty Bałtyckiej ZSRR, Marynarki Wojennej PRL i Ludowej Marynarki NRD.*

56 Pl. *Instrukcja o reżimie pływania okrętów i statków Floty Bałtyckiej ZSRR, Marynarki Wojennej PRL i Ludowej Marynarki NRD.*

57 Pl. *Instrukcja dla okrętów Floty Bałtyckiej ZSRR, Marynarki Wojennej PRL i Ludowej Marynarki NRD pełniących dozór.*

58 Pl. *Instrukcja o rozpoznawaniu między okrętami (statkami) Floty Bałtyckiej ZSRR, Marynarki Wojennej PRL i Ludowej Marynarki NRD wraz z załącznikami: Przepisy posługiwania się tabelami wzrokowych sygnałów rozpoznawczych na bałtyckim teatrze działań (ZOS BMT); Rozkład IO - 21 (Indywidualnego rozpoznawania) na I kw. 1963; Rozkład nr 1 (wzór); Tablica ZOS BMT - "A" (przykład).*

59 Pl. *Wytyczne o jednolitych reżimach pracy środków radioelektronicznych Floty Bałtyckiej ZSRR, Marynarki Wojennej PRL i Ludowej Marynarki NRD*; AWTOZG: sig. 3982/91/3, fol. 92.

60 Pl. *Instrukcja o współdziałaniu sił poszukująco-ratowniczych flot sojuszniczych państw członków Układu Warszawskiego.*

61 IPN BU: sig. 1420/81.

and visual means of reconnaissance: *Reconnaissance Instructions in the People's Navy of the GDR, Navy of the People's Republic of Poland, and the Baltic Fleet of the USSR.*[62] In parallel with the allied regulations, the Navy of the PRL developed national reconnaissance manuals used to supervise the maritime operational zone. In 1967, the *Instructions for NATO Ship Tracking*[63] became effective.[64] The undertaken actions served to improve the system for early detection of actions taken by NATO forces which could lead to the possible initiation of hostilities. At that time, the *Instructions for Mutual Notification of the Staffs of the People's Navy of the GDR, the Navy of the People's Republic of Poland and the Baltic Fleet of the USSR and Their Tactical Units*[65] was also in force.[66] The regulations described were refined throughout the whole period of the Warsaw Pact, as evidenced, for example, by the 1982 instruction on the movement of ships and reconnaissance regimes *Instrukciâ po uežimu plavaniâ korabliej j sudov NVMF, VMF PNR BF SSS v ûžnoj časti Baltijsgo Morâ* [*Инструкция по уежиму плавания кораблией й судов НВМФ, ВМФ ПНР БФ ССС в южной части Балтийсго Моря*].[67]

The situation with regard to the developing radio-electronic warfare was similar. In the described period of time the so-called *Principles of the Organisation and Conduct of Radio-electronic Warfare in Operations (Combat Operations) of the Unified Armed Forces of the Warsaw Pact Countries*[68] were in force, which contained recommendations on how to plan and conduct of radio-electronic warfare on the basis of experience gained during operational combat training.[69] To make cooperation more effective, signal tables common to the three navies were used.[70] The *Collection of Command Signals for Anti-submarine Warfare Forces of Allied Fleets of the People's Navy of the GDR, the Navy of the Polish People's Republic Navy and the Baltic Fleet of the USSR*[71] was introduced.[72] On the other hand, in order to improve the ship traffic system on the Baltic Sea, unified documents for the use of one fairway system were developed in 1980, e.g. *Edinaâ sistema farvterov i redstva navigacionogo oborudovaniâ v ûžnoj časti*

62 Pl. *Instrukcja rozpoznania w LMW NRD, MW PRL i FB ZSRR*; ibid.: sig. 1420/102.

63 Pl. *Instrukcja o prowadzeniu śledzenia okrętów NATO.*

64 AWTOZG: sig. 3982/91/10, fol. 68.

65 Pl. *Instrukcja o wzajemnym powiadamianiu sztabów LMW NRD, MW PRL i FB ZSRR i ich związków taktycznych.*

66 IPN BU: sig. 1420/68.

67 Ibid.: sig. 1420/62.

68 Pl. *Zasady organizacji i prowadzenia walki radioelektronicznej w operacji (działaniach bojowych) Zjednoczonych Sił Zbrojnych Państw Układu Warszawskiego.*

69 IPN BU: sig. 1420/58.

70 Ibid.: sig. 1420/206.

71 Pl. *Zbiór sygnałów dowodzenia siłami zwalczania okrętów podwodnych sojuszniczych flot LMW NRD, MW PRL, FB ZSRR.*

72 IPN BU: sig. 1420/194, fol. 362.

Baltijsgo Morâ [*Единая система фарвтеров и редства навигационого оборудования в южной части Балтийсго Моря*].[73] Despite the lack of surviving documents in this regard, it is reasonable to assume that documents with a similar function already existed earlier.

In an effort to improve combat operations, guidelines were introduced for the production of homogeneous combat documents – the *Instruction on the Use of Formalised Combat Documents.*[74] It defined the nature and purpose of formalised documents as well as how they should be prepared. It was used to standardise the system and how operational information was transmitted. Additionally, the *List of Classification Markings in Warsaw Pact Documents*[75] and *Templates of Reports to the General Staff and the Warsaw Pact Baltic Fleets*[76] were in force.[77]

Another area subject to regulation concerned the assessment of the effectiveness of task performance within the framework of the undertaken cooperation of navies – for this purpose a document entitled *Assessment of the Ratio of Forces in the Performance of Essential Tasks of Allied Fleets*[78] was introduced.[79] These solutions were intended to enable the analysis of processes that occur in operational training and the preparation of further recommendations based on them, described in publications such as: *Experience Gained from Unified Ship Squadron Training.*[80] The undertaken work represents a fragment of the organisational activities aimed at increasing the quality and effectiveness of forces and measures used in operational training. However, the rules of training were described in a number of separate documents, such as *Materialy operativnogo sbora rukovodâŝego sostava soûznyh flot Baltijskoj More* [*Материалы* оперативного *сбора руководящего состава союзных флот Балтийской Море*].[81] The process of training naval forces of the Warsaw Pact was subject to research and was comprehensively described, which enabled the procedures of military operations to be standardised.[82]

73 Ibid.: sig. 1420/61.
74 Pl. *Instrukcja o stosowaniu sformalizowanych dokumentów bojowych*; ibid.: sig. 1420/29; 1420/27; 1420/40.
75 Pl. *Wykaz oznaczeń klauzul tajności dokumentów Układu Warszawskiego.*
76 Pl. *Wzory sprawozdań do Sztabu Generalnego i ZFB.*
77 IPN BU: sig. 1420/64; 1420/203; AWTOZG: sig. 92/4046/8.
78 Pl. *Ocena stosunku sił przy wykonywaniu zasadniczych zadań flot sojuszniczych.*
79 IPN BU: sig. 1420/202.
80 Pl. *Doświadczenia wynikające ze szkolenia Zjednoczonej Eskadry Okrętów*; ibid.: sig. 1420/204.
81 Ibid.: sig. 1420/78; 1420/198.
82 Ibid.: sig. 1420/205; 1420/210.

In addition, documentation was produced on the use of training areas during missile and artillery firing.[83] Documents on training in raising combat readiness were prepared and introduced, which are described in *Kurs boevoj podgotovki častej RÈB Flota, as well as cooperation instructions entitled Instrukciâ po vzaimodejstviû cjl PVO voenno – morskih flotov s silami PVO primorskih ob'edinij c coedinenij PVO gosudarstv – učastnikov Varšavskogo Dogovora oraz Rukovodstvo organizacij i provedeniû sovmiestnyh učenij v ob'edinennyh vooružennyh silah gosudarstv – učastnikov Varšavskogo Dogovora* [*Курс боевой подготовки частей РЭБ Флота*, and cooperation instruction entitled *Инструкция по взаимодействию сйл ПВО военно – морских флотов с силами ПВО приморских обьединий с соединений ПВО государств – участников Варшавского Договора oraz Руководство организаций и проведению совмиестных учений в обьединенных вооруженных силах государств – участников Варшавского Договора*].[84]

Within the scope of the operational training of the allied naval forces, the *Instructions for the Operational Groups of the Navy of the People's Republic of Poland Addressed to Staff of the Allied Navies and Cooperating Operational Units of Other Types of the Unified Armed Forces*[85] was introduced and later improved.[86] It defined the basic principles concerning the composition and purpose of the operational groups, the rights and duties of the functional persons, as well as the organisation of their work during the operational development of fleets for peacetime and wartime, as well as planning and conducting operations and joint combat operations by the forces of the three fleets. Another type of documents developed for common use were the *Norms of Irrecoverable Losses of Armaments and Supply for the Military of the Warsaw Pact.*[87]

During the operational training, the executive documentation defined in the *Recommendations for Joint Actions of Allied Fleet Forces on the Baltic Sea*[88] and the *Principles of Air Defence Organisation*[89] was applied.[90] The guidelines concerning the organisation and principles of ship movement and dispersal of ships on the Baltic Sea in special conditions – i. e., in the event of a threat to the ships – as well as the actions to be undertaken during the transition to higher states of

83 Ibid.: sig. 1420/200.
84 Ibid.: sig. 1420/36; 1420/55; 1420/53.
85 Pl. *Instrukcja dla grup operacyjnych MW PRL kierowanych do sztabów flot sojuszniczych i współdziałających związków operacyjnych innych rodzajów Zjednoczonych Sił Zbrojnych.*
86 IPN BU: sig. 1420/75; 1420/33; 1420/32.
87 Pl. *Normy bezpowrotnych strat uzbrojenia, bojowej techniki materiałowej, zapasów w toku wojny i zgromadzonych zapasów w czasie pokoju dla Układu Warszawskiego*; ibid.: sig. 1420/ 213.
88 Pl. *Rekomendacje w sprawie wspólnych działań sił flot sojuszniczych na Morzu Bałtyckim.*
89 Pl. *Zasady organizacji obrony przeciwlotniczej.*
90 IPN BU: sig. 1420/90; 1420/88.

operational readiness, were also introduced into service. The document was entitled *Guidelines for Navigating on the Baltic Sea Theatre Following the Introduction of Special Conditions of Ship Movement.*[91]

Allied cooperation was also based on the documents that covered: *Instructions for the Unified High Readiness Forces for Combating Submarines; Scope of Tasks and Duties for the Staff of the Alert Joint State Political Directorate Unified Baltic Fleet; Instructions for the Duty Officer of the Joint State Political Directorate; Duty Obligations of the Assistant Duty Officer; The Role of Watch in Port; Instructions for Radar Guard-ships in the People's Navy of the GDR; The Navy of the People's Republic of Poland and the Baltic Fleet of the USSR.*[92]

Conclusions

Doctrinal and military documents that operated in the PRL constitute some of the most valuable and reliable historical sources that describe the operations performed for the benefit of its defence. The information contained therein concerns actions undertaken both domestically and on an international scale.

The documents described in the presented article reveal that they were drafted to function in a relationship based on cause and effect, in a system of actions that led from an idea to its implementation, and were coherent with each other. As a result of the adopted solution they formed one complete system of mutually correlated doctrinal documents. The activities defined therein were complimentary and formed a logical whole. The documents functioned in a hierarchical system, and were grouped into general documents, which described the concept for defending the PRL (prepared by the government), detailed documents, which defined the strategy of conduct, and executive documents, which determined a plan of action (the latter two groups were prepared by the military). The presented description unambiguously demonstrates that doctrinal and military documents were linked along the line of idea-doctrine-procedure, and presented the binding standard of drafting documents and the interdependence of all links that participated in the process, i.e., from central government bodies responsible for developing the idea of doctrine to the final individual executor acting on the basis of an instruction. Moreover, the conducted research confirmed the un-

91 Pl. *Wytyczne w sprawie żeglugi na bałtyckim morskim teatrze po wprowadzeniu specjalnych warunków pływania*; ibid.: sig. 1420/101.

92 Pl. *Instrukcja dla Zjednoczonych Dyżurnych Sił ZOP*; *Zakres zadań i obowiązków sztabu dyżurnej OGPU ZFB*; *Instrukcja oficera dyżurnego dyżurnej OGPU*, *Obowiązki służbowe pomocnika oficera dyżurnego*, *Obowiązki służbowe wachtowego przy trapie*; *Instrukcja dla okrętów dozoru LMW NRD, MW PRL, FB ZSRR*; ibid.: sig. 1420/64; 1420/63; 1420/15, fols. 220, 213.

equivocal adherence of the national security of the PRL to the participation in the Warsaw Pact, which resulted in total dependence on its russian command. All the described documents were influenced by confrontational factors that occurred during the Cold War between the Warsaw Pact and NATO.

[Translated by Tomasz Leszczuk]

Bibliography

Archival sources

Instytut Pamięci Narodowej Biuro Udostępniania: sig. 02958/79; 02958/79/80; 02958/79/81; 02958/79/82; 02958/79/83; 02958/79/425; 02958/86; 02958/105; 02958/106; 02958/107; 02958/123; 02958/164; 02958/162; 02958/163; 02958/165; 02958/167; 2603/1154; 1420/1; 1420/5; 1420/15; 1420/18; 1420/27; 1420/29; 1420/32; 1420/33;1420/36; 1420/40; 1420/53; 1420/55; 1420/58; 1420/61; 1420/62; 1420/63; 1420/64; 1420/68; 1420/64; 1420/78; 1420/75; 1420/81; 1420/88; 1420/90; 1420/101; 1420/102; 1420/194; 1420/198; 1420/200; 1420/202; 1420/203; 1420/204; 1420/205; 1420/206; 1420/210; 1420/213.

Archiwum Wojskowe w Toruniu Oddział Zamiejscowy w Gdyni: sig. 3533/75/92; 3533/75/192; 4109/99/3; 3982/91/13; 3982/91/10; 3982/91/3; 1420/81; 3982/91/10; 4046/92/8.

Centralne Archiwum Wojskowe: sig. 1596/29.

Literature

Burnetko, Krzysztof / Onyszkiewicz, Janusz / Bereś, Witold: *Onyszkiewicz ze szczytów do NATO.* 1999.

Chojnacki, Zenon: *Lotnictwo marynarki wojennej.* 2005.

Engerman, David: *Ideologia a geneza zimnej wojny 1917–1962*, in: Leffler, Paul Melvin / Westad, Odd Arne (eds.): *Historia zimnej wojny.* 2017/1, pp. 37–59.

Gaddis, John: *Teraz już wiemy… Nowa historia zimnej wojny.* 1997.

Gibianskij, Leonid Ânovič [Гибианский, Леонид Янович]: *Forsorovanie sovetskoj blokovoj politiki* [*Форсорование советской блоковой политики*], in: Egorova, Nataliâ Ivanovna, [Егорова, Наталия Ивановна] / Čubar'ân, Aleksándr Ogánovič [Чубарьян, Алексáндр Огáнович] (eds.): *Holodnaâ Vojna 1945–1963 gg. Istoričeskaâ retrospektva* [*Холодная Война 1945–1963 гг. Историческая ретроспектва*]. 2003, pp. 137–187.

Holloway, David: *Broń jądrowa i eskalacja zimnej wojny 1945–1962*, in: Leffler, Paul Melvin / Westad, Odd Arne (eds.): *Historia zimnej wojny.* 2017/1, pp. 359–379.

Jaruzelski, Wojciech: *Stan wojenny. Dlaczego…* 1992.

Jurek, Marian / Skrzypkowski, Edward: *Tarcza pokoju. XX-lecie Układu Warszawskiego.* 1975.

Kajetanowicz, Jerzy: *Polskie wojska operacyjne w systemie bezpieczeństwa w latach 1955–1975*, in: *Zeszyty Naukowe Akademii Obrony Narodowej.* 2008/2, pp. 152–169.

Kajetanowicz, Jerzy: *Wojsko Polskie w systemie bezpieczeństwa państwa 1945–2010.* 2013.
Lider, Julian: *Wojny i doktryny wojenne XX wieku.* 1966.
Linka, Henryk: *Zasadnicze rodzaje działań marynarki wojennej na otwartych i zamkniętych teatrach morskich*, in: *Myśl Wojskowa.* 1969/2, pp. 71–83.
Łuczak, Czesław: *Organizacja i prowadzenie przez marynarkę wojenną samodzielnych działań desantowych o charakterze taktycznym*, in: *Myśl Wojskowa.* 1984/3, pp. 145–154.
Mandat, Tadeusz / Serafin, Mieczysław: *Podstawy sztuki operacyjnej Marynarki Wojennej. Podręcznik.* 1976.
Matczak, Jerzy: *Zabezpieczenie tyłowe sił marynarki wojennej. Teoria ogólna tyłów marynarki wojennej.* 1976.
Miecznikowski, Ryszard: *Sztuka operacyjna marynarki wojennej. Zasady ogólne.* 1977.
Nowak, Jan Maria: *Od hegemonii do agonii. Upadek Układu Warszawskiego. Polska perspektywa.* 2011.
Pechantov, Vladimir Oleghovich: *Związek Radziecki i świat, 1944–1953*, in: Leffler, Paul Melvin / Westad, Odd Arne (eds.): *Historia zimnej wojny.* 2017/1, pp. 101–121.
Przybylski, Jerzy: *Marynarka Wojenna PRL w latach 1956–1980 (studium historyczno-wojskowe).* 1988/2.
Puchała, Franciszek: *Sztab Generalny Wojska Polskiego w latach 1945–1990.* 2010.
Rybak, Robert: *Doktryna wojenna Polskiej Rzeczypospolitej Ludowej – refleksje historyczne*, in: Bugajski, Dariusz / Rybak, Robert (eds.): *Siła i strategia bezpieczeństwa narodowego.* 2015, pp. 149–165.
Rybak, Robert: *Sztuka operacyjna marynarki wojennej. Analiza wybranych aspektów szkolenia operacyjnego w latach 1955–1990 w świetle dokumentów.* 2021.
Sztuka operacyjna marynarki wojennej. Obrona powietrzna na teatrze morskim. 1974.
Tobiasz, Stanisław: *Organizacja strefy obrony odpowiedzialności flotylli obrony wybrzeża*, in: *Myśl Wojskowa.* 1984/ 4, pp. 101–110.
Toczek, Marek: *Udział marynarki wojennej w obronie wybrzeża*, in: *Myśl Wojskowa.* 1985/ 1, pp. 102–107.
Tyły marynarki wojennej. 1974.
Veitch, Kim: *The Warsaw Pact Baltic Fleet.* 1984, in: URL: https://core.ac.uk/download/pdf/36712849.pdf [17.02.2021].
Zakatov, B. A. [Закатов, B. A.]: *O boevoj lužbe sil Sovetskogo VMF i period global'nogo protivostoâniâ v mirovom okeane v 1966–1986 gody. Istoričeskie očerki* [*О боевой лужбе сил Советского ВМФ и период глобального противостояния в мировом океане в 1966–1986 годы. Исторические очерки*]. 2016.
Zalewski, Bogdan: *Koncepcje dotyczące składu, rozwoju i zasad wykorzystania sił polskiej Marynarki Wojennej w koalicyjnym systemie działań morskich państw stron Układu Warszawskiego*, in: Centek, Jarosław / Krotofil, Maciej (eds.): *Od armii komputowej do narodowej. Problemy organizacyjne sił zbrojnych od XVI do XX wieku.* 2009/3, pp. 415–431.
Zasady obrony wybrzeża. 1978.

Marlena Jabłońska

The Environment of Contemporary Archives as the Context of Their Operations. An Area of Many Dimensions

Abstract
This article aims to discuss the factors that constitute the contemporary environment of archives in Poland, influence how they run and create the context in which they operate. This study was broken down into five aspects: socio-cultural, political and legal, economic, technological and international. While each of them raises separate issues, problems and challenges for archives, they are all areas that archives can influence. These considerations involved four groups of archives: public, institutional, community and commercial.
Keywords: archive environment; archives in Poland; public archives; state archives; social changes and archives

Institutions established to acquire, preserve, arrange and describe, and provide access to documentation operate worldwide. These are archives with different organisational structures, archival holdings, missions and work methodology; yet they share a common goal – to preserve the documentary heritage of their country. This goal is undoubtedly a noble one as it helps to cultivate the memory of a state and its citizens, but it is pragmatic too, as it ensures the continuous and smooth functioning of various types of entities. These institutions operate in a specific space, circumstances, time and place. Archives work in their own particular environment, which influences their structure and endeavours. Moreover, archives themselves interact with their environment.

This chapter aims to discuss selected factors that constitute the contemporary environment of archives in Poland, influence how they run and create the context in which they operate. This study was broken down into five aspects: socio-cultural, political and legal, economic, technological and international. Each of them raises separate issues, problems and challenges for archives. They are also all dimensions that archives can interact with, where they can make their presence felt and benefit from processes of exchange. These considerations involved

Assoc. prof. Marlena Jabłońska, Nicolaus Copernicus University in Toruń, ORCID: https://orcid.org/0000-0001-7189-9007.

four groups of archives: public, institutional, community and commercial. Each operates in an environment with a specific structure, which is influenced by the above-mentioned factors in a different way and to a different extent.

The environment of an institution is a set of factors and processes that directly and indirectly affect how it operates and determine development opportunities, as well as generate obstacles and threats. There is a feedback loop between the environment and the organisation itself, which creates space for processes of exchange. The environment is both internal in character – referring to the structure of the organisation and its resources – as well as external, in that its determinants, factors and processes are from outside, on which the organisation has limited influence. Environments may be divided into general and specific. For most organisations, a general environment has a socio-cultural, political, legal, economic, technological and international dimension, as will be discussed further in this text. A specific environment consists of the particular people, organisations or groups that can influence the organisation.[1]

The environment is characterised by dynamism – i.e., the intensity and predictability of changes.[2] Therefore, one may distinguish between a constant, changeable and turbulent environment. It is characterised by complexity – i.e., multiformity, diversity and variety. The more the external factors that affect the environment, the greater its diversity. This generates another feature, namely uncertainty, because the more complex and dynamic the environment is, the greater its uncertainty. A different feature, however, is the munificence of the environment, understood as a specific range of support for the organisation, its abundance, its wealth of partners, suppliers of goods and services, but also financial resources, opportunities for development and implementation of the organisation's plans. The features of an environment relate to both general and specific environments and have a significant impact on how an institution runs, no matter if the institution is a business or a not for profit.

Archives treated as organisations also function in their strictly defined environment, which is dynamic, diverse, uncertain, and of a particular munificence. However, they are not homogeneous since they differ in details, which means that the individual factors and processes that create their environment and characteristics will affect them to a different extent. The first group of archives are public – i.e., independent institutions established for the acquisition, long-term preservation, arrangement and description, and providing access to archival holdings of authorities, offices and public institutions.[3] These are institutions with a fixed organisational structure and a specific scope of autonomy. They are

1 Jabłońska 2014, p. 113.
2 Szymaniec-Mlicka 2014, p. 632.
3 Robótka 2002, p. 68.

often subordinate to bodies or higher-level institutions and form a network of organisations with a specific budget and fixed financing channels for their operation. These archives preserve both state and non-state national archival holdings, and their distinguishing feature is the constant and regular flow of archival materials guaranteed by certain provisions of law, as well as a genuine impact on the shape of their holdings.[4] The second group consists of institutional archives, which are organisational units of specific institutions or independent organisations that maintain close relations with one or more specific records creators.[5] What distinguishes this group is the fact that these archives have a specific source of financing and a constant supply of holdings. However, unlike the first group, they have very limited independence, and their decisions, scope and action plans depend in most cases on the consent of a governing body. Community archives and documentation centres constitute the third group. These are often non-governmental organisations of a voluntary nature which must obtain funds and actively seek out their holdings in order to function. They are often a bottom-up initiative and a response to the existing social demand and develop areas not covered by state institutions. Nowadays, this category of archives increasingly marks its presence in public space and enjoys growing interest and due respect. The literature contains numerous attempts to define this type of organisation as well as the entire phenomenon of community archiving.[6] However, it can be assumed that community archives are bottom-up documentary initiatives carried out by third sector organisations or informal groups that deal with the collection, preservation, processing and providing access to archives.[7] In the context of environment, the distinguishing feature of community archives is certainly the fact that they are largely dependent on social commitment, on the actions of people responsible for both financial issues and shaping the archival holdings. The final group of archives proposed for consideration are commercial.[8] These are companies that run back office services as part of their business. They are provided by outsourcing and involve records management, data processing and preserving joint archives. The latter is particularly relevant here because these archives perform the same tasks as the aforementioned archives, but they do so based on the principles of marketing and are focused on achieving financial gain. Therefore, they collect records, both for the short-term and long-term. They preserve it, often applying the highest possible standards and norms, process it, although this mainly boils down to keeping registers, and then finally make it available, satisfying the documentation and

4 Jabłońska 2016, p. 133.
5 Degen 2015, pp. 19–31.
6 Wiśniewska-Drewniak 2020, pp. 37–68.
7 Eadem 2018, p. 274.
8 Jabłońska 2016, p. 106.

information requirements of clients as well as individuals and institutions authorised to use the preserved holdings. From the point of view of the archive environment, this group is distinctively commercial in nature – i.e., there is a need to identify actual and potential contractors whose documentation will be preserved by the archive and these self-financing activities should generate profit from a defined perspective.

The first dimension that influences an archive environment is socio-cultural. Each of the above-mentioned institutions functions within its own social environment, which, just like society as a whole, evolves and changes over the years. The processes involved influence the way of thinking and the perception of archives as a synonym of the past, a space of *faits accomplis*, a storage room of events and people's lives. Regardless of whether the archive holdings are archival materials or records for temporary storage, social perception of the past, respect for artefacts and history will affect its environment and its image. Research in the field of sociology shows how much society changes over time and how its relationship to the present, past and future changes. The fourth law of sociology and time says that periods of intense and profound change, instability and discontinuity, perceived and felt as a turning point marking the end of one epoch and the beginning of another, induce individuals and collectivities to gaze into the past, to seek their shaky identity there, uncertain in the new circumstances.[9] This context of archives functioning as a synonym of the past may be witnessed in the countries of Central and Eastern Europe, where in the period of post-communist transformations a genuine turn towards the past was noticeable. The main aim was to fill the numerous "blank spots" – i.e., areas of ignorance, concealment and long-term taboos imposed by the previous political system, censorship, propaganda, and ideology. Real action taken by Poland in this regard was the establishment of the Institute of National Remembrance – Commission for the Prosecution of Crimes against the Polish Nation (*Instytut Pamięci Narodowej – Komisja Ścigania Zbrodni przeciwko Narodowi Polskiemu*, hereinafter: IPN).[10] Its basic responsibilities included, and still include, inventorying, collecting, sharing, managing and using documents of state security organs created and collected from 22 July 1944 until 31 December 1989, as well as of the security apparatus of the Third German Reich and Union of Soviet Socialist Republics (in 2016 the chronological scope of the Institute's historical research was extended from 8 November 1917 until 31 July 1990);[11] defining the procedure to be followed in the prosecution of Nazi, communist and other crimes against peace, hu-

9 Tarkowska 2016, p. 127.
10 Bednarek 2021, p. 21.
11 *Ustawa z dnia 29 kwietnia 2016 r. o zmianie ustawy o Instytucie Pamięci Narodowej – Komisji Ścigania Zbrodni przeciwko Nardowi Polskiemu oraz niektórych innych ustaw* 2016.

manity, as well as war crimes; protection of the personal data of victims; action in the field of public education.[12] Similar institutions were created in other countries of the Eastern bloc, and all of them set themselves a goal to meet social needs, to reclaim a mythologised and manipulated past, and to restore historical continuity. A period of change also marks a quest for points of reference for ambiguous and shifting identities, as well as mass interest in the past, which is reflected, among others, in initiatives of a biographical nature – in the publication of personal memories, accounts and diaries, and in conducting genealogical research. In Polish archives this is visible in the statistics of archival queries, in the development of the genealogical movement, and the formation of associations and companies dealing with genealogical research. One example is the structure of providing access to the holdings of the Central Archives of Historical Records (*Archiwum Główne Akt Dawnych*). Over the years 2009–2012, the percentage of genealogical queries in all performed queries increased successively from 65.1% to 70.8%.[13] An analysis of statistical data reveals that almost every third user of this archive conducted genealogical research, and almost 30% of the accessed archival materials are civil registers. A similar phenomenon may also be observed in the previous period across the entire network of state archives in Poland.[14]

Another important social phenomenon that influences the functioning of archives is the sociology of time theory that looks at memory in the context of the culture of the present. Contemporary culture is characterised by the growing role of the present, incorporating the past and the future, and shrinking the time horizon in the direction of both the past and the future.[15] These processes also relate to memory, finding expression in various new ways and mechanisms of bringing it closer to the present, and in fact incorporate it within the present. There are four areas of modernising the past by including it in the present: consumption, trade and market; art and artistic creation; individual and collective identity; and, finally, politics. Consumption, popular culture and the media are areas of particular activity. Archives appear here as a reservoir from which society draws the topics, threads and materials it deems necessary. As a kind of response to this phenomenon, observed as a change in the profile of someone who might use archival materials, contemporary archives conduct an open and very broad policy of providing access to archival materials, remove restrictions, develop archival aids that are commonly available in their form and content, and increasingly publish scans of archival materials online. One example

12 *Ustawa z dnia 18 grudnia 1998 r. o Instytucie Pamięci Narodowej – Komisji Ścigania Zbrodni przeciwko Nardowi Polskiemu* 1998.
13 Krochmal 2013, p. 135.
14 *Sprawozdania* [2022].
15 Tarkowska 2016, p. 127.

here may be the IPN, which gradually liberalises the rules whereby its archives may be shared, and demonstrating an increasing willingness to make materials available online.[16] Universal access to community archives collections is also one of the cornerstones for the operation of the Community Archives Centre (*Centrum Archiwistyki Społecznej*, hereinafter: CAS). It offers community archives broad organisational support, including a free database, an Open Archiving System (*Otwarty System Archiwizacji*), which facilitates the processing the collected materials, and enables them to be made available online. The Centre also tries to demonstrate the "usefulness" of the archives, how they may be used, their substantive and visual appeal as well as their value in terms of education, identity and integration. This is confirmed by the series of meetings under the slogan "Archives inspire!" organised by the CAS, where talks are held about the contemporary role of community archives, archivists and their work, as well as the artistic and commercial use of archives and information derived from them.[17] Commercialising the past and reducing historical events, people and artefacts to the status of product also carries risks, the main one being to trivialise the importance of events, break the sequences of history, take a story out of context and consolidate the theatricalisation of history in the social consciousness, told through reconstructions, para-documentaries or scenarios inspired by true stories. A characteristic feature of popular culture is the mixture of authenticity and imitation, actual and media reality, past and present, and learning through experience. Archives, noticing this change, once more adjust their operations to the expectations of the environment by interacting with actual and potential stakeholder groups. Educational activities, workshops and lessons on archives, engaging exhibitions, shows, presentations, as well as picnics, open-door days, field games, all serve to help discover the past through archival materials and the proactive approach taken by the archives themselves. This phenomenon sometimes evokes mixed feelings because it marks a departure from the sacred to the profane, from reflectivity to sensuality – a transition from the past as a "source of meaning" to the past as "an attractive and rich warehouse of signs, images and stylistic figures."[18] However, it is a sign of the times, a sign of the changes taking place in society, which the archives try and want to keep up with. This is because every shift that occurs in society affects the organisation and functioning of archives, and has a regional and global impact. It is in the interest of archives to keep up with the changes and make use of them wisely and profitably, to be better at adapting, recognising trends, reacting to new ones, allowing them to adapt to

16 *Udostępnianie dokumentów z Archiwum IPN on-line* [2022].

17 *Archiwa inspirują!* [2022].

18 "[…] atrakcyjnym i bogatym magazynem znaków, obrazów, figur stylistycznych." Krajewski 2003, p. 206.

their environment on the one hand and to shape, change and teach it on the other. Socio-cultural shifts take place over the long term, but are continuous, so archives are committed to researching them and incorporating the results into the organisation process.

The second dimension influencing archive space and functional scope is political and legal. Legislative changes particularly affect the scope of duties and organisation of archives in Poland.[19] The highest-ranking act is the Constitution of the Republic of Poland of 1997, which contains clauses relevant to archival work.[20] Article 73 establishes the freedom of scientific research, use of cultural goods, as well as teaching and artistic creation. According to article six, the public authorities are obliged to ensure appropriate conditions for dissemination as well as equal access to cultural goods. These freedoms are exercised in relation to accessing archival materials, for which purpose it is necessary to operate institutions specialised in their appropriate acquiring, preservation, processing and providing access to them. Moreover, with reference to some types of archives, the constitutional regulations establish the citizens' right to obtain information about the actions of public authorities and persons discharging public functions (article 61), as well as the right of all natural persons to access official documents and data files that concern them, to demand rectification and removal of information that is untrue, incomplete or collected in a manner inconsistent with the law (article 51). These provisions justify the need to organise archives in the public space and define their scope of responsibilities. On the one hand, the informative value of archival materials elicits the need to ensure special protection and, on the other hand, to enable their use both for scientific learning of the past and for satisfying other needs – administrative, educational, and cultural.[21]

The legal basis for archival operation in Poland is defined by the Act of 14 July 1983 on the national archival holdings and archives.[22] It has been amended 43 times, which indicates the instability of its provisions and the process of constant change, which, given the need for legal stability, undoubtedly impedes the functioning of archives in Poland.[23] Amendments to the provisions of the archive act were dictated, *inter alia*, by the need to adapt it to other statutory regulations and provisions of European law. This shows the close relationship between areas of public and private activity and their connection with the space in which archives function, both in institutional and documental terms. This may be confirmed by minor additions to the act between 2002–2018, followed by re-

19 Pęksa 2007, pp. 17–30.
20 Konstankiewicz 2019, pp. 339–340.
21 Ibid.
22 *Ustawa z dnia 14 lipca 1983 r. o narodowym zasobie archiwalnym i archiwach* 2019.
23 Konstankiewicz 2019, pp. 340–341.

peated amendments, provisions on how employers should proceed with personal and payroll records with a temporary preservation period, and on the commercial storage of such documentation. This demonstrates the direct impact of legal regulations on records management, but also on the functioning of two groups of archives – institutional and commercial.[24] They are also directly affected by all regulations relating to bureaucracy, including the use of modern technologies and electronic records management. They influence both the form of the documentation itself, which adopt archival traits over time, and the systems that process it.[25] Precise legal regulations are visibly lacking for the operation of private, especially community archives.[26] On the one hand, they are distinguished by a kind of freedom in the conduct of archival work, but on the other hand, a number of doubts exists as to the ownership of the collected materials and the possibility of their exploitation, sale, processing and providing access to them. The very issue of archival materials accessibility, regardless of archive type, is strongly related to regulations on access to public information and the re-use of public sector information. This is associated with a shift in the model of participation in social, cultural and scientific life or relations with the authorities, which is influenced by development in technology. On the other hand, legal regulations need to address the protection of privacy and personal data, including the right to be forgotten. Therefore, there is a necessity to reconcile the interests of the authors of records, its owners and users – i.e., those who wish to use archival materials. Both of these forces are concentrated in the custodians – i.e., in the archives, as depositories of the created documentation. This again indicates how strongly legal regulations influence the functioning of archives. Many rapid legal changes are dictated by the development of modern technologies, the adaptation of Polish law to the requirements of the European Union, as well as ongoing social changes. However, their roots lie in the political changes following 1989, related to the reconstruction of the legal system and public administration structures.

Changes in the area of politics include attitude to history, tradition and identity. Historical remembrance and the specific vision of its implementation is closely related to the organisation of archives as the depositaries of memory. This context should also be taken into account when discussing the environment of archives in Poland. This is more visible in relation to public archives, where state policy has a direct influence on the creation of archives and their organisation. This is evidenced by the recurring discussion on the liquidation of the IPN and its

24 Pepłowska 2011, p. 120.
25 Konstankiewicz 2016, p. 56.
26 Idem 2019, p. 346.

role in the historical policy of the state.[27] Different concepts and visions for nurturing the collective memory of Poles and building a historical identity clash. Politics also affects other archives. Local government authorities often financially support community archives, play an active role in events organised by state archives, and public administration offices keep their own institutional archives. Depending on the sensitivity of the administrators, their attitude to the past and historical awareness, this cooperation is more or less effective.

Another identified factor influencing the archive environment is the economic dimension. Archives, which are mostly nonprofit, must be maintained with external funding. This is especially relevant in the case of community archives, as they generally do not have institutional support, and their activity is based on grants, targeted subsidies, donations, and sometimes small revenues from membership fees and income from the sale of their own publications. Each year, these archives write at least a few applications for grant competitions announced by state and local government institutions, by domestic and foreign foundations, and from several to a dozen letters of intent encouraging potential commercial partners to cooperate.[28] Such dependence on sponsors means that the work that they plan must fall in line with the priorities of the announced competition, while at the same time appearing attractive. Archives carry out their duties in a rhythm and scope that depends on the support received.[29] Any decision not to fund an archive means difficulties in maintaining infrastructure and employees. Here lies the weakest link for project management, since this signifies that operational stability and comfort of work are lacking. However, it indirectly enforces the need for constant activity, self-publicity, working commitment, creativity and publicising actions undertaken for the benefit of science, education, local community, memory and identity. Thus, the influence of the economic factor on the activity of community archives is strong and indisputable. Due to the growing role of community archives in the public space, there are demands to include them in systemic solutions regarding financing.[30] Therefore, public archives maintained from the state budget are in a much better situation. Their income is officially established, relatively stable and predictable, which enables planning ad hoc as well as strategic action. In 2019, 8.5% of all planned expenditures on culture and protection of national heritage were allocated for the operation of state archives from the state budget.[31] Thus, the budget allocated to

27 Leszczyński [2022].

28 Michałowska 2015, p. 73.

29 Wiśniewska-Drewniak 2018, p. 276.

30 Konstankiewcz 2015, p. 56.

31 The structure of state budget expenditures on cultural institutions in 2019: museums 32.6%; art and culture centres 10.3%; protection and care of historical monuments 8.1%; theatres

the state archives network amounted to PLN 219,127,861 including capital expenditure of PLN 58,104,410, which is a significant increase compared to the previous year.[32] These are funds allocated for the basic operation of archives, employee remuneration, and the maintenance, modernisation and expansion of infrastructure. In addition, as cultural institutions, archives can apply for subsidies under European Union programs and thus obtain external funding.[33] This budget stability ensures a calm working environment where issues related to financial liquidity recede into the background. It is similar in the case of institutional archives, which base their activities on the budget of the institution in which they operate. However, for commercial archives, the financial aspect is highly relevant. These are business organisations, established to carry out specific tasks and earn tangible profits. Their operations are subordinated to commercial goals and this has a key impact on the organisation.

The development of modern technologies is another factor that has had a real impact on how archives function in Poland. Since the 1980s, measures have been taken to popularise the use of computers in the work of archivists and the operation of archives.[34] Research centres have played an important role in this process. The conceptual work, analyses and studies of systems carried out by academics laid the foundations for the development of an archival information system for the network of state archives in Poland. This system has evolved over the years, transforming in character from local and non-standardised to integrated, standardised and available online.[35] In this way, the archives gained new opportunities to boost the efficiency of their work and users gained convenient tools for searching the holdings. Digitisation is closely associated with the process of archive computerisation. The transition from a traditional or analogue document, as it is commonly known, to a digital format is another area of archive operations that has been strongly influenced by modern technology. Digitisation of archival materials is a new generation tool that supports the preservation and providing access to archival materials. It makes the vision of open archives achievable, offering high-quality remote access to information contained in archival materials, and facilitates the preservation of these materials for future generations in the form of digital backups, using modern technologies.[36] The first digital copies of materials from the holdings of state archives were made in 1997, while large-scale digitisation began ten years later. The digitisation strategy de-

8.5%; archives 8.5%; libraries 4.7%; philharmonics, orchestras, choirs and bands 3.8%; radio and television activities 1.4%; other 22.1% – compilation based on: Ilczuk 2020, p. 19.

32 *Budżet 2019* [2022].

33 *Programy unijne dla archiwów państwowych* [2022].

34 Barczak 1982, pp. 27–38.

35 Jabłońska 2011, pp. 89–157.

36 *Strategia digitalizacji* 2017, p. 3.

fined five goals that set the directions for the work to be carried out, and outlined a vision of the development of the network of state archives in this respect. Focus turned towards expanding the digital availability of the holdings, maintaining open and free access to digital copies on the szukajwarchiwach.pl website, building the image of state archives as institutions providing sources of knowledge, and finally providing digital access to archival materials and supporting the permanent preservation of archival materials, including in the form of digital copies.[37] Therefore, this process is associated with a whole catalogue of new duties that the archives have decided to take on. Nevertheless, digitisation, is not only the domain of public archives, as community and commercial archives are also increasingly taking this path. For some community archives, digital copies of material are their bread and butter. Some do not even keep originals or collect traditional materials, but build their collections based on copies made available. Community archives are also eager to publish their collections on the Internet, using digital materials collected or created for the purpose of preservation and providing access. For commercial archives, digitisation means the ability to quickly transfer information gathered in stored documentation; it is an archive at the touch of a button that speeds up accessing to the shortest possible time. Often, it also presents a competitive advantage and helps with advertising.

Modern records are increasingly digital. Electronic documents are slowly becoming the norm, fully acceptable, and in some areas even a required method of documentation. This is experienced both in everyday and institutional life. To create and use such documents, appropriate equipment (computer, tablet, mobile phone) and software is required, and they must be stored on a digital data carrier. The permanence of such records is particularly important from the point of view of archives and long-term and free access to their contents. State archives, which are responsible for the permanent preservation of archival materials, regardless of their form, are therefore faced with the need to develop and then improve methods of dealing with such documentation, account for technological advances, seek solutions to new problems, and learn to work with digital records.[38] Moreover, a huge challenge facing archives is the need to influence at least some of the digital information world so that electronically recorded content may be created and stored in a way that allows access to it. Without this relationship, without an awareness of the threats, it will not be possible to preserve Poland's digital heritage. That is why there is so much talk about security, authenticity, data integration, and systems for electronic document management that take into account the traditional and electronic form. Poland is currently in the process of digital transformation, which applies to what may be broadly

37 Ibid., p. 6.
38 Czerniak / Orszulak 2017, p. 9.

understood as administration, including archives of all types, in particular state archives. They perform public tasks and are offices that, on the one hand, manage their own documentation and, on the other hand, are appointed to acquire, preserve, process and provide access to records of historical value. So, there is a visible point of contact between bureaucracy and archives which should care about the quality of the produced records. The connection between these two worlds, the present with the past, has always existed, but never before has it been so relevant from the point of view of preserving documentary heritage as it was in the era of digital transformation. Electronic records and electronic records management constitute a challenge for archives and archivists, for administration and management, for users and the society which actively participates in the documenting process. This is why it would seem to be particularly relevant to develop a good legal basis and implement electronic systems based on IT knowledge and archival experience. Paying attention to this issue in government records is also of great importance. The National Integrated Informatisation Programme (*Program Zintegrowanej Informatyzacji Państwa*) assumes the implementation of uniform Electronic Records Management for Public Administration (*Elektroniczne Zarządzanie Dokumentacją w Administracji Publicznej*, EZD RP).[39] This is to be a modern and universal tool for electronic records management, used universally in Polish offices, setting standards for this class of systems. This clearly translates into the functioning of institutional archives and the work of government offices and institutions of other types. The aspect of records management emerges here and emphasises the role of the office coordinator, which is often the archivist themselves. The above-mentioned document also assumes the implementation of the Archive of Electronic Records (*Archiwum Dokumentów Elektronicznych*, ADE), which is a tool for acquiring archival materials in electronic form created in the public sector, including those produced in all available e-services that are or will be provided therein in the future. Additionally, the system enables the acceptance, storage and preservation of archival materials in electronic form from non-state archival holdings. Modern technology also means modern solutions in terms of security and storage as well as processing of the holdings.[40] There is more and more talk about using not only computer databases in archives, but also artificial intelligence, which will help the work of archivists and facilitate archival searches, improve the process of archival appraisal, as well as protect the integrity and authenticity of items of digital archival heritage.[41] Modern technology also offers an easier and faster way to communicate, a tool for archival outreach, cooperation with the media, the

39 *Program zintegrowanej informatyzacji państwa* 2019, p. 40.
40 Żyła 2021, pp. 33–43.
41 Stępień 2021, p. 69.

presence of archives on the Internet through commonly available communication channels, and finally the issue of Web archiving. As may be easily observed, the influence of modern technologies on the organisation and functioning of modern archives is vast and multi-area. Archives draw from this transformation, but also give experience, knowledge and awareness of the need to implement specific changes, to document the processes occurring and be vigilant when it comes to adopting proposed solutions.

The final dimension that creates the context for the operation of modern archives in Poland is the international environment, which influences the area of work organisation and archival holdings. It is a model of best practice and often an inspiration for action, but also serves to standardise processes. This influence is very clearly visible in the commercial activity of archives. The United States of America is the cradle of archival outsourcing. There, in 1951, Iron Mountain was founded, the first company in the world to provide documentation services for private enterprises and local administration.[42] With time, more and more entrepreneurs in the world began to notice the financial potential in records management and archival outsourcing. Domestic companies as well as branches of foreign enterprises have also started operating in Poland. Examples include ArchiDoc SA, located in Gorzów, one of the largest companies in this industry in Poland, operating since 1994; Iron Mountain Polska Sp. z o.o., an American company in Poland since 2003 and located in Reguły, which has its own numerous branches; Rhenus Data Office Polska Sp. z o.o., based in Nadarzyn, which has been on the Polish market since 2001 as part of Rethmann AG & Co. KG. These are the largest companies of this type in Poland, which define the standard of archival services and, on the one hand, compete with smaller entities. On the other hand, they inspire innovative solutions and operational area expansion.

An important factor influencing how archives operate internationally is their participation in various types of organisations and projects aimed at transferring knowledge and experience, and above all, conducting a common and coherent policy to protect the world's documentary heritage. One example here may be the presence of Polish representatives in the structures of the International Council of Archives, the European Council of National Archivists, EURASICA (a forum for archives from Eastern European and Asian countries), as well as UNESCO and the UN.[43] Polish public archives also benefit from active participation in projects such as *Memory of the World* or *Information for All*, run by UNESCO to foster a knowledge society and preserve memory. A coherent European policy is also an important factor in the development of Polish archives.[44] They should definitely

42 Stryjkowski / Stryjkowska 2017, pp. 49–51.
43 Stępniak 2000, pp. 27–38.
44 Idem 2008, p. 23.

be an item of concern for politicians, and the regulations drafted should be conducive to the acquiring, preservation and providing access to archival holdings. It is a similar story with archival processing, which is strongly influenced by standardisation, especially in terms of archival description. One should mention here the ISAD (G) standard from 1993, which in many countries became the basis for developing national standards or served as a model for the development of forms to describe archival materials, as was the case in Poland. This is supplemented by the ISAAR (CPF) standard for authority control records. Equally important is the EAD standard, developed in cooperation with the Society of American Archivists and the Library of Congress, which was created for archives to facilitate searching for information within an IT system.[45] Both ISAD (G) and EAD were the basis for the development of the Polish Integrated Archive Information System (*Zintegrowany System Informacji Archiwalnej*, ZoSIA), which is run by the network of state archives.[46]

Internationally, an important area that influences on how Polish archives operate is the forging of a professional identity, the sense of an archivist community, and shared responsibility for records and memory that they serve to perpetuate. Meetings, conferences, joint scientific ventures, which are plentiful in the world of archives, serve this purpose well. One might mention, for example, the International Archives Congress, the European Archives Conference or the regular *Colloquia Jerzy Skowronek dedicata* Polish conference of international scope. In 2007 alone, Polish archivists attended over 70 international conferences, seminars, meetings of working groups for archives in the European Union, which fostered an exchange of information on digitised and digital records, creating digital libraries, modern methods of information management and mass data storage.[47] Many important issues relating to the digitisation and conservation of archives are discussed on an ongoing basis in working group meetings within the EU. The following may be mentioned: High Level Expert Group on Digital Libraries; Advisory Committee on the Collection of Private Archives by the European University Institute in Florence; European Archives Group. During the meetings, Polish archivists can learn about the work done by their foreign colleagues as well as share their own experience and professional knowledge. The information obtained can be put to practice in Polish archives. These meetings help to bring the archive world closer together and make problems easier to solve. Therefore, archivists share common challenges as well as their common values. Evidence of this may be the Polish community of archivists' adoption of the Code of Ethics for Archivists drafted in 1996 at the

45 Płoszajski 2008, p. 31.
46 *ZoSIA* [2022].
47 *Współdziałanie polskich archiwów z archiwami Unii Europejskiej* [2022].

13th International Archives Congress in Beijing, which takes into account the supranational principles of ethical conduct and for years has been the basic interpretation of the applicable standards.[48] The annual archive celebrations also serve to integrate the whole community. A series of events around the world are organised on 9th June within the scope of the International Archives Day – established during the 16th International Archives Congress in Kuala Lumpur in 2007 and a permanent fixture in the calendar of archival events. It is celebrated by institutions of various types that have the common need to acquire, preserve, process and provide access to documentary evidence of the past.

The environment of contemporary archives in Poland is shaped by a multitude of factors, whose roots may be found in the rich history of our country, in social attitudes, as well as political, legal and cultural circumstances. Their development is influenced by economic and legal factors, technological development as well as numerous international relations. The space in which they function determines their scope of work and attitudes, determines the possibilities and sets limitations. However, it is partially dependent on them. Indeed, archives can influence society by shaping its documentary awareness and historical sensitivity; politics and law by lobbying for archives; economics by presenting an open and committed attitude, also while raising funding for their operation; technology by sharing their experience and expertise; finally, the international community of archives, playing an active role in all its manifestations. However, it is important that archives are aware of this interdependence and take advantage of the opportunities to mark their presence and agency.

[Translated by Steve Jones]

Bibliography

Printed sources

Ilczuk, Dorota: *System finansowania instytucji kultury w Polsce. Opinie i ekspertyzy OE-319*. 2020.

Program Zintegrowanej Informatyzacji Państwa, in: *Załącznik do Uchwały Rady Ministrów nr 109/2019 z dnia 24 września 2019 r.* [Annex to the Resolution of the Council of Ministers No. 109/2019 of 24 September 2019].

Sprawozdzania, in: *Naczelna Dyrekcja Archiwów Państwowych*, URL: https://www.archiwa.gov.pl/pl/o-nas/naczelna-dyrekcja-archiw%C3%B3w-pa%C5%84stwowych/sprawozdania [15.01.2022].

48 *Kodeks etyczny archiwisty* 1997, pp. 10–14.

Strategia digitalizacji zasobu archiwów państwowych na lata 2018–2023. Warszawa 2017, in: *Załącznik do Zarządzenia nr 79 Naczelnego Dyrektora Archiwów Państwowych z dnia 25 października 2017 r. w sprawie wprowadzenia Strategii digitalizacji zasobu archiwów państwowych na lata 2018–2023* [Annex to Order No. 79 of the Chief Director of the State Archives of 25 October 2017 on the introduction of the Strategy for Digitisation of the State Archives' Resources for 2018–2023].

Ustawa z dnia 14 lipca 1983 r. o narodowym zasobie archiwalnym i archiwach, in: *Dziennik Ustaw Rzeczypospolitej Polskiej*. 2019, item 553, as amended.

Ustawa z dnia 18 grudnia 1998 r. o Instytucie Pamięci Narodowej – Komisji Ścigania Zbrodni przeciwko Narodowi Polskiemu, in: *Dziennik Ustaw Rzeczypospolitej Polskiej*. 1998, No. 155, item 1016.

Ustawa z dnia 29 kwietnia 2016 r. o zmianie ustawy o Instytucie Pamięci Narodowej – Komisji Ścigania Zbrodni przeciwko Narodowi Polskiemu oraz niektórych innych ustaw, in: *Dziennik Ustaw Rzeczypospolitej Polskiej*. 2016, item 749.

Literature

Archiwa inspirują!, in: *Centrum Archiwistyki Społecznej*, URL: https://www.facebook.com/watch/live/?ref=watch_permalink&v=879915372691205; https://www.facebook.com/watch/live/?ref=watch_permalink&v=369551021593323 [15.01.2022].

Barczak, Henryk: *Informatyka w archiwach*, in: *Archeion*. 1982/74, pp. 27–38.

Bednarek, Jerzy: *Wokół pamięci i historii. Działalność archiwalna Instytutu Pamięci Narodowej w latach 2000–2016*. 2021.

Budżet 2019, in: Naczelna Dyrekcja Archiwów Państwowych, URL: https://ndap.bip.gov.pl/budzet/budzet-2019.html [15.01.2022].

Czerniak, Sebastian / Orszulak, Jarosław: *Dokument elektroniczny. Przewodnik i katalog dobrych praktyk*. 2017.

Degen, Robert: *Archiwa bieżące. Pojęcie i systematyzacja*, in: Jabłońska, Marlena (ed.): *Archiwa bieżące. Zagadnienia teoretyczne i praktyczne rozwiązania*. 2015/6, pp. 11–34.

Jabłońska, Marlena: *Dokumentacja specjalna w archiwach. Opis tradycyjny i komputerowy*. 2011.

Jabłońska, Marlena: *Nowe wyzwania archiwów. Komunikacja społeczna i public relations*. 2016.

Jabłońska, Marlena: *Otoczenie archiwów w Polsce – projekt badawczy*, in: *Archiwa – Kancelarie – Zbiory*. 2014/5 (7), pp. 111–123.

Jabłońska, Marlena: *Outsourcing archiwalny – nowy wymiar usług archiwalnych*, in: Drzewiecka, Dorota / Jabłońska, Marlena (eds.): *Archiwa przejściowe i zbiorcze w Polsce. Organizacja i funkcjonowanie*. 2016, pp. 105–120.

Kodeks etyczny archiwisty uchwalony na XIII Międzynarodowym Kongresie Archiwów w Pekinie, in: *Archiwista Polski*. 1997/1, pp. 10–14.

Konstankiewicz, Marek: *Aspekty teoretyczne i prawne działalności archiwalnej organizacji pozarządowych*, in: Czarnota, Tomasz / Konstankiewicz, Marek (eds.): *Archiwa organizacji pozarządowych w Polsce*. 2015, pp. 51–61.

Konstankiewicz, Marek: *Kształtowanie podstaw prawnych działalności archiwalnej w Polsce na przełomie XX i XXI w.*, in: *Archeion.* 2019/120, pp. 337–366.

Konstankiewicz, Marek: *Zarządzanie dokumentacją w polskim prawie*, in: Degen, Robert / Jabłońska, Marlena (eds.): *Zarządzanie dokumentacją. Badania i dydaktyka.* 2016/7, pp. 59–76.

Krajewski, Marek: *Kultury kultury popularnej.* 2003.

Krochmal, Jacek: *Program "Przywracanie pamięci o Polakach z Kresów Wschodnich"*, in: Walczak, Wojciech / Łopatecki, Karol (eds.): *Stan badań nad wielokulturowym dziedzictwem dawnej Rzeczypospolitej.* 2013, pp. 131–144.

Leszczyński, Adam: *Lewica chce zlikwidować IPN i powołać Instytut Ochrony Konstytucji.* 2021, in: URL: https://oko.press/lewica-chce-zlikwidowac-ipn-i-powolac-instytut-ochrony-konstytucji/ [15.01.2022].

Michałowska, Joanna: *Archiwum społeczne w organizacji pozarządowej – sytuacja obecna i szanse rozwoju na podstawie działalności Archiwum Ośrodka KARTA*, in: Czarnota, Tomasz / Konstankiewicz, Marek (eds.): *Archiwa organizacji pozarządowych w Polsce.* 2015, pp. 71–75.

Pepłowska, Katarzyna: *Dokumentacja osobowa i płacowa*, in: Robótka, Halina (ed.): *Współczesna dokumentacja urzędowa.* 2011/2, pp. 115–150.

Pęksa, Władysław: *Prawo archiwalne – wprowadzenie do zagadnienia*, in: Robótka, Halina (ed.): *Prawo archiwalne. Stan aktualny i perspektywy zmian.* 2007, pp. 17–30.

Płoszajski, Grzegorz: *O digitalizacji dziedzictwa kulturowego*, in: Płoszajski, Grzegorz (ed.): *Standardy w procesie digitalizacji obiektów dziedzictwa kulturowego.* 2008, pp. 24–71.

Programy unijne dla archiwów państwowych, in: *Naczelna Dyrekcja Archiwów Państwowych*, URL: https://archiwa.gov.pl/pl/o-nas/programy-unijne-dla-archiw%C3%B3w-pa%C5%84stwowych [15.01.2022].

Robótka, Halina: *Wprowadzenie do archiwistyki.* 2002.

Stępień, Robert: *Możliwości zastosowania sztucznej inteligencji i blockchain w działalności archiwalnej. Przegląd doświadczeń zagranicznych*, in: *Archeion.* 2021/122, pp. 69–93.

Stępniak, Władysław: *Archiwa w polityce europejskiej. Uwagi wstępne*, in: Poraziński, Jarosław / Stryjkowski, Krzysztof (eds.): *Archiwa w nowoczesnym społeczeństwie. Pamiętnik V Zjazdu Archiwistów Polskich, Olsztyn 6–8 września 2007.* 2008, pp. 23–43.

Stępniak, Władysław: *Organizacje międzynarodowe jako przedmiot zainteresowania archiwistyki*, in: Basta, Jan / Zamoyski, Grzegorz (eds.): *Historia. Archiwistyka. Ludzie. Księga pamiątkowa w pięćdziesiątą rocznicę powołania Archiwum Państwowego w Rzeszowie.* 2000, pp. 27–38.

Stryjkowski, Krzysztof / Stryjkowska, Sylwia: *Usługi archiwalne i outsourcing oraz ich wpływ na działalność i zasób archiwów*, in: *Archeion.* 2017/118, pp. 48–68.

Szymaniec-Mlicka, Kamila: *Charakterystyka otoczenia organizacji publicznych*, in: *Zeszyty naukowe Politechniki Śląskiej. Organizacja i zarządzanie.* 2014/73, pp. 631–640.

Tarkowska, Elżbieta: *Pamięć w kulturze teraźniejszości*, in: *Kultura i Społeczeństwo.* 2016/60/4, pp. 121–141.

Udostępnianie dokumentów z Archiwum IPN on-line, in: *Instytut Pamięci Narodowej*, URL: https://ipn.gov.pl/pl/dla-mediow/komunikaty/143810,Udostepnianie-dokumentow-z-Archiwum-IPN-on-line.html [15.01.2022].

Wiśniewska-Drewniak, Magdalena: *Inaczej to zniknie. Archiwa społeczne w Polsce – wielokrotne studium przypadku.* 2020.

Wiśniewska-Drewniak, Magdalena: *Wpływ projektowego finansowania na działalność archiwów społecznych jako możliwy problem badawczy*, in: *Zarządzanie w kulturze.* 2018/19/3, pp. 273–286.

Współdziełanie polskich archiwów z archiwami Unii Europejskiej, in: *Naczelna Dyrekcja Archiwów Państwowych*, URL: https://archiwa.gov.pl/pl/604-wsp%C3%B3%C5%82dzie%C5%82anie-polskich-archiw%C3%B3w-z-archiwami-unii-europejskiej [15.01.2022].

ZoSIA, in: *Narodowe Archiwum Cyfrowe*, URL: https://www.nac.gov.pl/archiwum-cyfrowe/systemy-i-infrastruktura-it/zosia/ [15.01.2022.].

Żyła, Adriana: *DNA: prawie niezniszczalny i najbardziej pojemny nośnik danych*, in: *Archeion.* 2021/122, pp. 33–43.

Katarzyna Pepłowska

The European Union Policy Regarding the Re-use of Public Sector Information and Its Legal Impact in Poland

Abstract
The EU policy in force for many years regarding access to public sector information, its re-use and opening up of data affects the legal order in the Member States, including Poland. These issues are closely related to the operation of archives, since they are responsible for managing the most valuable resources, including those that are public. The chapter presents EU actions regarding community law and their impact on Polish archival law in terms of the re-use of archival materials constituting public sector information made available by Polish state archives.
Keywords: open data; access to archives; re–use of public sector information; Directive 2003/98/EC

Introduction

Access to information is a fundamental right and a constitutional norm. Its international context is guaranteed not only by the *Universal Declaration of Human Rights* of 1948,[1] the *International Covenant on Personal and Political Rights* of 1966,[2] but also by Article 10 of the *European Convention for the Protection of Human Rights and Fundamental Freedoms* of 1950[3] and Article 11 of the *EU Charter of Fundamental Rights.*[4]

For years, the structures of united Europe have been determined by the need to create a common, harmonised internal market. To this end, numerous actions have been undertaken that significantly affect the economic, social and cultural situation of the Member States, including Poland. Areas impacted include the access, exploration and use of information, as the EU considers information to be

Dr Katarzyna Pepłowska, Nicolaus Copernicus University in Toruń, ORCID: https://orcid.org/0000-0001-5364-684X.

1 *Universal Declaration of Human Rights* 1948.

2 *International Covenant on Civil and Political Rights* 1966.

3 *European Convention for the Protection of Human Rights and Fundamental Freedoms* 1950.

4 *Charter of Fundamental Rights of the European Union* 2012.

an economically valuable commodity. Endeavours undertaken since the 1980s have resulted in a number of EU solutions to open up data and offer unfettered access for every European. This determines the need to harmonise the law in the context of Community regulations, which directly affects the operation of state archives in Poland.

The EU's policy on re-using public sector information (hereinafter: PSI) and opening up data offers unprecedented possibilities for combining information and creating new meanings for documents. Common knowledge states that each document is created for a specific purpose that, for its creator, is clearly defined. As a rule, this purpose is not the same as the motives of a later user who seeks and uses this document in different circumstances at another time. The collection of topics and variety of objectives for which documents are created offer an almost infinite number of combinations. Depending on the times and the goals, those interested may explore archival holdings in different contexts and different realities, which often determine specific actions and how the sources are used. These dependencies combined with the information potential of archival holdings allow users to create new meanings and contexts, give them a second life and derive some benefit thereof. For years, the EU's PSI re-use policy has been devoted to these objectives.

The main objective of this chapter is to examine the major law-making operations and stages involved in EU regulation for the re-use of PSI, including archival materials, through an analysis of Community law, and to evaluate its impact on Polish archival law.

In order to achieve the assumed goal, two research techniques were used. The first overarching method involved a critical analysis of texts, scientific literature, EU norms and Polish legal acts. The second was comparative analysis which, in basic terms, helped assess the form of Polish legal regulations and the context of their amendment. The second part of the chapter referring to the impact of EU law on Polish archival law does not represent a complete analysis, but is more contributory in character.

EU policy on the re-use of PSI and open public data

EU policy for the development of an information society and open data has quite a long history, dating back to the 1980s. Even then, the European Commission made efforts to make PSIs widely available for re-use.[5] In 1999, on the basis of the *Public Sector Information: A Key Resource for Europe* commonly known as the green paper, EU bodies indicated the fundamental role of PSI as the basis for

5 Janssen / Dumortier 2003, p. 184.

the proper functioning of the internal market and the free circulation of goods, markets and people. It was also emphasised that easily accessible administrative, legislative, financial, public and economic data can, and should, be the foundation for making fully informed decisions, including transparency in public life.[6] The green paper also indicated the need to develop synergies between public and private sectors to create a competitive European information-based industry.[7] These assumptions were repeated in the *eEurope 2002. An Information Society for All. Action Plan.*[8] Moreover, it was highlighted that a digital knowledge-based economy is a powerful engine of growth, competitiveness, jobs and creates unprecedented circumstances for improving quality of life. The directive on PSI re-use, designed on this basis, was not only part of this scheme, but according to the EU legislator, was also to be the basis for the implementation of EU goals in electronic administration and digital content.

The re-use of PSI, according to its creators, means not only unlocking the potential of data, but most of all economic growth and strengthening the competitiveness of European companies compared with American ones,[9] creating new jobs and common, uniform rules for unleashing the potential of data and using them across borders. According to the adopted legislation, PSI should be considered "any content or part thereof, irrespective of the method of recording, in particular in paper, electronic, audio, visual or audiovisual form, which is in the possession of an obliged entity."[10] Re-use, as defined by law, means "the use by persons or legal entities of documents held by public sector bodies, for commercial or noncommercial purposes other than the initial purpose within the public task for which the documents were produced."[11] Interpretation of the above definition requires the application of a pro-EU interpretation, according to which re-use should be considered to be the use of PSI for economic and non-economic purposes, for the creation of products and services with added

6 *Public Sector Information: A key Resource for Europe. Green Paper on Public Sector Information in the Information Society* 1999.

7 Piskorz-Ryń 2015 (2), pp. 37–38.

8 The eEurope 2002 Action Plan is an integral part of the Lisbon strategy for making the European Union the world's most dynamic knowledge-based economy by 2010; cf.: *eEurope 2002* [2022].

9 Piskorz-Ryń 2015 (1), pp. 34–35.

10 "Informacja sektora publicznego – każda treść lub jej część, niezależnie od sposobu utrwalenia, w szczególności w postaci papierowej, elektronicznej, dźwiękowej, wizualnej lub audiowizualnej, będącą w posiadaniu podmiotu zobowiązanego." *Ustawa z dnia 11 sierpnia 2021 r. o otwartych danych i ponownym wykorzystywaniu informacji sektora publicznego* 2021, Art. 2, item 8.

11 *Directive 2003/98/EC of the European Parliament and of the Council of 17 November 2003 on the Re-use of Public Sector Information* (hereinafter: Directive 2003/98/EC) 2003, Art. 2, item 4.

value. This enables the creative use of data by combining them and giving a new context, regardless of their source.

One of the main objectives of the enactment of *Directive 2003/98/EC on the Re-use of Public Sector Information* (hereinafter: Directive 2003/98/EC)[12] was to exploit the full economic potential of a key documentary resource. It is worth emphasising that the objectives for which the directive was introduced should be split into economic and non-economic, bearing in mind that the former played a key role in shaping it.[13] While economic goals formed the basis of the regulation, non-economic objectives were raised later, only after criticism from the Commission,[14] which began to stress that unlocking the potential of public data is an equally important element of the democratic system and the development of an information and scientific society.[15] Importantly, the critique stated that "the directive is the result of adopting a US-centric point of view, based primarily on the need to commercialise PSI, without providing a sufficient counterbalance to information access."[16] At this point, it is worth considering the so-called "American-centric point of view", which assumes that, contrary to EU law and jurisprudence, gaining access to public data on the basis of the provisions on freedom of information automatically permits its re-use even for commercial purposes. This should be regarded as a natural consequence of gaining access. As rightly mentioned in the literature, it is related to the rather strong American tradition and culture related to the commercialisation of PSI. The European model, different from the American one, assumes differentiation in terms of access to information and its re-use,[17] which is crucial for analysing the transposition of EU law to Poland, for example, in this respect. This definition also has the advantage of distinguishing between both information rights (access to public information and re-use).[18]

Nevertheless, a general legal framework has been standardised across the EU, specifying the minimum degree of harmonisation. In the original form of the 2003 directive, archival holdings were excluded from its effect, and this state of affairs only changed upon its amendment, which brought in some quite significant adaptations. In the original wording of Directive 2003/98/EC, Article 1 (2) (f), documents "held by institutions such as museums, libraries, archives,

12 Directive 2003/98/EC.
13 Piskorz-Ryń 2015 (2), p. 37.
14 Eadem 2017, p. 87.
15 Directive 2003/98/EC, recital 1.
16 "[...] dyrektywa jest wynikiem przyjęcia amerykańsko-centrycznego punktu widzenia, opartego przede wszystkim na potrzebie komercjalizacji informacji sektora publicznego, bez zapewnienia wystarczającej przeciwwagi dla dostępu do informacji." Piskorz-Ryń 2017, p. 87.
17 Eadem 2015 (2), pp. 36–37.
18 Fischer et al. 2019, pp. 38–47.

orchestras, operas, ballets and theatres" were excluded from the right of re-use.[19] In seeking the reasons for this state of affairs, one may surmise, *inter alia*, the burden of the above-mentioned administrative obligations of institutions, the fact that much of the collections are still subject to third party copyrights, and the fear that private entities being permitted to re-use the collections will harm the financial state of those entities that have so far obtained revenues from providing direct, as well as indirect, access to them.[20] While these arguments mentioned in the legal literature should be considered justified, in the case of archives, it would appear that some of them did not apply. In the case of archives, the vast majority of their holdings are not covered by third party intellectual property rights, due to the expiry of the protection period or the exclusion from protection of official documents and materials. Nevertheless, before the 2003 amendment to the directive was adopted, it was revised a few years after it came into force. In 2009, EU bodies drew attention to the still apparent differences in the laws of the Member States and practical solutions. It had been noticed that certain obstacles existed that hindered the cross-border use of official documents, and that they could not be eliminated by Member States alone.

In 2013, a pan-European discussion, community objectives focusing on the development of a knowledge-based economy, an open data policy, a need to unlock the full economic potential of public resources and the implementation of the European Digital Agenda,[21] led to an amendment of the Directive 2003/98/EC[22] which, as previously mentioned, brought in some significant changes. One of them, from the point of view of the topic under consideration, was of major significance as its scope was extended to libraries, including university libraries, museums and archives. The arguments in favour of the above change included the valuable collections of the above-mentioned institutions, an increasingly wider range of EU and national digitisation projects, which *de facto* created greater opportunities for EU enterprises to make use of public cultural heritage and contributed to economic growth and the creation of new jobs.[23] The growing economic importance of PSI was not without significance. The total, direct and indirect financial gain from PSI applications and use across the entire EU-27

19 Directive 2003/98/EC, Art. 1 (2) (f).

20 Felchner 2014, p. 30.

21 *Communication from the Commission to the European Parliament, the Council, The European Economic and Social Commitee and the Committee of the Regions. A Digital Agenda for Europe* 2010.

22 *Directive 2013/37/EU of the European Parliament and of the Council of 26 June 2013 Amending Directive 2003/98/EC on the Re-use of Public Sector Information* 2013 (hereinafter: Directive 2013/37/EU).

23 Ibid., recital 15 of the preamble.

economy was estimated in 2010 to amount to EUR 140 billion per year.[24] It should be emphasised that the wider use of PSI was, and is, also consistent with other EU activities, such as the competition policy, integrated maritime policy, common transport policy, the need to promote open access to scientific information and the policy on digitisation and cultural heritage.[25] As of 2013, the latter of these activities, the digitisation policy, was subject to comprehensive EU regulations imposing appropriate obligations on the Member States. The three EU documents adopted at that time on the digitisation of cultural heritage largely relate to endeavours undertaken by archives.[26] According to their fundamental assumptions (defining how to solve legal, financial and organisational issues), the digitisation of collections, including archives that constitute part of Europe's cultural heritage, is an important means of ensuring greater access to cultural material, thereby increasing economic opportunities.

This generally outlined background of the amendments to the Directive 2003/98/EC not only broadened its subjective scope, including archives, but the new provisions retain the right of access to public information as the exclusive competence of Member States, introducing a fundamental change, making re-use their obligation.[27] Due to the confines of this chapter, selected aspects related to the re-use of PSI by archives will be discussed later as well as their impact on Polish archival law.

The Directive 2003/98/EC, along with its 2013 amendment, was in force for another 6 years. Pursuant to Article 13 of the amended Directive 2003/98/EC, five years after its adoption, the European Commission performed an evaluation and review of its operation under the regulatory fitness and performance program. Due to the need for further changes and in order to ensure regulatory clarity, the Directive 2003/98/EC was repealed and replaced by *Directive (EU) 2019/1024 of the European Parliament and of the Council of 20 June 2019 on Open Data and the Re-use of Public Sector Information* (hereinafter: Directive (EU) 2019/1024).[28] This amendment was dictated by the remaining barriers to large-scale re-use and the imperative to further harmonise the law in the light of advances in digital

24 *Proposal for a Directive of The European Parliament and of the Coucil Amending Directive 2003/98/EC on Re-use of Public Sector Information* 2011, p. 3.

25 Ibid.

26 *European Parliament Resolution of 5 May 2010 on 'Europeana – the Next Steps'* 2011; *Commission Recommendation of 27 October 2011 on the Digitisation and Online Accessibility of Cultural Material and Digital Preservation* 2011; *Council Conclusions of 10 May 2012 on the Digitisation and Online Accessibility of Cultural Material and Digital Preservation* 2012.

27 *Proposal for a Directive of The European Parliament and of the Coucil Amending Directive 2003/98/EC on Re-use of Public Sector Information* 2011.

28 *Directive (EU) 2019/1024 of the European Parliament and of the Council of 20 June 2019 on Open Data and the Re-use of Public Sector Information* 2019 (hereinafter: Directive (EU) 2019/1024).

technologies so as to stimulate digital innovation to a greater extent, especially in the field of artificial intelligence.[29] Furthermore, the main motives include the evolution towards a knowledge-based society, the demand for intelligent use of data, including its processing in artificial intelligence. These actions, according to the EU legislator, could have groundbreaking results for all sectors of the economy, while striving to make data more widely available through generally available platforms for the entire European community.

The very concept of open data refers to data in an open format that can be freely re-used and shared for any purpose, while the EU open data policy has an important role to play in terms of initiating and stimulating the development of new services based on innovative ways of combining and using such information,[30] which is particularly important in the context of the topic discussed. In the five star system of data openness, the final 5th star involves linking data to other data to provide context.[31] As we know, the context of the data and, to use the language of archivists, the context of the sources in this case will be determined by user needs or the justified integration of data, documents or sources, independent of their original purpose of production.

This short overview of the EU's policy on the extensive use of documents, data or collections, including archives has quite a long history. Further development is to be expected, as data is a commodity whose economic value rises proportionally to its growth. It is worth emphasising that the operation of archives fall within the field of culture, and the cultural policy of the European Union is recognised as an important area of economic activity, as reflected in the policy regarding the re-use of PSI.[32]

How EU law on the re-use of PSI and open data has influenced archival law in Poland

For years, the role of EU law has had a significant impact on the legal regulations of the Member States, including Poland. This impact has grown rapidly from year to year, for example in the regulatory field of Polish archival law.[33] According to the position of Polish scholarship, archival law should be considered as all the legal norms regulating archival activity. The most important legal motion was the Act of 14 July 1983 on the National Archival Holdings and Archives (*Ustawa z*

29 Ibid., recital 3.
30 Ibid., recital 16.
31 *Otwieranie danych* [2021], pp. 11–12.
32 For more on the impact of EU policy on archive activities in the context of culture, cultural heritage, and cultural goods, cf.: Stępniak 2007, pp. 23–44; Styjkowska 2017, pp. 43–53.
33 Pęksa 2007, pp. 20–21.

dnia 14 lipca 1983 r. o narodowym zasobie archiwalnym i archiwach, hereinafter: Archives Act).[34] It is not the only source of law, and the provisions that constitute the core of archival law are dispersed throughout numerous legal acts belonging to all types of universally binding sources of law specified in the Constitution.[35]

Legal acts enacted by the EU, including directives that impose obligations to regulate specific matters in national legal systems, constitute an important element of the Polish legal order. One example of this regulation is the right to access archives, taking into account the citizens' rights regarding information. This area of regulation includes the issue of re-using PSI and public open data kept in state archives, discussed in this chapter.

Due to the limited thematic scope of the issues discussed, the transposition of EU law within the scope indicated refers to PSI in accordance with its legal definition, located in the holdings of state archives, as obliged entities. The adoption of such a solution is justified, because pursuant to Article 22 of the Archives Act, the legislator, when defining the state archival network, constructed it on the basis of an enumeration of its components (i. e., state, separated and institutional archives).[36] Therefore, due to different legal regulations regarding the scope of access to archival materials located in the archives that make up the state archival network, the analysed impact of EU law on the right to re-use PSI has been limited to state archives.

State archives, as units of the public finance sector, hold both public information and PSI. Archives not only create information about their activities, but also store information given to them, including documentation created by other entities. For this reason, public information (which includes registers of archival materials and finding aids, among others) should be distinguished from PSI (which also consists of archival materials).[37]

The Directive 2003/98/EC came into force on 31 December 2003, but was only adopted by the Polish legal system on 1 May 2004, with Poland's accession to the EU. As demonstrated above, its original wording excluded archival materials from the material scope of the law on the re-use of PSI, and archives from the subjective scope. The implementation of the Directive 2003/98/EC was the subject of proceedings by the European Court of Justice, which ruled in 2011 that Poland had failed to comply to transpose this legal regulation.[38] It was implemented the same year through the amendment to the Act of 6 September 2001 on Access to

34 *Ustawa z dnia 14 lipca 1983 r. o narodowym zasobie archiwalnym i archiwach* 2019.
35 For more on this topic, cf.: Konstankiewicz 2020, pp. 15–67.
36 Niewęgłowski / Konstankiewicz 2016, p. 335.
37 Fischer et al. 2019, p. 452.
38 *Judgment of 27 October 2011, Case C-362/10.* 2011; Piskorz-Ryń 2015 (2), pp. 35–39.

Public Information.[39] In accordance with the provisions of the amended act on access to public information in force at that time, the re-use of PSI was defined and the procedure in this respect was specified. Pursuant to the Directive 2003/98/EC, state archives were excluded from the provisions on the re-use of PSI with regard to archival materials at their disposal.[40] One ought to bear in mind that public information is an important component of state archival holdings, and the broadly understood disclosure of archival materials partially overlaps with the implementation of Article 61 of the Constitution on the right of access to public information. It has been rightly noted in the literature that public information constitutes any existing information on public matters, regardless of its date of production, and this applies to the vast majority of archival materials.[41] The rules for making available archival materials constituting public information during the period in question (from 2003 to 2016) were regulated by the Archives Act. Thus, archival materials that are public information (within the meaning of the Act on access to public information), by virtue of the principle expressed in Article 1 (2), gave legislative priority to the Archives Act. The legal basis in this case was the *lex specialis derogat legi generali* collision rule. The Archives Act should be treated as a special piece of legislation, which had a significant impact, for example, due to the closed period in force at that time, i.e., a period of 30 years after which, as a rule, archives could be made available during the period in question.[42] The closed period for access to archival materials that had been in force since 1983 presented a specific obstacle. Despite the fact that the legislator, by virtue of executive regulations, provided for exceptions for early disclosure, the closed period seriously hindered access to files. It also contradicted the constitutional norm. The closed period that was in force at that time was in conflict with article 61 (2) of the Constitution establishing the citizens' right to obtain information about the activities of public authorities and persons discharging public functions, including the right to access documents. A constitutional limitation imposed on the implementation of the above-mentioned right was the freedom and rights of other persons and business entities, as well as the protection of public order, security or important economic interest of the state, defined in the statutes. Thus, the exclusion of access to archival materials on the grounds of the closed period, regardless of their content, was contrary to the

39 *Ustawa z dnia 16 września 2011 r. o zmianie ustawy o dostępie do informacji publicznej oraz niektórych innych ustaw* 2011.

40 *Ustawa z dnia 6 września 2001 r. o dostępie do informacji publicznej* 2020, Art. 23 (a). This article was added at the end of 2011 and was in force until the 2016 Act on the re-use of public sector information came into force (Pl. *Ustawa z dnia 25 lutego 2016 r. o ponownym wykorzystaniu informacji sektora publicznego* 2019).

41 Niewęgłowski / Konstankiewicz 2016, pp. 261–264.

42 *Wyrok Naczelnego Sądu Administracyjnego z 22 września 2016 r. w sprawie I OSK 371/15* 2016.

constitutional norm.[43] This was the state of affairs until mid-2016. The form of the changes was influenced by the implementation of the 2003 directive on PSI re-use, amended in 2013, which extended its scope of application to archives, obliging the Member States to implement it by 1 July 2015.[44] Due to the need for numerous changes in the legislation and earlier proceedings by the Court of Justice, Poland decided to transpose it by adopting a law. Its draft was submitted in December 2015, and after a few months, the Act of 25 February 2016 on the re-use of public sector information was passed and came into force on 16 June 2016.[45]

Referring to the previous analysis of the amendment to the Directive 2003/98/EC and its transposition, it is important to distinguish between the implementation of the right of access to PSI and the re-use of information obtained in this way. As the legislator rightly asserts, access to public information, specified in the act on access to public information, is an implementation of the principle of openness expressed in Article 61 of the Constitution. However, with regard to re-use, its economic and social aspect is emphasised. Therefore, re-use does not infringe the right to public information and the freedom to disseminate it. The act adopted in 2016 defined the subjective and objective scope, as well as re-use and PSI, which, with reference to archival holdings, may be reproductions of archival materials within the meaning of Article 1 of the Archives Act, as well as the content of these materials.[46] The act also established the conditions for re-using PSI, the procedure for availability on request, fees for re-use and the rules for their collection. It also introduced a number of changes, including in archival law.

Due to the implementation of the EU directive (extending the material scope of PSI re-use to include archival materials), the legislator duly established the rules regarding access to archival materials. In connection with the above, some significant changes were introduced to the Archives Act. One of the most significant was the introduction of the principle of universal access to state archival holdings (Article 16a (1)) and the principle of free access (Article 16c (1)). The adoption of universal access to the holdings meant waiving the 30-year closed period.

Currently, access to archival materials is limited to the extent and on the terms specified in the provisions on the protection of classified information and other secrets safeguarded by law, and with a view to securing personal rights and personal data. Access to materials may also be limited due to the need to maintain the integrity of the state archival holdings from the risk of damage,

43 Niewęgłowski / Konstankiewicz 2016, p. 266.

44 Directive 2003/98/EC, Art. 12.

45 *Ustawa z dnia 25 lutego 2016 r. o ponownym wykorzystaniu informacji sektora publicznego* 2019.

46 Ibid., justification of the project.

destruction or loss (Article 16b (1)). The legislator introduced temporary protection for archival materials with regard to the nature of the information contained therein, and their categories were outlined in the act. Other, equally important changes include an indication of the entities obliged to make information available (Article 16a), a definition of the scope of obligations charged to the obliged entities and the meaning of the concept of "making available archival materials" by listing the forms in which this may be executed (Article 16a (2)). Similarly, the legislator listed the forms and purposes for which archival materials may be used (Article 16a (4)), an example of which is the re-use of archival materials (contents or reproductions) for purposes other than those for which they were produced or originally collected, including for commercial purposes (Article 16 (3)). This provision offers any interested parties the opportunity to commercially explore the information obtained via access to archival materials.[47] So, from 16 June 2016, it has been possible to use archival holdings for commercial purposes – in line with PSI re-use – in new contexts, different circumstances and forms.

The amendments to the Archives Act, in force since mid-2016, are valid in the same version.[48] It is worth emphasising that this was the thirty-fifth amendment to the Archives Act and, at the same time, one of the three most significant changes in terms of the depth of the changes made.[49]

The 2016 act on the re-use of PSI that brought in the directive amended in 2013 has been repealed. By implementing Directive (EU) 2019/1024 on open data and the re-use of public sector information, Poland has transposed it by adopting the new Act of 11 August 2021 on open data and the re-use of public sector information.

In adopting Directive (EU) 2019/1024, the Polish legislator asserted the need to update the existing legal framework for PSI re-use in order to adapt it to ongoing changes in digital technologies and to ensure the full use of PSI potential for the European economy and society, thereby increasing the amount of data.[50] In line with EU law, this made it possible to distinguish new categories of data, including high-value and dynamic. The former means documents that would, if re-used, offer significant benefits for society, the environment and the economy. The latter signifies digital documents that are updated frequently or in real time, in particular due to their changeability or rapid obsolescence.[51] The act reiterates that archives are entities obliged to make available or transfer PSI for re-use.

47 Niewęgłowski / Konstankiewicz 2016, pp. 223, 266; Fischer et al. 2019, pp. 451–454.

48 The legal status as of January 2022.

49 Konstankiewicz 2016, p. 5.

50 *Ustawa z dnia 11 sierpnia 2021 r. o otwartch danych i ponownym wykorzystaniu informacji sektora publicznego* 2021, justification of the project.

51 Directive (EU) 2019/1024.

The only limitation in the right to re-use, reiterated vis-a-vis the previous regulations in the case of state archives, concerns state archival holdings whose original proprietary copyrights or related rights are owned by entities other than the obliged entities (i. e., archives or, more broadly the State Treasury), and the duration of these rights have not expired.

Poland's participation and readiness in the policy of data openness has been measured in comparison with other EU Member States since 2015. Analysis of the annual reports leads to the conclusion that over the 7 years after implementing the basic assumptions, Poland has risen to become a trend-setting country in this area. 2021 Perhaps this is due to the adoption of solutions that go beyond the scope of the 2019 directives on data openness and PSI re-use.[52]

Summary

The changes introduced in the Archives Act, effective from 16 June 2016, are directly related to the implementation of the directive. The scope of changes and the direct impact of EU law on the shape of the amendments introduced will be subject to detailed analysis planned by the author of this chapter. It must be stated that the discussed amendment was related to the implementation of EU law and remodelled access to archives in Poland. The scope of the changes introduced in the Archives Act at that time exceeded their application to EU law.[53]

Therefore, the discussed problem directly and indirectly influences the operation of archives in Poland, while for many years the literature has been raising the importance of EU regulations on how archives work. The period of legal harmonisation is a continuous process, and we stand at its center as an integral part of it. Besides, every balance sheet features a profit side and a loss side, and these should be a problem of research into a detailed analysis of the transposition of EU law into the shape of archival law in Poland.

The institution of re-use focuses on harnessing the economic value of PSI as a raw material for the development of new products and services, whose scope is growing rapidly. Not without significance is also that the directives analysed in this chapter were adopted on the basis of Article 114 TFEU (ex Article 95 TEC). Since they involve the free movement of services and the proper functioning of the internal market, the aim of the regulation was and is to provide conditions that will enhance the potential benefits of re-using public data resources in Europe.

52 *Open Data Maturity* [2022].

53 Konstankiewcz 2016, p. 6.

Regardless of the intentions of the EU legislator, the right to re-use PSI and data openness must also be examined from the perspective of national and regional development in terms of culture, transparency of public life and the development of modern technologies. We, the people of Europe, are evolving from a knowledge-based society. Therefore, the openness of collections, including the openness of archival holdings, can only be seen as beneficial.

[Translated by Steve Jones]

Bibliography

Printed sources

Charter of Fundamental Rights of the European Union, in: *Official Journal of the European Union*. 2012, 2012/C 326/02.

Communication from the Commission to the European Parliament, the Council, The European Economic and Social Commitee and the Committee of the Regions. A Digital Agenda for Europe. COM (2010) 245, in: EUR-Lex, URL: https://eur-lex.europa.eu/legal-content/EN/TXT/?uri=CELEX%3A52010DC0245R%2801%29 [15.01.2022].

Directive (EU) 2019/1024 of the European Parliament and of the Council of 20 June 2019 on Open Data and the Re-use of Public Sector Information, in: *Official Journal of the European Union*. 2019, 2019/L 172/56.

Directive 2003/98/EC of the European Parliament and of the Council of 17 November 2003 on the Re-use of Public Sector Information, in: *Official Journal of the European Union*. 2003, 2003/L No. 345, as amended.

Directive 2013/37/EU of the European Parliament and of the Council of 26 June 2013 Amending Directive 2003/98/EC on the Re-use of Public Sector Information, in: *Official Journal of the European Union*. 2013, 2013/L 175/1.

European Convention for the Protection of Human Rights and Fundamental Freedoms. 1950.

International Covenant on Civil and Political Rights. 1966.

Proposal for a Directive of the European Parliament and of the Coucil Amending Directive 2003/98/EC on Re-use of Public Sector Information. COM (2011) 877, in: *European Parliament*, URL: https://www.europarl.europa.eu/meetdocs/2009_2014/documents/com/com_com(2011)0877_/com_com(2011)0877_en.pdf [13.01.2022].

Proposal for a Directive of the European Parliament and of the Council on the Re-use and Commercial Exploitation of Public Sector Documents. COM (2002) 207, in: *EUR-Lex*, URL: https://eur-lex.europa.eu/legal-content/NL/HIS/?uri=CELEX:32003L0098# [14.01.2022].

Public Sector Information: A Key Resource for Europe. Green Paper on Public Sector Information in the Information Society. COM (1998) 585, in: *Publications Office of the European Union*, URL: https://op.europa.eu/en/publication-detail/-/publication/599834ce-7a43-44fe-8cd8-334b3c19feba [21.04.2022].

Universal Declaration of Human Rights. 1948.

Ustawa z dnia 11 sierpnia 2021 r. o otwartych danych i ponownym wykorzystywaniu informacji sektora publicznego, in: *Dziennik Ustaw Rzeczypospolitej Polskiej*. 2021, item 1641.

Ustawa z dnia 14 lipca 1983 r. o narodowym zasobie archiwalnym i archiwach, in: *Dziennik Ustaw Rzeczypospolitej Polskiej*. 2019, item 553, as amended.

Ustawa z dnia 16 września 2011 r. o zmianie ustawy o dostępie do informacji publicznej oraz niektórych innych ustaw, in: *Dziennik Ustaw Rzeczypospolitej Polskiej*. 2011, No. 2014, item 553, as amended.

Ustawa z dnia 25 lutego 2016 r. o ponownym wykorzystywaniu informacji sektora publicznego, in: *Dziennik Ustaw Rzeczypospolitej Polskiej*. 2019, item 1446, as amended.

Ustawa z dnia 6 września 2001 r. o dostępie do informacji publicznej, in: *Dziennik Ustaw Rzeczypospolitej Polskiej*. 2020, item 2176, as amended.

Wyrok Naczelnego Sądu Administracyjnego z 22 września 2016 r. w sprawie I OSK 371/15, in: *Centralna Baza Orzeczeń Sądów Administracyjnych*, URL: https://orzeczenia.nsa.gov.pl/doc/81993D46CE [10.01.2022].

European Parliament Resolution of 5 May 2010 on 'Europeana – the Next Steps', in: *Official Journal of the European Union*. 2011, 2011/C 81 E/04.

Commission Recommendation of 27 October 2011 on the Digitisation and Online Accessibility of Cultural Material and Digital Preservation, in: *Official Journal of the European Union*. 2011, 2011/L 283/39.

*Judgment of 27 October 2011, European Commission v Republic of Poland (Failure of a Member State to Fulfil Obligations – Directive 2003/98/EC – Re-use of Public Sector Information – Incorrect Transposition of or Failure to Transpose Certain Articles Within the Period Prescribed), Case C-362/*10, in: *Official Journal of the European Union*. 2011, 2011/C 370/21.

Council Conclusions of 10 May 2012 on the Digitisation and Online Accessibility of Cultural Material and Digital Preservation, in: *Official Journal of the European Union*. 2012, 2012/C 169/02.

Literature

eEurope 2002, in: *EUR-Lex*, URL: https://eur-lex.europa.eu/legalcontent/EN/TXT/?uri=LEGISSUM:l24226a [19.01.2022].

Felchner, Krzysztof: *Biblioteki, archiwa, muzea w świetle nowelizacji przepisów o ponownym wykorzystywaniu informacji publicznej*, in: *Europejski Przegląd Sądowy*. 2014/7, pp. 30–36.

Fischer, Bogdan / Piskorz-Ryń, Agnieszka / Sakowska-Baryła, Marlena / Wyporska-Frankiewicz, Joanna: *Ustawa o ponownym wykorzystywaniu informacji sektora publicznego. Komentarz*. 2019.

Janssen, Katleen / Dumortier, Jos: *Towards a European Framework for the Re-use of Public Sector Information: a Long and Winding Road*, in: *International Journal of Law and Information Technology*. 2003/2, pp. 184–201.

Konstankieiwcz, Marek: *Zmiany w zakresie udostępniania materiałów archiwalnych, wchodzące w życie 16 czerwca 2016 r., w ustawie z 1983 r. o narodowym zasobie i archiwach*, in: *Archiwista Polski.* 2016/83/3, pp. 5–20.

Konstankiewicz, Marek: *Regulacja prawa polskiego mające znaczenie dla działalności archiwalnej*, in: *Archeion.* 2020/121, pp. 15–67.

Niewęgłowski, Adrian / Konstankiewicz, Marek: *Narodowy zasób archiwalny i archiwa. Komentarz.* 2016.

Open Data Maturity in Europe 2015. Insights into the European State of Play, in: *European Data Portal*, URL: https://tinyurl.com/2p84z74y [01.02.2022].

Otwieranie danych. Podręcznik dobrych praktyk, in: *Ministerstwo Cyfryzacji*, URL: https://dane.gov.pl/media/ckeditor/2018/11/22/otwieranie-danych-podrecznik-dobrych-praktyk.pdf [25.01.2022].

Pęksa, Władysław: *Prawo archiwalne - wprowadzenie do zagadnienia*, in: Robótka, Halina (ed.): *Prawo archiwalne. Stan aktualny i perspektywy zmian.* 2007, pp. 17–30.

Piskorz-Ryń, Agnieszka: *Hybrydowy charakter prawa do ponownego wykorzystywania – wybrane zagadnienia*, in: *Samorząd Terytorialny.* 2017/1–2, pp. 83–93.

Piskorz-Ryń, Agnieszka: *Pojęcie ponownego wykorzystywania informacji sektora publicznego w świetle dyrektywy 2003/98/EC*, in: *Samorząd Terytorialny.* 2015/ 4, pp. 34–42. (1)

Piskorz-Ryń, Agnieszka: *Prawo dostępu do informacji a ponowne wykorzystywanie informacji sektora publicznego. Glosa do wyroku TS z dnia 27 października 2011 r., C-362/10*, in: *Europejski Przegląd Sądowy.* 2015/5, pp. 35–39. (2)

Stępniak, Władysław: *Archiwa w polityce europejskiej. Uwagi wstępne*, in: Porazinski, Jarosław / Stryjkowski, Krzysztof (eds.): *Archiwa w nowoczesnym społeczeństwie. Pamiętnik V Zjazdu Archiwistów Polskich, Olsztyn 6–8 września 2007.* 2008, pp. 23–43.

Stryjkowska, Sylwia: *Problematyka ochrony dóbr kultury w prawie Unii Europejskiej*, in: *Archiwista Polski.* 2017/1–2, pp. 43–53.

Liisi Taimre / Aigi Rahi-Tamm / Sven Lepa / Tõnis Türna

From Community Involvement to Research Interests: Crowdsourcing Projects of the National Archives of Estonia[1]

Abstract
Involving volunteers in the description of archival sources through different crowdsourcing projects has become a common feature of the rapidly developing digital culture. Creating new digital resources has built on the interest of various audiences and research goals, yet the success of the aims set depends on diverse factors. The chapter analyses the results of users' surveys of people involved in the crowdsourcing projects at the National Archives of Estonia as well as broader issues related to the involvement of communities.
Keywords: crowdsourcing; digital culture; Estonian Archives; involvement of volunteers; users surveys

In 2020, the National Archives of Estonia celebrated its 100th anniversary. Such milestones make us look both backwards and forwards, to estimate what has been done and set goals for the future. In 2005, when the use of archival sources from home computers became possible in Estonia, SAAGA – the environment for digital images and AIS, the electronic catalogue of archival registers – was opened, the number of visitors soared. Priit Pirsko, the state archivist, has acknowledged that if an archival source is not accessible online, it does not exist. The involvement of volunteers in the description of archival sources through crowdsourcing projects is another manifestation of the digital boom in the field of Estonian archives.[2] In order to give a "voice" to archival sources, we not only have to digitise them but also contribute to their efficient use. Crowdsourcing is a great opportunity for the involvement of users in the enhancement of diverse

Liisi Taimre M. A., National Archives of Estonia.
Prof. Aigi Rahi-Tamm, University of Tartu, ORCID: https://orcid.org/0000-0001-8792-860X.
Sven Lepa M. A., National Archives of Estonia.
Tõnis Türna B. A., National Archives of Estonia.
1 The article was written in the framework of the project *National Program: Estonian Language and Culture in the Digital Age (EKKD29)* financed by the Estonian Ministry of Education and Research.
2 Pirsko 2020, p. 6.

databases and making them more user-friendly.[3] A wide circle of users with different interests enjoys this work and the results of these efforts.

Community involvement in the collection of cultural heritage is not a new idea for Estonian society. At the end of the 19th and at the beginning of the 20th centuries, about 122,000 pages of Estonian folklore were collected by about 1,400 people from all over the country.[4] Letters of the people who were engaged in this campaign to Jakob Hurt (1839–1907), initiator of the enterprise, shed light on several problems that have risen with involving people in different times and therefore received our attention. Like crowdsourcing today, the actions of documenting people's oral memory more than a hundred years ago were motivated by a similar common spirit – to do something for the benefit of the nation.

The year 2020 was declared the year of digital culture by the Estonian Ministry of Culture with the aim of paying more attention in society to the impact of the digital world and its diverse manifestations. The changes to historical culture and the relationship of society with the past – from academic studies to computer games inspired by historical events – were also highlighted. Besides state-financed mass digitisation of cultural heritage,[5] new opportunities for historical research – including stakeholders through digital crowdsourcing – were discussed.[6] The rapid development of digital technologies contributes to the acquisition of digital competencies and participatory culture, which is increasingly shaping our relationship with the past.[7]

Although crowdsourcing in its contemporary form has been implemented since the 21st century, the concept itself is not so original. The success of crowdsourcing depends on several factors, one of the most important of which is developing the interest of volunteers and their effective involvement. To understand these processes better, we conducted a survey among people who participated in the last two crowdsourcing projects and asked what motivated the volunteers to contribute to these initiatives and what has proved to be a hindrance. Mia Ridge, who has studied digital heritage, said:

> Building a successful crowdsourcing project requires an understanding of the motivations for initial and on-going participation, the characteristics of tasks suited to crowdsourcing and the application of best practices in design for participation, content validation, marketing and community building.[8]

3 Howe 2006.
4 Põldmäe 1989, p. 10.
5 *Kultuuripärandi digiteerimise tegevuskava* [2021].
6 Tamm 2020, p. 29.
7 Galani / Mason / Arrigoni 2020.
8 Ridge 2017, p. 2.

These principles also served as the basis for our feedback survey. This chapter gives an overview of the crowdsourcing projects carried out at the Estonian National Archives – primarily focusing on the last two projects – describes the results of the user surveys and analyses the experiences acquired by involving volunteers.

On the first crowdsourcing projects (2014–2018)

Since 2014, four crowdsourcing projects have been launched at the National Archives. They were inspired by similar projects in other countries. The motto of the Citizen Archives of the US National Archives – "One day all of our records will be online. You can help make it happen" – was especially inspiring.[9] Furthermore, the crowdsourcing environment Vele Handen links different memory institutions in Holland,[10] and the Australian arcHIVE enables users to enter both paper registers and diverse, primarily biographical, sources under the auspices of digital volunteering.[11] The project of the name index of parish registers that began in 2005 can be regarded as the first attempt of crowdsourcing in Estonia. For this project, the National Archives developed a special online environment and volunteer genealogists started to compile a name index of digitised parish registers. By today, more than a million entries have been inserted into the name register.[12]

Setting up a database of Estonian soldiers who participated in World War I in 2014 became the first full-scale crowdsourcing project. Until then, the knowledge of recruits from Estonia had been based on estimates. As a result of the contribution by 300 volunteers, a database with 194,000 personal descriptions, combining information from different sources (885 archival files), was composed that made the personal data of people who participated in the war as well as a wide circle of conscripts easily available for those interested in family history and also provided rich material for historians for further studies and in-depth analyses.

Next, the National Archives called for the help of the volunteers in 2017 to combine the data of the citizens of Tartu, documented by the census on 2 March 1867, when Estonia belonged to the czarist Russian Empire, with the online application of the city map. The citizens' lists (eleven archival documents containing data of about 21,000 people) provide a detailed survey of the population including all social groups. An interactive map of the historical properties of

9 *Citizen Archives Dashboard* [2021].
10 *VeleHanden* [2021].
11 *Digital volunteering at the National Archives* [2021].
12 *Luteri koguduste personaalraamatute nimeregister* [2021].

Tartu enables the users to experience the past through contemporary urban space. Each volunteer (70 people participated) could choose a place he/she liked, or which had a special personal significance, and start to write down the persons who once lived there from the source.[13] The first two projects were completed in 2018.

Currently, the third and fourth crowdsourcing projects are ongoing. As a continuation of the World War I project, in 2020 the volunteers were invited to contribute to the next database of the soldiers who participated in the War of Independence. Before that, in 2019, the project of rewriting and labelling parish court protocols was launched. Participants in this project also shared their opinions with us on their crowdsourcing experience.

Current crowdsourcing projects (since 2019)

Parish courts

In Estonia, the first parish courts, as institutions of the estate of peasants for regulating their mutual relations, were established in the late 18th century. As well as trials, the courts fulfilled local administrative functions. With the 1868 parish reform, the self-government system of peasants was established, and the parish court became the first legal authority in the system of peasant courts. It was primarily a conciliation court, the priority of which was not conviction but solving legal issues. As such, protocols of the parish courts describe the everyday life of the peasants, various problems with farms, land, property transactions, all sorts of violations and dysfunctions to the normal order of life, including family and moral problems, and the general mentality in the village society of the era. The protocols also provide interesting material for studying language history as they reflect the process of the development of Estonian written language. In the protocols, the dialects of those times and the still developing written language are mixed. This rich source material began to come to the attention of scholars in the 1970s[14] but more intensive use alongside the digitalisation of databases began in the 1990s.[15]

More than 2,200 protocol and contract books of parish courts from the czarist period (1818–1917) are kept in the National Archives. These were first made available for users in SAAGA, the online environment of digitised archival

13 *Tartu 1867* [2021].
14 Linnus 1970.
15 Türna 2004.

sources.[16] This database contains about 235,000 digital images of the protocols. Yet, to find relevant information, the researchers had to read them all through, page by page, and line by line. Since the protocols are used by a wide range of people from academic scholars to amateurs interested in the history of their native place and family, a common project of the historians and linguists of the University of Tartu and the National Archives was launched for rewriting the protocols word by word and as close to the originals as possible through crowdsourcing. In the crowdsourcing environment, each participant can choose a region and protocol. To facilitate the searches, the text of the protocol has to be grouped thematically and the place names and personal names have to be labelled. Words or paragraphs that are difficult to read are also labelled.

Media coverage on radio, television, in the papers and social media as well as various promotional events invited friends of the archives to contribute to this initiative. In 2021, 222 volunteers participated in the project, and more than 68,000 court protocols were recorded. It is worth mentioning that the most active volunteer recorded more than 12,000 protocols. Considering that about 600,000 protocols have been preserved, there is enough work for this crowdsourcing project for years to come.

The War of Independence

For Estonians, World War I broke out in 1914 but did not end in 1918 as it continued as the War of Independence until 1920 in the form of battles with Soviet Russia and Baltic Germans who had seized power in Latvia (the so-called *Landeswehr* War), resulting in the birth of the independent nation-state. At its peak, 74,506 soldiers, belonging to the Estonian People's Army, participated in the War of Independence.[17] In almost every Estonian family, a relative participated in the War of Independence, yet their personal data is fragmentary. In 2020, when a hundred years had passed since the end of the war, a crowdsourcing project was launched in order to gather the data about the soldiers in the documents of the military units into a common database. The slogan of the action – "Let us sign up all the soldiers!" (*Paneme kõik sõjamehed kirja!*) – speaks for itself. The participants' task was to enter the data of persons found in the digitised documents into the database with a respective reference to the original document. This collection of data was similar to that of the project *Estonians in World War I.* Since several participants of the War of Independence had also taken part in the world war, their documents contain information on their earlier

16 *VAU* [2021].
17 Vahtre 2020, p. 389.

service that will also be recorded during the project. This crowdsourcing project mainly includes two sets of documents: first, the personal files of reservists kept in the staff of military operations commands, and, second, personnel documents drawn up during the war in the army (various lists, certificates, orders of the day, etc.). Until now, finding personal data in these documents has been rather complicated. Although the project is still ongoing, the first results have enabled persons about whom there was no information available before to be identified. The contribution of the volunteers has improved the availability of data and opened up the content of poorly described sources to a wide range of interested parties, including for academic research. In 2021, 174 volunteers, who recorded data about more than 77,000 people, contributed to the project. Unfortunately, this crowdsourcing initiative has not advanced as quickly as was initially planned.

Feedback study on participation in crowdsourcing

As mentioned, crowdsourcing is largely based on the contribution of volunteers. All the crowdsourcing initiatives have revealed the same pattern of behaviour: many people give it a try but most of the work is done by a few devoted participants. The feedback survey helped us understand the motives for active participation. It was conducted via e-mail and on a voluntary basis. In the case of the parish courts project, the survey questionnaire was sent to all participants who had made at least one entry to the crowdsourcing environment; in the case of the War of Independence project, it was sent to everyone who had logged into the environment at least once. The survey aimed to study the background of the volunteers, their motives, the problems that had arisen and their expectations towards the development of the project and other suggestions. 44 volunteers, who had contributed with at least one entry to the parish courts project, and 110 people, who had logged into the environment at least once, answered the questionnaire. In the case of the parish court project, this accounted for about a quarter of all the contributors (222 participants altogether). About seven per cent of those who had registered in the portal of the War of Independence project (altogether 1649 people) participated in the survey. Although our expectations towards the activity of the respondents were higher, the answers enabled us to map the general tendencies quite well and make certain conclusions.

General profile of the users

More than a half of the respondents of both surveys belonged to the age group 50–70. 15% of the users were under 40. As for the age group 40–50, there were some differences as they accounted for 27% of the respondents to the parish court survey and 10% of the respondents to the War of Independence survey. A comparison of these data with the user satisfaction survey, conducted by the National Archives in 2019, which aimed to identify their main clients, revealed that the main users belonged to the age group 50–70 years.[18]

Involvement

First, we asked how the volunteers had discovered the crowdsourcing projects, especially focusing on the permanent users of the archives. It is apparent that the success of the crowdsourcing projects primarily depends on participation. 46% of respondents to the parish court survey discovered crowdsourcing via the website of the National Archives; 68% of respondents to the War of Independence survey followed the same pattern. All permanent users who participated in the War of Independence project learned about this opportunity via the website of the National Archives; in the case of this group, other channels of communication were insignificant. Yet, the fact that a number of those who initially just tested the environment have become permanent users, proves the significance of media coverage. From the eight people who learned about the parish courts crowdsourcing via the media, six have become permanent users of the archives. Students and pupils who were encouraged to participate in the projects at school have also contributed to the projects, especially the parish courts project. For quite a few of them, a compulsory task has become a voluntary hobby.

Likewise, students were among the top-thirty of the list of participants in the World War I project.[19] On the other hand, some criticism has been voiced by those who see crowdsourcing primarily as entertainment and deplore the practice of compulsory study tasks.[20] Indeed, crowdsourcing projects should not be based on the contribution of pupils and students only, but participation in crowdsourcing might be a part of secondary school and university curricula. Considering the increasing spread of crowdsourcing initiatives, they offer a good opportunity to acquire practical experience in historical studies.

18 *Rahulolu-uuringu tulemused* [2021].
19 Tooming 2019, p. 113.
20 Davies / Looseley 2015.

Motivation

What urges people to participate in crowdsourcing? The following factors emerged as most significant: personal interest in history, family relationships and a sense of mission. Several contributors have emphasized their personal relationship with the material, including a family relationship with persons mentioned in the sources. Their comments, which reflect an in-depth interest in the fate of their ancestors, also indicate the significance of family stories. For example, a woman in her 50s has written the following comments about her personal curiosity that drove her to participate in the project:

> The eldest brother of my grandmother was killed in the War of Independence (actually, in the War of *Landeswehr*) in the battle of Võnnu (he served in the 7th platoon of the narrow-track armoured train with his compatriots from Pärnumaa). They held the Iron Division at the manor of Heidelbergshof. 17 of the 24 men were killed. Three young men from his native village Kaisma (Aleksander Weber (Weeber/Veber), Lilienthal + 1) fell in this battle – this is the reason for my curiosity.[21]

The work of the Estonian Genealogical Society has remarkably promoted genealogical studies,[22] through which several members of the society have taken an interest in crowdsourcing. Studying family tradition has not only stimulated interest and raised new questions but also motivated people to fill in the gaps in the sources – crowdsourcing projects have also proved this.[23] A 40-year-old woman, who is participating in the parish court crowdsourcing project, commented on her interest:

> I have also studied my family tree a lot; thus, there are connections between the names in the parish court archives and the names in my family. In the stories of my native place, I can see the links with the farms as well as family names. I have shared the best stories with my friends and relatives, and they also like it a lot.[24]

21 "[…] Mu vanaema vanim vend hukkus Vabadussõjas (täpsemalt Landeswehri sõjas) Võnnu lahingus (oli II kitsarööpmelise soomusrongi 7. rühmas koos kaasvõitlejatega Pärnumaalt), kes hoidsid kinni Rauddiviisi Heidelbergshofi mõisas. 24 mehest hukkus 17. Tema kodukohast, Kaismalt, hukkus 3 noort meest (Aleksander Weber (Weeber/Veber), Lilienthal + 1) – see ongi minu seos uudishimuga." Rahvusarhiiv (hereinafter: RA): *Crowdsourcing of the War of Independence, Survey on motives for participation*; user 97, female, working, Harju County, age group 50–60, 30.10.2021.

22 *Activities* [2021].

23 Jaago / Jaago 1998.

24 "[…] Olen ka sugupuud palju uurinud, vallakohtute arhiivides tekivad juba sugupuu uurimisel nähtud nimedega seosed. Kodukoha lugudes tekib seos nii talude kui ka perekonnanimedega. Toredamaid lugusid jagan sõprade-sugulastega, ka neile väga meeldib." RA: *Crowdsourcing of parish courts, Survey on motives for participation*; user 29, female, working, Harju County, age group 50–60, 15.12.2021.

Indeed, 8.9% of the participants in the user survey of the parish court project joined crowdsourcing on the recommendation of their friends.

A sense of mission or a wish to be part of something bigger may also be motivating factors. As participants in the crowdsourcing project related to the use of the heritage of philosopher Jeremy Bentham said, they wish to take part in something which will ultimately benefit the wider community.[25] Participants in the crowdsourcing projects of the National Archives expressed similar ideas. They wish to make contribution, however tiny that might be.[26] They also welcome making the material available for many people.[27] A woman in her 70s wrote: "As an elderly person, I can contribute to something which in my opinion is important and necessary to the history of our culture and learn myself about the life and environment of my predecessors – this is fascinating!"[28] For some volunteers the work has become really enthralling: "I read a story about a horse thief. It was like watching a movie. I was looking forward to the continuation. […] Unfortunately, the case went over from the parish court to the bridge court (*Ordnungsgericht*) and finally I could not find out what the verdict was."[29]

Thus, diverse factors are at play in crowdsourcing. As the survey results indicate, gender also plays a certain role. Gender differences were quite clearly manifested in the comparison of the parish court and War of Independence projects. Whereas 80% of the respondents to the survey of the parish courts were women, in the case of the War of Independence project, their percentage was 43. It seems that the material concerning everyday life captured the enthusiasm of women more than the military content of the War of Independence database, although three women who, at the end of 2021, had made more than 53% of the entries (41,439 of 77,776 entries) are at the top of the list of contributors.[30] Obviously, the topics of the crowdsourcing projects motivate social groups differently. Furthermore, the personal connection with one's native place and relatives, which is characteristic to participants of the Estonian crowdsourcing projects, need not be similar to those of other countries. Thus, regional and other differences have to be taken into account when considering potential topics for crowdsourcing.

25 Causer / Terras 2017, p. 67.

26 RA: *Crowdsourcing of parish courts, Survey on motives for participation*; user 3, female, working, Jõgeva County, age group 50–60, 15.12.2021.

27 Ibid.; user 43, female, retired, Lääne County, age group 70+, 15.12.2020.

28 "[…] Vanainimesena panustan sisestamisega midagi, minu arvates olulist ja vajalikku meie kultuuri ajalukku ja tutvun ise oma eelkäijate elu ja olemisega, mis on väga huvitav." Ibid.; user 13 female, retired, Võru County, age group 70+, 15.12.2020.

29 "[…] Sisestasin üht hobusevarguse lugu. Film hakkas justkui silmade ees jooksma. Ootasin põnevusega järge. […] Kahjuks läks asi vallakohtust üle sillakohtusse ja ma ei saanudki teada mis lõpuks sai." Ibid.; user 20, female, working, Tartu County, age group 50–60, 15.12.2020.

30 *Kasutajate edetabel* [2021].

Obstacles

When estimating the success of crowdsourcing, we also have to take into account possible obstacles and problems. 11% of those who answered the survey questionnaire had discontinued their work. In the case of both surveys, the major obstacles mentioned were problems related to reading the sources, like bad handwriting or incomprehensible abbreviations. Some also mentioned more specific problems like identifying the terms of units of measurement.

About 10% of the respondents to both surveys complained about an uncomfortable data entry environment. They found it disturbing when they could not see enough of the source on the screen and had to scroll the image back and forth too frequently. To avoid this problem, the users were advised to leave the margins of the entry environment as narrow as possible.

Although a sense of mission was mentioned above as a motivating factor, in some cases it may prove to be a problem. For example, a retired person in his 60s has described the following situation: "I was looking for data about my relative Paul-August Hirv (he was awarded the Cross of Freedom) and did not find anything from other sources. Yet, I did not dare to enter him into the database as I do not consider myself competent enough."[31] Therefore, we can see that what is written into sources may sometimes inspire excessive awe.

The team working on the development of the crowdsourcing environment is grateful for all kinds of feedback that helps to improve the design of further projects and, more broadly, offers food for thought on how to prepare digitised sources for the users so that the voluntary work would not become bogged down with linguistic or calligraphic barriers and would meet the needs of diverse interest groups.

The interests of the researchers

Of the four crowdsourcing initiatives, the project of parish courts has been most closely related to academic researchers. The digital resource created in the framework of the project and supported by crowdsourcing is being used to solve different research tasks. 24% of the respondents of the feedback survey saw the potential of the entered texts mainly for research. The same amount of re-

31 "[…] Otsisin andmeid oma sugulase Paul-August Hirve (Vabadusristi kavaler) kohta, muudest allikatest andmeid ei leidnud. Aga andmebaasi sisestada ka ei julgenud, kuna ei loe end kompetentseks." RA: *Crowdsourcing of the War of Independence, Survey on motives for participation*; user 14, female, retired, Saaremaa County, age group 60–70, 30.09.2021.

spondents emphasized the need to introduce the topic for a wider audience and publish materials and studies.

Language technologists, who apply methods of automatic linguistic analysis to the texts of parish court protocols, are looking for innovative ways of adapting the new resource for contemporary users and develop new possibilities for analysis. In language technology and digital humanities in general, automatic analysis of historical texts and modelling linguistic changes are increasingly topical trends. Several reasons have hindered the automatic processing of historical texts. First, the usually hand-written text has to be digitised. Yet historical texts often vary a lot because norms in the written language were not harmonised, and several norms may have been in use simultaneously. Furthermore, regional dialects have considerably shaped the written language: the meanings of words have changed over time; the texts may contain unknown words for contemporary people, etc.[32] Of course, all these factors make the study of language interesting, but on the other hand they complicate the processing of historical texts and text search. On the processing of historical texts written in variable language and the methods applied, we advise others to read studies by Maarja-Liisa Pilvik, Kadri Muischnek, Gerth Jaanimäe, Liina Lindström, and Siim Orasmaa.[33]

For historians, parish court protocols are sources of unique value for studying 19th-century peasant society,[34] for which crowdsourcing has offered new fascinating opportunities. The focus of the sources on persons and places as well as their narrative style enable us to study different stories and social developments on the microlevel. Providing the body of the text with linguistic, geographical, and thematic information and making it searchable has not only broadened the range of potential users but has also opened up new opportunities for in-depth analysis of the everyday life and social networks of those times. Labelling the personal names of the judges, applicants, defendants, and parish clerks and connecting them with other sources (court files, parish registers, documents of parish archives, newspapers, memories, etc.) has enabled the mutual contacts between villagers and their relationships to be studied. The database of parish court clerks, which was compiled during the research project linked to crowdsourcing in which different types of sources are connected, enables a group of parish officials, who were regarded as "first men" or "souls of the parish" due to their education and competence in legal or administrative matters, to be portrayed. Kersti Lust and Tõnis Türna, who have been leading the studies based on parish court materials, have published several interesting articles.[35]

32 Piotrowski 2021, pp. 1–157.
33 Pilvik et al. 2019, pp. 139–158; Lindström et al. 2019, pp. 155–193.
34 Traat 1980; Must 1998, pp. 93–108; Kaaristo 2006, pp. 49–62.
35 Lust / Türna 2021, pp. 10–32; Lust 2021, pp. 74–99.

All projects have presented challenges for processing, linking, and analysing the databases created by crowdsourcing. For example, comparing the databases of Estonian men who fought in World War I and the War of Independence with later data concerning World War II and the postwar repressions, have motivated Aigi Rahi-Tamm and Liisi Esse to investigate the war experience of Estonians in a long-term perspective all through the 20th century.[36] Furthermore, working with diverse sets of data helps scholars in the field of humanities to acquire new methods and technical competence and increase the effectivity of interdisciplinary cooperation.

Conclusions on the experience of crowdsourcing

User surveys of the two crowdsourcing projects clearly indicated the importance of motivation for the success of the project. Of course, to keep the volunteers interested, various obstacles have to be eliminated; the user environment has to become friendlier. We have to consider the difficulties related to reading the texts in the sources and mitigate these issues by adapting the environment or making the manuals or aids user-friendly. 62% of the respondents to the parish courts survey confirmed that they have looked at and read materials entered by other users. Presenting illustrative cases that link the topics not only incites curiosity but also has educational value.

Keeping up the users' motivation is the most important guarantee of successful crowdsourcing. This begins with the successful choice of a topic that is relevant for the broader audience and also offers connections to the community involved on a personal level. The relationship of the material with the home, region, or family concerns both people's self-consciousness and historical memory and increases the wish to contribute to a common enterprise. Genealogists using the archive's online resources on a regular basis are very interested in contributing their time to projects related to their research.

Since most of the work is done by enthusiastic permanent users of the archives, their motivation is especially important. The work is also valued through feedback from the managers of the crowdsourcing projects. The same is valid for other initiatives of collection and mediation at memory institutions, such as life story competitions carried out by the Association of Estonian Life Histories[37] or the participation campaigns of the Network of Correspondents of the Estonian National Museum.[38] Already, the campaigns of collecting folk heritage during the

36 Rahi-Tamm / Esse 2022; eidem 2014, pp. 391–411.
37 Hinrikus 2003, pp. 171–213.
38 Metslaid 2021.

time of Jakob Hurt in late 19th – early 20th centuries made the factors related to the involvement of people manifest. Hurt's co-workers were certainly motivated by a deep sense of mission as well as various examples,[39] but direct communication with the organisers was not insignificant either. Hurt sustained the interest of the collectors by thanking and encouraging them: he sent them letters of appreciation, his photos and books, published lists of most active contributors in the press, corresponded with many of them and even tried to help solve their personal problems.[40] Such methods still work today.

In the conclusions made at the end of the World War I project, analysing the experiences gathered over four years, it was stated that making midterm reviews had a positive impact on data entering, but sharing the ranking of contributors on the website created excitement and motivated people to work faster. Appreciation events, handing out souvenirs and media coverage have also had a positive effect. Yet, there is one more factor which is sometimes forgotten: direct communication with project leaders or managers who can encourage the contributors and would be ready to help them with their problems either in oral or written form. When collaboration between the initiators and participants is smooth, even hardly readable sources in foreign language do not seem frightening and people do not give up easily. As a rule, those volunteers who are able to read the sources keep going. Solving problems may even be fascinating, yet the participant must feel and know that there is someone – even if he or she is behind the screen – who cares for the work being done, who is willing to help and who values the contribution given.

The involvement of communities in collecting cultural heritage and making it available for the public and different interest groups have become a common phenomenon of participatory culture. The wish to address sources and make them available, inspiring people to participate in a common enterprise as well as innovative methods of using the documents, enable us to experience history in a more personal manner. Nevertheless, maintaining the curiosity and interest created by the archives, the media, the researchers and some other groups active in the social environment requires additional effort, diverse activities supporting the community, active collaboration between the leaders of the project and the participants or those involved in some other way, in order to create further knowledge through joint efforts.

[Translated by Anu Kannike]

39 Laar 2006, p. 166.
40 Hurt / Lepp / Rahi-Tamm 2017.

Bibliography

Archival sources

Rahvusarhiiv:
- *Crowdsourcing of parish courts* (project documentation, without file number);
- *Crowdsourcing of the War of Independence* (project documentation, without file number).

Literature

Activities, in: *Eesti Genealoogia Selts*, URL: https://genealoogia.ee/en/activities/ [31.12.2021].

Causer, Tim / Terras, Melissa: *"Many Hands Make Light Work. Many Hands Together Make Merry Work" Transcribe Bentham and Crowdsourcing Manuscript Collections*, in: Ridge, Mia (ed.): *Crowdsourcing our Cultural Heritage.* 2017, pp. 57–88.

Citizen Archives Dashboard, in: *National Archives*, URL: https://www.archives.gov/citizen-archivist [31.12.2021].

Davies, Ally: *The School as the Crowd. Adventures in Crowdsourcing with Schools*, in: *MW2015: Museums and the Web 2015*, URL: https://mw2015.museumsandtheweb.com/paper/the-school-as-the-crowd-adventures-in-crowdsourcing-with-schools [31.12.2021].

Digital volunteering at the National Archives, in: *National Archives of Australia*, URL: https://transcribe.naa.gov.au/ [31.12.2021].

Galani, Areti / Mason, Rhiannon / Arrigoni, Gabi (eds.): *European Heritage, Dialogue and Digital Practices (Critical Heritages of Europe).* 2020.

Hinrikus, Rutt: *Eesti elulugude kogu ja elulugude uurimise perspektiive*, in: Krikmann, Arvo / Olesk, Sirje (ed.): *Võim ja kultuur.* 2003, pp. 171–213.

Howe, Jeff: *The Rise of Crowdsourcing*, in: *Wired*, URL: https://www.wired.com/2006/06/crowds/ [12.12.2021].

Hurt, Mihkel / Lepp, Anu / Rahi-Tamm, Aigi: *Jakob Hurda korrespondentide kirjavahetus.* 2017 (typescript, in the possession of the authors).

Jaago, Tiiu / Jaago, Kalev: *See olevat olnud… Rahvaluulekeskne uurimus esivanemate lugudest.* 1996.

Kaaristo, Maarja: *Vägivald loomade vastu. Inimene ja koduloom Lõuna-Eesti külas 19. sajandi II poolel vallakohtute protokollide näitel*, in: *Mäetagused.* 2006/31, pp. 49–62.

Kasutajate edetabel, in: *Rahvusarhiiv*, URL: https://www.ra.ee/vabadussoda/user/index?sort=-soldiers_inserted&page=1&per-page=50 [31.12.2021].

Kultuuripärandi digiteerimise tegevuskava, in: *Kultuuriministeerium*, URL: https://www.kul.ee/kultuurivaartused-ja-digitaalne-kultuuriparand/digitaalne-kultuuriparand/kultuuriparandi [27.12.2021].

Laar, Mart: *Äratajad. Rahvuslik ärkamisaeg Eestis 19. sajandil ja selle kandjad.* 2006.

Lindström, Liina / Pilvik, Maarja-Liisa / Ruutma, Mirjam / Uiboaed, Kristel: *On the Use of Perfect and Pluperfect in Estonian Dialects. Frequency and Language Contacts*, in:

Björklöf, Sofia / Jantunen, Sandra (eds.): *Multilingual Finnic – Language Contact and Change.* 2019, pp. 155–193.

Linnus, Jüri: *19. sajandi talurahvakohtute materjalid rahvakultuuri uurimise allikana*, in: *Emakeele Seltsi Aastaraamat.* 1970/16. pp. 231–242.

Lust, Kersti / Türna, Tõnis: *Valdade iseseisvumise raske algus. Vallakirjutajad 1866–1891*, in: *Tuna. Ajalookultuuri ajakiri.* 2021/3 (24), pp. 10–32.

Lust, Kersti: *A Not so Undesirable Status? Widowhood Options and Widows' Living Conditions in Post-emancipation Rural Estonia*, in: *The History of the Family.* 2021/26/1, pp. 74–99.

Luteri koguduste personaalraamatute nimeregister, in: *Rahvusarhiiv*, URL: https://www.ra.ee/dgs/addon/nimreg/ [31.12.2021].

Metslaid, Marleen: *Seminar "Kirjasaatjatest ühisloomeni: kaasavate kogude olevik ja tulevik"*, in: *Eesti Rahva Muuseumi ajaveeb*, URL: https://blog.erm.ee/?p=15175 [31.12.2021].

Must, Kadri: *Tori vallakohtu protokollid ajalooallikana*, in: *Ajalooline Ajakiri.* 1998/3, pp. 93–108.

Pilvik, Maarja-Liisa / Muischnek, Kadri / Jaanimäe, Gerth / Lindström, Liina / Lust, Kersti / Orasmaa, Siim / Türna, Tõnis: *Möistus sai kuulotedu: 19. sajandi vallakohtuprotokollide tekstidest digitaalse ressursi loomine*, in: *Eesti Rakenduslingvistika Ühingu aastaraamat.* 2019/15, pp. 139–158.

Piotrowski, Michael: *Natural Language Processing for Historical Texts*, in: *Synthesis Lectures on Human Language Technologies.* 2012/5/2, pp. 1–157.

Pirsko, Priit: *Eesti arhiivinduse arengufaasid*, in: *Tuna.* 2020/1, pp. 2–7.

Põldmäe, Rudolf: *Materjale J. Hurda vanavara kogumise loost*, in: *Paar sammukest eesti kirjanduse uurimise teed. Uurimusi XII. Jakob hurda 150. sünniaastapäevaks.* 1989, pp. 10–40.

Rahi-Tamm, Aigi / Esse, Liisi: *"In Spite of Everything, Life is Still Beautiful!" War and Postwar Experiences in Estonia Through the Example of Oskar Nõmmela's Life Story (1893–1969)*, in: *Journal of Baltic Studies.* 2022/2 (in print).

Rahi-Tamm, Aigi / Esse, Liisi: *Sõjaveteranid NKVD ees: Esimese maailmasõja peegeldused veerand sajandit hiljem*, in: *Eesti Ajalooarhiivi toimetised (Acta et commentationes Archivi Historici Estoniae).* 2014/22 (29), pp. 391–411.

Rahulolu-uuringu tulemused: 90% arhiivikasutajatest peab Rahvusarhiivi veebiteenuseid väga heaks, in: *Rahvusarhiiv*, URL: https://www.ra.ee/rahulolu-uuringu-tulemused-90-arhiivikasutajatest-peab-rahvusarhiivi-veebiteenuseid-vaga-heaks/ [12.12.2021].

Ridge, Mia: *Crowdsourcing Our Cultural Heritage. Introduction*, in: Ridge, Mia (ed.): *Crowdsourcing our Cultural Heritage.* 2017, pp. 1–13.

Tamm, Marek: *Digitaalse ajalookultuuri sünd*, in: Ibrus, Indrek / Tamm, Marek / Tiidenberg, Katrin (eds.): *Eesti digikultuuri manifest.* 2020, pp. 23–31.

Tartu 1867, in: *Rahvusarhiiv*, URL: https://www.ra.ee/tartu1867/index.php/site/preamble [31.12.2021].

Tooming, Kadri: *Ühisloomealgatus "Eestlased Esimeses maailmasõjas" jõudis finišisse*, in: Tannberg, Tõnu / Tamman, Helina (eds.): *Rahvusarhiiv 2017–2018.* 2019, pp. 111–113.

Traat, August: *Vallakohus Eestis 18. sajandi keskpaigast kuni 1866. aasta reformini.* 1980.

Türna, Tõnis: *1860.–80. aastate Lõuna-Eesti vallakohtute protokollid. Massiliste täistekst-andmebaaside loomise, publitseerimise ja kasutamise metoodika.* 2004 (Bachelor thesis, Tartu Ülikool: Library of Institute of History and Archaeology).

Vahtre, Lauri: *Vabadussõja eellugu. Punaväe sissetung ja Eesti vabastamine*, in: Vahtre, Lauri (ed.): *Eesti Vabadussõja ajalugu.* 2020/1.

VAU, in: *Rahvusarhiiv*, URL: https://www.ra.ee/vau/index.php/en [31.12.2021].

VeleHanden, in: *VeleHanden*, URL: https://velehanden.nl [31.12.2021].

Krzysztof Kopiński

Die unendliche Bearbeitung und Evidenzführung (von der altpolnischen Urkunde zum elektronischen Dokument in Polen)

Abstract
The Craze for the Recording of Documentary Evidence (From Old Polish Documents to Electronic Documents in Poland)
From time immemorial, people have tended to commit aspects of the world around them to writing. However, do archivists and documentation managers consider the changes occurring in how materials and documentation of interest are described? The author observes a lack of general reflection in Poland that might clarify how archival materials and documentation is compiled and recorded. At the same time, we forget that we live in a world where documentation is produced on a mass scale. We have not learned to react logically to this fact.
Keywords: compilation of archival materials; filing; documentation; mass documentation; detailed description

Die Behauptung mag trivial klingen, der Mensch hat jedoch seit uralten Zeiten die Tendenz dazu, allerlei Dinge sehr sorgfältig aufzulisten und zu notieren. In Umberto Ecos Buch *Die unendliche Liste* gibt es sehr viele Beispiele für verschiedene „Verzeichnisse“, die man in der Belletristik und Kunst finden kann.[1] Bereits im Vorwort zu dieser Publikation vermerkte Eco, dass sie ausschließlich mit der Wendung „und so weiter“[2] enden kann, da er auf sehr viele Aufzählungen gestoßen ist und einen Teil davon unberücksichtigt lassen musste. Der Titel des vorliegenden Beitrags knüpft an die herangezogene Arbeit von Umberto Eco an. Der Text stellt einen Versuch dar, eine Reflexion über die Veränderungen in der Beschreibung des Archivgutes und der Dokumentation sowie über den Kontext ihres Auftretens vorzunehmen. Es soll von vornherein vermerkt werden, dass ein gewisses Unbehagen mehr durch das Fehlen einer allgemeinen Reflexion als durch den Mangel an einer detaillierten, analytischen hervorgerufen wird, die

Prof. Dr. Krzysztof Kopiński, Nikolaus-Kopernikus-Universität Toruń, ORCID: https://orcid.org/0000-0002-4379-9217.

1 Eco 2009.

2 Ebd.

darauf ausgerichtet ist, präzisere Verfahrensweisen für die Bearbeitung des Archivgutes und Evidenzführung der Dokumente sowohl in sogenannter traditioneller als auch elektronischer Form zu entwickeln.

Im vorliegenden Text werden ausgewählte Fälle von Erstellung einer archivischen Beschreibung in Bezug auf die Effizienz ihres Funktionierens und die informative Qualität erörtert. Gegenstand der Analyse bilden hier historische, deutschsprachige archivische Hilfsmittel, die das Archiv der Stadt Thorn (*Archiwum Miasta Torunia*) beschreiben (und anschließend von polnischen Archivaren ergänzt und weiterentwickelt wurden). Wesentliche Bedeutung für den vorliegenden Text hat der Wandel der allgemeinen Gestalt der Bearbeitung in den polnischen Archiven, der durch die Einführung vereinfachter Bearbeitungsmethoden und den Beginn eines Retrokonversionsprogramms für archivische Hilfsmittel bedingt wurde. Die Analyse wurde um die Problematik der Erstellung von Beschreibungen elektronischer Dokumente im Kontext der Massenhaftigkeit der zeitgenössischen Dokumentation ergänzt.

Alte Urkundeninventare trifft man in den Archiven relativ oft. Allein für das Archiv der Stadt Thorn sind bis Ende des 18. Jahrhunderts neun Inventare und Verzeichnisse von Stadtakten erhalten geblieben. Karola Ciesielska, die beste Kennerin dieses Themas, stellte fest: „Diese Inventare und Verzeichnisse sind ferner unmittelbare Beispiele für Evidenz, die zu verschiedenen Zeiten geführt wurde, das heißt dafür, wie Dokumente und Korrespondenz registriert wurden, für deren Beschreibung, die verwendete Sprache, das Alphabet usw.“[3] Ein im 18. Jahrhundert entstandenes Beispielinventar, in dem sich Abschriften von Urkunden zur Geschichte Polens und Preußens befinden, enthält folgende Informationen:

- Regest;
- Datum;
- Ort der Urkundenausstellung;
- außerdem oft Angaben über hinzugefügte Siegel.[4]

Von neun analysierten Inventaren haben nicht weniger als acht kurze Regesten, die jedoch ausreichende Informationen über den Inhalt vermitteln. Nur eines der Inventare hat ausführlichere Regesten, die detailliertere Angaben enthalten. Der Bearbeiter dieses Inventars war jedoch bei der genauen Beschreibung der Dokumente nicht konsequent, daher kann man in seinem Inventar auch Regesten finden, die in Bezug auf den Inhalt sogar bescheidener ausfallen als jene, die in

3 „Inwentarze te i spisy są również bezpośrednimi przykładami ewidencji prowadzonej w różnym czasie, tj. sposobów rejestrowania dokumentów i korespondencji, ich opisu, używanego języka, alfabetu itp.“ Ciesielska 1990, S. 72.

4 Ebd., S. 75.

den übrigen acht Inventaren enthalten sind. Es sei am Rande vermerkt, dass die meisten Regesten in lateinischer Sprache verfasst wurden. Deutsch verwendete man in vereinzelten Fällen bei der Beschreibung von Urkunden, die zwischen dem 14. und dem 18. Jahrhundert in deutscher Sprache erstellt wurden.[5]

Karola Ciesielska verglich auch, anhand verfügbarer Literatur, den Inhalt der Thorner Register mit den Inventaren, die im Archiv der Stadt Danzig (*Archiwum Miasta Gdańska*) und im Archiv der Stadt Elbing (*Archiwum Miasta Elbląga*) erhalten geblieben sind. Aus der durchgeführten Untersuchung ergab es sich, dass der Genauigkeitsgrad der Elbinger und Danziger Inventare niedriger als derjenige der in Thorn aufbewahrten Inventare war.[6]

Der Bestand des Thorner Archivs wurde in den Jahren 1878–1880 neugeordnet und inventarisiert. Diese Arbeiten wurden zunächst von Rudolf Philippi, einem Archivar aus Königsberg, geleitet. Für ihre Fortsetzung sorgte der Stadtsyndikus Georg Bender, dem Ernst Kestner und Joseph Tietzen halfen. In dieser Zeit entstanden vier Kataloge: der erste (I) erfasste Urkunden und Briefe, der zweite (II) Bücher und Akten, der dritte (III) Zunftbriefe, die man auch als Geburtsbriefe bezeichnete, und der vierte (IV) Zunftakten.[7] Die Kataloge I und II werden in den Forschungsräumen des Thorner Archivs nur zum Teil benutzt. Sie werden vor allem von Wissenschaftlern aus Deutschland und Vertretern der älteren Generation der Thorner Forscher verwendet. In den letzten Jahren wurden diese Kataloge teilweise durch Inventarkarten erschlossener Serien ersetzt: der Serie *Urkunden und Briefe* (*Dokumenty i listy*) und der Serie *Bücher und Akten* (*Księgi i akta*) aus dem Bestand *Akten der Stadt Thorn* (*Akta Miasta Torunia*) aus altpolnischer Zeit von den Teilungen Polens. Die Bearbeitung dieser Karten vollendete und ergänzte in den Jahren 2001–2007, nach den Arbeiten einiger Archivarsgenerationen (Karola Ciesielska, Bogusław Dybaś, Beata Herdzin, Irena Janosz-Biskupowa, Piotr Oliński, Andrzej Radzimiński, Janusz Tandecki), der selige Dr. Witold Szczuczko. Es sei am Rande vermerkt, dass die archivischen Arbeiten an den zwei erwähnten Aktenserien noch nicht abgeschlossen sind, da die wissenschaftlichen Einführungen dazu nicht verfasst wurden. Es scheint auch, dass die Inventarkarten an sich, die von verschiedenen, im Thorner Archiv nach dem Zweiten Weltkrieg tätigen Archivaren erstellt worden sind, gewisser Vereinheitlichungen und einer gründlichen Durchsicht bedürfen. Die erwähnten Inventarkarten wurden nach den geltenden methodischen Empfehlungen vorbereitet. Anfangs wurden die Karten auf Formularen mit neun Rubriken erstellt, die für Urkunden, Bücher und Akten bestimmt wa-

5 Ebd., S. 81.
6 Ebd., S. 85.
7 Dies. 1978, S. 18–19.

ren.[8] Mit der Zeit begann man in staatlichen Archiven im Falle von Urkunden und Briefen die von Józef Płocha vorgelegten Empfehlungen und die von ihm vorgeschlagene Inventarkarte mit elf Rubriken zu benutzen.[9]

Der erwähnte Katalog III, der Zunftbriefe umfasst, ist, nach etwa 140 Jahren, bis heute das einzige archivische Hilfsmittel im Thorner Staatsarchiv für 2.794 Archivalieneinheiten aus den Jahren 1339–1939.[10] Der Zunftakten umfassende Katalog IV ist wiederum das einzige dieser Hilfsmittel, das nicht mehr aktuell ist. Anfang der 80er Jahre des 20. Jahrhunderts bearbeitete Janusz Tandecki die Inventare der Thorner Zunftakten, der sich auch mit der Konkordanz der im Katalog IV vorkommenden Signaturen mit den Signaturen von Akten im neuen Inventar beschäftigte.[11] An dieser Stelle möchte ich auf den Umstand hinweisen, dass von der Vorbereitung des Katalogs IV durch deutsche Archivare bis zur Vorbereitung des archivischen Inventars der Thorner Zünfte, das den Richtlinien der sich nach dem Zweiten Weltkrieg entwickelnden archivischen Methodik entspricht, über 100 Jahre vergingen.

Es wäre immens wichtig, den Informationsgehalt der Kataloge I und III, das heißt der Findmittel, die über Urkunden aus altpolnischer Zeit informieren, unter die Lupe zu nehmen. Die Bearbeiter des Katalogs I erfassten folgende Angaben zu den von ihnen geordneten Dokumenten:
- Nummer (das heißt Signatur);
- Datum (das heißt Datum der Urkundenausstellung);
- Aussteller und Inhalt der Urkunde.[12]

Es sollte erwähnt werden, dass sich das Regest des Dokumentinhalts in den meisten Fällen auf einen Satz beschränkt. Gleichzeitig stellt die Information über den Aussteller des Dokumentes einen integralen Teil (den Anfang) dieses Regestes dar. Demgegenüber sah die Urkundenbeschreibung im Katalog III folgendermaßen aus:
- Nummer;
- Datum;
- Empfänger, Ort, Aussteller und Inhalt der Urkunde – ein Regest wurde jedoch nicht erstellt;

8 Die Karten mit neun Rubriken wurden anhand eines geringfügig erweiterten Kartenformulars (mit 13 Rubriken), das von Adam Wolff vorgeschlagen wurde, erarbeitet; Wolff 1948, S. 159; Vgl. Konarski 1951, S. 91–93; Kwiatkowska 2010, S. 123–124.

9 Płocha 1985.

10 Die Übersetzungen des Katalogs III ins Polnische, die von Mateusz Superczyński im Rahmen der Retrokonversionsarbeiten angefertigt wurden und die Beschreibungsfelder wie Signatur, Titel, Äußere Daten enthielten, werden hier nicht berücksichtigt.

11 Archiwum Państwowe w Toruniu (im Folgenden: APT): *Registratura własna*, Tandecki 1980.

12 APT: *Registratura własna*, Katalog II, S. 1.

- Bemerkungen;
- Schrank (das heißt der Aufbewahrungsort);
- Nachträge.[13]

Nach dem Zweiten Weltkrieg wurden Empfehlungen in Bezug auf die Bearbeitung von Papier- und Pergamenturkunden, wie bereits erwähnt, von Józef Płocha erstellt. Die dazu bestimmten Inventarkarten enthielten folgende Rubriken:

1. Abkürzung des Namens des Archivs, in dem die Urkunde aufbewahrt wurde;
2. Name des Bestandes oder der Sammlung, aus der die Urkunde stammte;
3. Aktuelle Signatur;
4. Regest der Urkunde, in dem man, außer dem Inhalt, auch Informationen über den Aussteller und Empfänger des Dokumentes angeben sollte. Darüber hinaus sollte man vermerken, ob es sich dabei um eine Bestätigung oder Wiederholung einer anderen Urkunde handelte. Im unteren Teil der analysierten Rubrik sollte die Information über die Sprache vorkommen, in der das Dokument verfasst wurde;
5. Datum und Ort der Urkundenausstellung. Die Datierung sollte nach heutiger Zeitrechnung aufgelöst werden. Wenn das Datum fehlte, wurde der Versuch empfohlen, es zu bestimmen;
6. Physische Beschreibung der Urkunde (Format des Dokumentes, Material, auf dem es erstellt wurde, Erhaltungszustand, verwendete Schrift, im Falle von Papierurkunden Informationen über das angebrachte Wasserzeichen. An dieser Stelle sollte auch das oder die Siegel beschrieben werden, die am Dokument befestigt waren);
7. Platz für Vorsignaturen und Informationen über die auf dem Dokument vermerkten Eigentümerkennzeichen;
8. Platz für Informationen über Editionen des Dokumentes oder Publikationen, in denen es in quellenkundlicher oder diplomatischer Hinsicht detailliert behandelt wird;
9. Platz für zusätzliche Anmerkungen.

Die verso-Seite der Inventarkarte enthielt:

10. Dorsalnotizen, die man abzuschreiben oder zusammenzufassen hatte;
11. Platz für die Information über Kanzleinotizen.[14]

Bearbeitete Karten wurden, nachdem die Dokumente richtig angeordnet waren oder ihre Anordnung wiederhergestellt worden war, anschließend ins traditionelle Buchinventar eingetragen, zu dem man eine Einleitung erstellte, die den von

13 APT: *Registratura własna*, Katalog III.
14 Płocha 1985, S. 11.

Kazimierz Konarski im Jahre 1952 vorgelegten Grundsätzen folgte.[15] Man sollte hier hinzufügen, dass diese Einleitung, die sehr synthetisch und nicht eine Monographie des Bestandes sein sollte, doch sehr viel Arbeit seitens der Archivare erfordert. Das Ziel der Einleitung war, dem Archivnutzer den Aufbau und den Inhalt des Archivbestandes näherzubringen. Kazimierz Konarski vertrat die Ansicht, dass die Einleitung aus folgenden Teilen bestehen sollte:

I. Geschichte der Aufbauorganisation der Behörde
II. Geschichte des Bestandes
III. Archivische Charakteristik des Bestandes
IV. Inhalt des Archivbestandes
V. Analyse der Methoden des Ordnens und der Inventarisierung des Bestandes.[16]

Für den Archivar bedeutet dies zeitraubende Studien. Bevor er mit der Arbeit an der Inventareinleitung beginnen kann, muss er sich nämlich mit der Aufbauorganisation der Behörde, bei der die Akten entstanden, und den kanzleispezifischen und archivischen Fragen, die mit dem Bestand verbunden sind, gründlich auseinandersetzen. Im Rahmen der Analyse von Methoden des Ordnens und der Inventarisierung des Bestandes soll man wiederum den Ablauf der in diesem Bereich ausgeführten Arbeiten darstellen, mit besonderer Berücksichtigung der Probleme, die dabei auftraten. Diese Aufgaben setzen ohne Zweifel große Erfahrung der Archivare voraus.

An dieser Stelle drängt sich einerseits die Frage auf, wie es möglich ist, dass die deutschen Archivare innerhalb von drei Jahren Hilfsmittel bearbeitet und geschaffen hatten, die dann im Thorner Archiv über 100 Jahre lang mit Erfolg eingesetzt wurden. Andererseits sollte man erwägen, warum es den polnischen Archivaren bis jetzt nicht einmal gelang, anhand der Anfang der 50er Jahre des 20. Jahrhunderts ausgearbeiteten Richtlinien mit der Bearbeitung der Urkunden und Briefe aus dem Bestand *Zunftbriefe* (*Listy cechowe*, Katalog III) zu beginnen und warum sie in bestimmten Fällen Bearbeitungen – Serie *Urkunden und Briefe* (*Dokumenty i listy*) in den Akten der Stadt Thorn (*Akta miasta Torunia*) – nicht vollenden konnten. Die Antwort auf diese Frage ist ohne Zweifel sehr komplex. Nicht zu übersehen ist aber die Abhängigkeit zwischen der Einfachheit der Beschreibung von Urkunden und Briefen in den deutschen Katalogen und dem nicht langen Zeitraum (zwei oder drei Jahre), in dem sie entstanden sind. Mit Sicherheit war diese Bearbeitungsweise nicht so aufwendig wie die von Adam Wolff vorgeschlagene, von Konarski optimierte, und schließlich von Płocha auf Urkunden und Briefe ausgeweitete Beschreibung. Es scheint, dass man heutzu-

15 Konarski 1952, S. 192–201.

16 „I Dzieje ustrojowe urzędu, II Dzieje zespołu, III Charakterystyka archiwalna zespołu, IV Zawartość zespołu, V Analiza metod porządkowania i inwentaryzacji zespołu.“ Ebd., S. 193–194.

tage eine genaue und präzise archivische Information, insbesondere die, die sich auf Urkunden und Briefe aus Zeit vor den Teilungen Polens bezieht, will und braucht, was eine besondere Anforderung an die Archivare darstellt. Gleichzeitig verurteilen wir uns auf diese Weise dazu, diese Information jahrzehnte- oder sogar jahrhundertelang nicht zu erlangen, da man sie nicht in relativ kurzer Zeit bereitstellen kann.

In polnischen Staatsarchiven wurden Veränderungen unternommen, die die Optimierung des Prozesses der Bearbeitung und des Ordnens von Archivalien, insbesondere in Bezug auf einen Teil der Archivbestände aus dem 19.–21. Jahrhundert, zum Ziel hatten. 2002 wurden methodische Richtlinien eingeführt, die eine vereinfachte Bearbeitung von in den Staatsarchiven aufbewahrten Beständen betreffen. Das Archivgut aller polnischen Staatsarchive wurde in drei Beständegruppen: A1, A2, A3 gegliedert. Im Falle von Beständen der Gruppe A1, darunter denjenigen, deren Vorlaufzeit vor Ende des 18. Jahrhunderts beginnt, und den Aktenbeständen der Staats-, Kirchen- und Gerichtsbehörden, Parteien und Vereine der zentralen Stufe sowie Beständen mit einzigartigem Charakter, zum Beispiel kartographischen, fotografischen und ikonografischen Sammlungen und Kollektionen, wurden keine Veränderungen eingeführt. Verkürzt wurden einzelne Teile der Inventareinleitung im Falle von Beständen, die zur Gruppe A2 gezählt wurden. Dazu gehörten Aktenbestände der Staats- und Kirchenbehörden, Parteien und Vereine der landkreisübergreifenden Stufe, Stadtakten aus dem 19. und 20. Jahrhundert, Akten der Standesämter, Geburts- und Taufurkunden sowie Akten von Unternehmen und Institutionen mit wesentlicher Bedeutung für den Staat oder die Region. Für die Bestände der Gruppe A3, das heißt die übrigen Bestände aus dem 19.–21. Jahrhundert, sollte man eine kurze Informationsnotiz anfertigen, die in knapper Form Angaben erfasste, die sich bislang in der Einleitung zum Inventar befanden. Ein Hilfsmittel für so einen Bestand konnte nicht nur ein Buchinventar, sondern auch ein korrekt erstelltes Übergabeverzeichnis sein, das die Bereitstellung von Archivalien ermöglichte.[17]

Die Archivare reagierten auf die oben besprochenen Veränderungen der methodischen Richtlinien mit gewissen Vorbehalten oder Kritik.[18] Wiesława Kwiatkowska überlegte sogar, in welche Richtung die Erweiterung der Beschreibung von einzelnen Archivalieneinheiten gehen sollte, und wies zudem auf Möglichkeiten hin, die in den methodischen Hinweisen steckten, die Irena Radtke für die Anfertigung archivischer Inventare der zur Zeit der Sachakten-

17 *Decyzja nr 20 Naczelnego Dyrektora Archiwów Państwowych* 2002, S. 61–67; Krochmal 2002 (1), S. 9–22; ders. 2002 (2), S. 26–60.

18 Kwiatkowska 2002, S. 57–60; Herdzin 2002, S. 51–56; Auch der Autor des vorliegenden Beitrags hat sich dazu kritisch geäußert, vgl. Kopiński 2008, S. 473–482, und auf eine unterschiedliche Anwendung der implementierten Entscheidung in den Staatsarchiven in Polen hingewiesen.

kanzlei (19.–20. Jahrhundert) entstandenen Aktenbestände (-sammlungen) ausgearbeitet hatte.[19] Kwiatkowska setzte jedoch gleich danach hinzu:

> Das Postulat, die Beschreibung des Akteninhalts auf der Basisebene in einem noch größeren Ausmaß zu vertiefen, ist heutzutage unausführbar, wenn man die Möglichkeiten der Archive, die es realisieren sollen, in Betracht zieht. Die Rolle eines grundlegenden archivarischen Hilfsmittels sollte dem Buchinventar zukommen, das mit Benutzung der Computertechnik erstellt und in dem die Beschreibung der Archivalieneinheiten um Schlüsselwörter erweitert werden sollte.[20]

Heutzutage können sich wohl nicht viele Menschen an die damaligen Probleme erinnern. Die nicht ganz logische Weise, das Archivgut zu gliedern, verfestigte sich in der polnischen archivischen Methodik wohl ebenso wie ein inkonsequentes Verfahren bei der Bearbeitung in verschiedenen Staatsarchiven, in denen die der Gruppe A3 zugeordneten Bestände aufbewahrt werden. Es scheint, dass diese Veränderungen nicht mehr rückgängig zu machen sind. An dieser Stelle sollte vermerkt werden, dass die vereinfachte Bearbeitung des Archivgutes wohl in gewissem Sinne eine Reaktion darauf darstellte, dass man in den Staatsarchiven mit der Beschreibung und den nach dem Zweiten Weltkrieg in der polnischen Archivistik ausgearbeiteten Grundsätzen der Bearbeitung nicht zurechtkam. Man versuchte also die Folgen und nicht die Ursache zu beheben.

Im Juli 2016 startete der Hauptdirektor der Staatsarchive (*Naczelny Dyrektor Archiwów Państwowych*) das *Programm zur Retrokonversion archivischer Hilfsmittel* (*Program retrokonwersji pomocy archiwalnych*), dessen Ziel darin bestand, die in diesen Hilfsmitteln gespeicherten Angaben zu den Beständen der Archive in Polen in möglichst breitem Ausmaß im Internet zur Verfügung zu stellen. In den Jahren 2017–2018 sollten die Staatsarchive 13.000.000 Beschreibungen von Archivalieneinheiten, die anhand der für 35.000 Archivbestände erstellten traditionellen Papierhilfsmittel (Übergabeverzeichnisse, Buchinventare, Karteninventare) zugänglich gemacht wurden, ins Integrierte System der Archivinformation (*Zintegrowany System Informacji Archiwalnej*, im Folgenden: ZoSIA) übertragen und schließlich im Internet zur Verfügung stellen. Zu den Grundsätzen des Retrokonversionsprogramms gehörte die Forderung, dass „die Retrokonversionsarbeiten einen ausschließlich redaktionellen und nicht einen methodischen Charakter annehmen sollten" (sie sollten nicht mit Wiederer-

19 *Pismo okólne nr 2 Naczelnego Dyrektora Archiwów Państwowych* 2001, Nr. 183.

20 „Postulat pogłębienia na poziomie podstawowym opisu zawartości akt w stopniu jeszcze większym jest dzisiaj nierealny z uwagi na możliwość jego realizacji przez archiwa. Rolę podstawowej pomocy archiwalnej powinien pełnić inwentarz książkowy sporządzony z wykorzystaniem techniki komputerowej, w którym opis jednostek archiwalnych zostałby poszerzony o słowa kluczowe." Kwiatkowska 2002, S. 58.

schließungsarbeiten verbunden sein).[21] Die Beschreibungen von Archivalien sollten stufenweise auf dem Portal www.szukajwarchiwach.gov.pl bereitgestellt werden. Gleichzeitig wurde die lang erwartete Entscheidung getroffen, das System ZoSIA – eine zur Anfertigung einer archivischen Beschreibung auf mehreren Ebenen der Struktur des Archivgutes dienende Applikation – in den Staatsarchiven zu implementieren. Die Idee einer breiten Bereitstellung von archivischen Beschreibungen ist an sich mit Sicherheit beachtenswert. Bereits in den Beschreibungen dieses Unternehmens fallen jedoch einige Dinge auf. Erstens lesen wir Folgendes: „Zu den führenden Archiven, die den durch den Hauptdirektor der Staatsarchive angeordneten Plan realisieren, gehören [außer dem Staatsarchiv in Posen (Poznań)] die Archive von Stettin (Szczecin), Radom, Petrikau (Piotrków Trybunalski) und Oppeln (Opole).“[22] Einer anderen Information über das realisierte Programm, bei der es sich um die Zusammenfassung des ersten Halbjahres der Arbeiten handelt, entnimmt man, dass 55 % des Plans realisiert worden sind und dass zu den Spitzenreitern die Archive in Breslau (Wrocław), Warschau (Warszawa), Lodz (Łódź), Oppeln (Opole) und Siedlce gehören.[23] Man erfährt außerdem, dass die Hauptdirektion in Abstimmung mit den Staatarchiven Normen festgelegt hat, die das Abschreiben von Hilfsmitteln für die Informationsrecherche betreffen. Für eine Person innerhalb einer Stunde sind es:

> a) mindestens 50 Beschreibungen von Archivalieneinheiten in polnischer Sprache, das heißt 350 Beschreibungen täglich unter Annahme von sieben Stunden Arbeit, b) mindestens 30 Beschreibungen von Archivalieneinheiten in einer Fremdsprache, das heißt 210 Beschreibungen täglich unter Annahme von sieben Stunden Arbeit.[24]

In ihrem Grundton scheinen diese Informationen an Zeitungsberichte aus einer, wie man meinen könnte, unwiderruflich vergangenen Zeit anzuknüpfen. Es drängt sich die Frage auf, wie es zu diesem wahrhaft an die Stachanow-Bewegung

---

21 „[...] prace retrokonwersyjne mają przybrać tylko i wyłącznie charakter redakcyjny, a nie metodyczny.“ Naczelna Dyrekcja Archiwów Państwowych (in Folgenden: NDAP): *Program retrokonwersji pomocy archiwalnych – cele i założenia*, Aktenzeichen: DA.812.1.2016, Anhang Nr. 1.

22 „Wśród czołówki archiwów realizujących plan wskazany przez Naczelnego Dyrektora Archiwów Państwowych znalazły się także [oprócz Archiwum Państwowego w Poznaniu] archiwa ze Szczecina, Radomia, Piotrkowa Trybunalskiego i Opola.“ *Aktualności NDAP z dn. 01.02.2017 r.* [2018]; vgl. auch NDAP: *Registratura własna, Pismo Naczelnego Dyrektora Archiwów Państwowych Wojciecha Woźniaka z dn. 29 lipca 2016 r. do dyrektorów archiwów państwowych*, Aktenzeichen: DA.812.1.2016; Ebd., *Program retrokonwersji pomocy archiwalnych – cele i założenia*, Aktenzeichen: DA.812.1.2016, Anhang Nr. 1.

23 *Aktualności NDAP z dn. 17.07.2017 r.* [2018].

24 „a) co najmniej 50 opisów j.a. w języku polskim, tj. dziennie 350 opisów przy założeniu siedmiu godzin pracy, b) co najmniej 30 opisów j.a. w języku obcym, tj. dziennie 210 opisów przy założeniu siedmiu godzin pracy.“ NDAP: *Registratura własna, Pismo Naczelnego Dyrektora Archiwów Państwowych Wojciecha Woźniaka z dn. 9 listopada 2016 r. do dyrektorów archiwów państwowych*, Aktenzeichen: DA.812.1.2016.

erinnernden Arbeitstempo kam, warum auf die Staatsarchive in dieser Hinsicht so ein Druck ausgeübt wurde und wieso man bei dieser Angelegenheit die Atmosphäre eines Wettstreits kreierte. Das Abschreiben diverser Papier-Hilfsmittel, in denen es gelegentlich sehr umfangreiche Beschreibungen geben kann, die noch dazu in verschiedenen Fremdsprachen verfasst worden sind, ist mit Sicherheit keine einfache Aufgabe. In einer so delikaten Materie sollte es keinen Wettstreit und keine Eile geben. Das ehrgeizig angelegte Programm erweckt also ernsten Verdacht, dass bei der Retrokonversion Fehler begangen wurden. Am meisten beunruhigt jedoch die Tatsache, dass man sich im Rahmen der weit angelegten „redaktionellen" Arbeiten nicht darum kümmerte, Redakteure zu beschäftigen, die die Qualität der Abschrift archivarischer Hilfsmittel geprüft und verifiziert hätten. In letzter Zeit kam mir aus verschiedenen Archiven die Information zu Ohren, dass die „Papier"-Hilfsmittel auch von Praktikanten, Freiwilligen und Mitarbeitern in der Probezeit abgeschrieben wurden und die Ergebnisse ihrer Arbeit keinerlei Analyse unterzogen, sondern lediglich oberflächlich überprüft wurden.

Im vorliegenden Text wurden bereits einige Male Übergabeverzeichnisse von Archivalien erwähnt, deren Informationswert in den letzten Jahren in den Staatsarchiven mit Sicherheit gestiegen ist. Diese Verzeichnisse können unter anderem die Grundlage für die Einordnung eines Bestandes als bearbeitet bilden, falls dieser Bestand in die Gruppe A3 eingeordnet worden ist. Während der Retrokonversion wurden auch die Übergabeverzeichnisse abgeschrieben. Die informative Qualität der Verzeichnisse ist ohne Zweifel niedriger als die der Hilfsmittel, die während der Bearbeitung in den Archiven entstanden.

Das Formular eines Archivalien-Übergabeverzeichnisses besteht aus fünf Rubriken:
- Ordnungszahl;
- Mappenkennzeichen (Symbol aus dem Aktenplan);
- Titel der Mappe (Stichwort, unter dem die Archivalien im Aktenplan klassifiziert worden sind);
- die äußeren Daten von – bis;
- Anmerkungen.

Für die weiteren Erörterungen ist es von Bedeutung, dass man eine allgemein bekannte Tatsache in Erinnerung bringt: dass als Position in diesem Formular eine Mappe gilt, die eine Archivalieneinheit darstellt, die nach Sachgesichtspunkten gegliedert ist, denen wiederum die relevanten Dokumente zugeordnet worden sind. Damit nähern wir uns langsam den elektronischen Dokumenten, die im Titel des Beitrags erwähnt wurden. Ein Übergabeverzeichnis elektronischer Dokumente, die an ein Staatsarchiv überwiesen werden sollen, besteht aus sieben Positionen:

- Ordnungszahl;
- Sachzeichen;
- Stichwort, unter dem die Archivalien in einem dem Sachzeichen entsprechenden Aktenplan klassifiziert worden sind;
- Sachtitel;
- Beginn der Laufzeit;
- Ende der Laufzeit;
- Anzahl der für den Vorgang relevanten Dokumente.

Besonderes Augenmerk sollte man an dieser Stelle auf die Tatsache richten, dass als Position im Verzeichnis in diesem Fall eine Sache gilt, dass wir also de facto eine Ebene tiefer im Verhältnis zur Beschreibung traditioneller Dokumentation absteigen. Das System der Elektronischen Dokumentationsverwaltung (*Elektroniczne Zarządzanie Dokumentacją*, im Folgenden: EZD) oder sein Modul unterstützt natürlich die Bildung von derartigen Verzeichnissen elektronischer Dokumente. Den Ausgangspunkt für die korrekte Vorbereitung der Verzeichnisse bildet nichtsdestoweniger eine zuverlässige Beschreibung elektronischer Dokumente mittels Metadaten, die in der Verordnung des Innen- und Verwaltungsministers vom 30. Oktober 2006 bestimmt worden sind.[25] Zum automatischen, halbautomatischen oder manuellen Ausfüllen einer Beschreibung von elektronischen Dokumenten im EZD-System müssen die Organisationseinheiten unter der Aufsicht des staatlichen Archivdienstes, die sich für derartige Führung von Vorgängen entschieden haben, sieben Pflicht-Metadaten eingeben (Identifikator, Bildner, Titel, Erstellungsdatum, Format, Zugang, Typ); weitere sieben Metadaten werden fakultativ geführt (Beziehung, Empfänger, Gruppierung, Qualifikation, Sprache, Beschreibung, Befugnisse).[26] Falls sich eine Organisationseinheit entscheiden würde, die Beschreibung eines elektronischen Dokumentes mit fakultativen Metadaten zu ergänzen, müsste sie die erwähnten Metadaten an die Staatsarchive überweisen. Die Metadaten sollten dem Dokument beigefügt werden oder seinen integralen Bestandteil bilden.[27] An dieser Stelle sollte man darauf hinweisen, dass die EZD-Systeme die Mitarbeiter der Organisationseinheiten bei der Beschreibung elektronischer Dokumente mittels Metadaten zwar stark unterstützen, dass sie jedoch auf diesem Feld den Menschen nicht ganz ersetzen werden. Das Problem könnte man so in Worte fassen, dass der „Titel“ des Dokumentes das Sorgenkind unter den Metadaten war, bereits seitdem man begonnen hatte, die Problematik elektronischer Dokumente auf polnischem Boden zu implementieren, da man diese Angabe in elektroni-

25 *Dziennik Ustaw Rzeczypospolitej Polskiej*. 2006/97, Stelle 1517.
26 Schmidt 2007, S. 17–19.
27 Baniecki 2009, S. 12–13.

schen Systemen „manuell" beschreiben muss. Kazimierz Schmidt befürchtete sogar, dass es in dieser Hinsicht in den Organisationseinheiten zu gewissen Manipulationen kommen könnte, denen man entgegenwirken sollte.[28] Dies bedeutet, dass wir bei der Evidenzführung elektronischer Dokumente und deren Übergabe an die Staatsarchive sehr viel Arbeit haben werden. Wir ziehen auch keine Schlüsse daraus, dass die Anzahl der Dokumente in unserer Welt ständig steigt und dass man von ihrer Massenhaftigkeit schon seit langem spricht. Eine natürliche Reaktion auf dieses Problem wäre die Vereinfachung der Beschreibung elektronischer Dokumente. In dieser Überzeugung sollte uns der Umstand bestätigen, dass wir bislang auch mit der Beschreibung von Dokumenten im traditionellen „Papier"-System nicht besonders gut zurechtkamen. In diesem Fall handeln wir jedoch anders, wir gehen von der Beschreibung auf der Ebene der Mappe zugunsten der Beschreibung auf der Ebene der Sache ab und noch dazu berücksichtigen wir darin sehr viele Details. Die Zukunft wird zeigen, ob das die richtige Verfahrensweise ist. In dieser Arbeitsphase werden die Staatsarchive vor allem dadurch gerettet, dass die Pflicht, die elektronischen Dokumente zu beschreiben, den Bildnern des Schriftguts obliegen wird. Inwiefern die Staatsarchive diese Beschreibung mit eigenen Metadaten ergänzen werden, bleibt zu diesem Zeitpunkt wohl eine Sekundärfrage.

In der abschließenden Reflexion zu diesem Text sollte man das Augenmerk auf einige Fragestellungen richten. Erstens sollte man bedenken, dass auch eine einfache, unkomplizierte Beschreibung Grundinformationen in Bezug auf die Archivalien vermittelt. Eine ausgebaute, detaillierte Beschreibung verursacht wiederum, dass man jahrzehntelang überhaupt nicht imstande ist, die Dokumentation in ausreichendem Maße zu bearbeiten und zu ordnen. In einer Materie, die viel Ruhe erfordert – die Staatsarchive gehören doch zu den wichtigsten Kultur- und Wissenschaftseinrichtungen – handeln wird sehr oft unbesonnen, zu rasch, und sehen nur kurzfristige Ziele. Man sollte schließlich auch bemerken, dass wir nicht aus den begangenen Fehlern lernen und uns in der Ära der Massendokumentation für eine sehr detaillierte und anspruchsvolle Beschreibung elektronischer Dokumente entscheiden.

[Übersetzung: Katarzyna Szczerbowska-Prusevicius]

28 Schmidt 2007, S. 16.

Bibliografie

Archivalische Quellen

Archiwum Państwowe w Toruniu: *Registratura własna* [Eigene Registratur]:
- Katalog I;
- Katalog II;
- Katalog III;
- Katalog IV;
- Tandecki, Janusz: *Inwentarz Akt cechów toruńskich.* 1980 (maschinenschriftliches Exemplar).

Naczelna Dyrekcja Archiwów Państwowych: *Registratura własna* [Eigene Registratur]:
- *Pismo Naczelnego Dyrektora Archiwów Państwowych Wojciecha Woźniaka z dn. 9 listopada 2016 r. do dyrektorów archiwów państwowych*, Aktenzeichen: DA.812.1.2016;
- *Pismo Naczelnego Dyrektora Archiwów Państwowych Wojciecha Woźniaka z dn. 29 lipca 2016 r. do dyrektorów archiwów państwowych*, Aktenzeichen: DA.812.1.2016;
- *Program retrokonwersji pomocy archiwalnych – cele i założenia*, Aktenzeichen: DA.812. 1.2016, Anhang Nr. 1.

Gedruckte Quellen

Decyzja nr 20 Naczelnego Dyrektora Archiwów Państwowych z dnia 10 grudnia 2002 r., wyd. Naczelny Dyrektor Archiwów Państwowych (ZNA-021-7/02), in: *Archeion.* 2002/104, S. 61–67.

Dziennik Ustaw Rzeczypospolitej Polskiej. 2006/97, Stelle 1517.

Pismo okólne nr 2 Naczelnego Dyrektora Archiwów Państwowych z 28 maja 1984 r. w sprawie wprowadzenia wskazówek metodycznych do sporządzania inwentarzy archiwalnych zespołów (zbiorów) akt wytworzonych w okresie kancelarii akt spraw (XIX–XX w.), in: Tarakanowska, Maria / Rosowska, Ewa (Bearb.): *Zbiór przepisów archiwalnych wydanych przez Naczelnego Dyrektora Archiwów Państwowych w latach 1952–2000.* 2001, Nr. 183.

Literatur

Aktualności NDAP z dn. 01.02.2017 r., in: *Naczelna Dyrekcja Archiwów Państwowych*, URL: https://tinyurl.com/bde3mn4r [07.05.2018].

Aktualności NDAP z dn. 17.07.2017 r., in: *Naczelna Dyrekcja Archiwów Państwowych*, URL: https://tinyurl.com/7rk4tnnc [07.05.2018].

Baniecki, Adam: *Dokument elektroniczny*, in: *Archiwista Polski.* 2009/15/3 (55), S. 7–32.

Ciesielska, Karola: *Zarys dziejów Archiwum Toruńskiego*, in: *Zapiski Historyczne.* 1978/43/4, S. 7–42.

Ciesielska, Karola: *Dawne inwentarze Archiwum Miasta Torunia*, in: *Archeion*. 1990/7, S. 71–99.

Eco, Umberto: *Die unendliche Liste*. 2009.

Herdzin, Beata: *„Projekt kierunków zmian archiwalnych przepisów metodycznych" – omówienie i próba oceny*, in: *Archiwista Polski*. 2002/7/1 (25), S. 51–56.

Konarski, Kazimierz: *Podstawowe zasady archiwistyki*, in: *Archeion*. 1951/19–20, S. 19–104.

Konarski, Kazimierz: *Wstęp do inwentarza zespołu archiwalnego. Zasady opracowania*, in: *Archeion*. 1952/21, S. 192–201.

Kopiński, Krzysztof: *Z problemów zarządzania informacją naukową w archiwach państwowych – próba oceny skutków uproszczonego opracowania zespołów archiwalnych*, in: Porazinski, Jarosław / Stryjkowski Krzysztof (Hg.): *Archiwa w nowoczesnym społeczeństwie. Pamiętnik V Powszechnego Zjazdu Archiwistów Polskich Olsztyn 6–8 września 2007 r.* 2008, S. 473–482.

Krochmal, Jacek: *Propozycja nowych zasad opracowania zasobu archiwalnego*, in: *Archiwista Polski*. 2002/7/2 (26), S. 9–22. (1)

Krochmal, Jacek: *Zasady uproszczonego opracowania zasobu archiwalnego*, in: *Archeion*. 2002/104, S. 26–60. (2)

Kwiatkowska, Wiesława: *Kilka uwag do „Projektu kierunków zmian archiwalnych przepisów metodycznych"*, in: *Archiwista Polski*. 2002/7/1 (25), S. 57–60.

Kwiatkowska, Wiesława: *Tradycyjny model opracowania zasobu archiwalnego i jego znaczenie w dobie współczesnej*, in: *Archiwa – Kancelarie – Zbiory*. 2010/1 (3), S. 107–129.

Płocha, Józef: *Wytyczne opracowywania dokumentów pergaminowych i papierowych*. 1985.

Schmidt, Kazimierz: *Dokumenty elektroniczne w podmiotach publicznych: struktura, postępowanie i przekazywanie do archiwów państwowych. Co wynika z nowych rozporządzeń MSWiA wydanych na podstawie ustawy archiwalnej?*. 2007, in: *Naczelna Dyrekcja Archiwów Państwowych*, URL: https://www.archiwa.gov.pl/images/docs/o_rozporzadzeniach_MSWiA.pdf [07.05.2018].

Wolff, Adam: *Archiwalne karty inwentarzowe*, in: *Archeion*. 1948/17, S. 151–163.

Magdalena Wiśniewska-Drewniak

Archival Appraisal in Community Archives

Abstract
Archival appraisal is one of the basic functions of archives. This chapter provides an initial analysis of the contexts in which community archives make appraisal decisions. The author draws attention to the different degrees of archival selection, how archival selection is perceived by community archivists, the importance of the human factor in this activity and how value is attributed to documentation. The chapter applies methods of analysis of texts and data from semi-structured interviews with community archivists.
Keywords: community archives; archival appraisal; archival selection

Community archives – and this means independent documentary initiatives – are becoming an increasingly important component of archival heritage. Growing in number (in Poland, at least several hundred are estimated to exist),[1] they are increasingly studied at university and researched.[2] At the same time, community archives are becoming more and more recognisable as a phenomenon of cultural heritage. However, they are still relatively obscure, including in terms of how they function on a daily basis and how they create their own archival collections.

The aim of this text is to present the issue of constructing archival collections by community archives, and more specifically, how their archival appraisal is made. In community archives, this process is informal and extremely diverse, unlike in state archives. At the same time, it is a highly relevant context for the functioning of community archives and a key factor influencing how their collections are shaped. Very often this context is hidden (albeit unintentionally) from the potential user, so it is important to be aware of its existence and possible consequences.

Dr Magdalena Wiśniewska-Drewniak, Nicolaus Copernicus University in Toruń, ORCID: https://orcid.org/0000-0001-9119-1372.

1 *Baza archiwów społecznych* [2021].

2 Czarnota 2017.

The analysed data originates in particular from interviews with archivists involved in the work on independent community archives, conducted between 2015–2018 within the scope of the *Community archives in Poland – multiple case study* research project. The descriptive (in a sense, "encyclopaedic") objective of this project was to learn about a wide range of aspects regarding the functioning of community archives, such as methods of collecting, preserving, processing and providing access to archives, the characteristics of archival collections, the people involved in creating archives, methods of financing or the problems faced by archives.[3] One element of the specific research question concerning the collection of archival materials by community archives was also the issue of archival appraisal. However, due to the time constraints of the project, this was only one of many issues raised, and it received insufficient attention during the cross-case analysis stage, which is addressed in this chapter. Secondary analysis of semi-structured interviews conducted directly, on site (in most cases at the archive headquarters) was supplemented with an analysis of the literature and existing data.

The chapter looks at the practices and mechanisms of selection in community archives in Poland. Indeed, they provided empirical material and it is the context in which they function that is of particular interest here. However, the results may to some degree extend beyond this geographic location, especially since they were to some extent contextualised with the findings of Anglo-Saxon literature.

Due to their huge variety, community archives are difficult to define – as both Polish[4] and English-speaking authors[5] tend to agree. In Poland, the term "community archive" dates back to the 1990s.[6] It began to gain special attention in 2012, when the KARTA Centre (the largest independent archive in Poland) stepped up its operations regarding other community archives. Currently, this term is promoted by the Community Archives Centre (*Centrum Archiwistyki Społecznej*) – an organisation co-created by the KARTA Centre (*Ośrodek KARTA*) and the Ministry of Culture and National Heritage.[7] It is worth noting that the Polish version of the term "community archive" is *archiwum społeczne*, which in direct translation means "social archive" and does not refer to any community, but instead to the society. In this sense, "social" means:

> Relating to society or part of it; produced by society and owned by it as common property; [...] working selflessly for the good of a community; concerning the attitudes

3 Wiśniewska-Drewniak 2016.
4 Czarnota 2011, p. 15; Ziętal [2022], p. 3; Wiśniewska 2015 (1) p. 222; eadem 2016, p. 195.
5 *Listening to the Past* 2004, p. 43; Flinn 2007, p. 152; idem 2011, pp. 5–6; Gilliland / Flinn 2013, p. 2; Flinn 2015; Welland / Cossham 2019; Poole 2020.
6 Gluza 2002.
7 *Zarządzenie Ministra Kultury i Dziedzictwa Narodowego* 2020.

or actions of the majority of the society; organised by a community independently, without the participation of the state.[8]

According to the regulations regarding the community archives database, currently run by the Community Archives Centre (previously by the KARTA Centre), community archives are "organisations that arose as a result of grassroots, deliberate civic activity in terms of collecting, processing and providing access to archival materials."[9]

In Polish-language literature, the most common features of community archives are: grassroots,[10] non-state, very often associated with non-governmental organisations,[11] intended for the permanent storage of collected materials,[12] social and civic motivation to operate the archive.[13]

The operation of community archives is both varied and complex, encompassing both the classic roles of archives (such as acquiring/collecting or processing archives) as well as activities beyond the archive mainstream (e.g., project financing of core activity). This chapter focuses on one classic role of historical archives – archival appraisal, although the context of its use in the case of community archives is definitely different than in other types of archives (e.g., state archives).

In this chapter, "appraisal" will be understood according to the Society of American Archivists Dictionary of Archives Terminology as "the process of identifying materials offered to an archive that have sufficient value to be accessioned"[14] – i.e., determining whether a given document or documents have any archival value that qualifies them for long-term (permanent) preservation.

The first level of selection (though not yet the selection of documents) occurs very early in community archives, already at their creation stage. The creators of an archive declare what thematic, territorial or chronological scope they are interested in to such an extent as to collect archival materials or copies thereof. Otherwise, they state that the official narrative presented by mainstream heritage institutions is unsatisfactory for them (as incomplete or incorrect), and so they decide to document a given topic (or a social group) on their own terms.[15]

8 "[…] odnoszący się do społeczeństwa lub jego części; wytworzony przez społeczeństwo i będący jego wspólną własnością; […] pracujący bezinteresownie dla dobra jakiejś społeczności; dotyczący postaw lub działań większości członków społeczeństwa; zorganizowany przez jakąś społeczność samodzielnie, bez udziału państwa." *Społeczny* [2021].

9 "[…] organizacje, które powstały w wyniku oddolnej, celowej działalności obywatelskiej gromadzące, opracowujące i udostępniające materiały archiwalne." *Regulamin bazy* [2021].

10 Cf. Ziętal 2012; Wiśniewska 2013; Czarnota 2014; Giziński 2016.

11 Cf. Ziętal 2012; Wiśniewska 2013; Czarnota 2013.

12 Cf. Czarnota 2011; Wiśniewska 2014; Ziętal 2014; Wiśniewska-Drewniak 2019.

13 Czarnota 2014; Ziętal 2014; Wiśniewska 2015 (1).

14 *Appraisal* [2021].

15 Caswell et al. 2017.

Therefore, community archivists, in giving a certain topic archival value, make a decision – even if at this point it is not yet possible to speak of appraising documents. Moreover, the decision to select a particular topic does not necessarily have to be made only once, at the outset of an archive. Archivists may add another theme to the original concept of the archive that, for various reasons, interested them later, or they might change the chronological, geographic, physical or formal nature of the material collected.

One of the basic principles of archival selection, developed decades ago by archival methodology in Poland, is to select records creators first, and then appraise the records.[16] In some cases, the practice of community archives can refer to this principle, albeit to a very limited extent.

Sometimes community archives decide to announce campaigns to collect materials for their collections (or (co)create them, e.g., by recording oral history interviews). Such campaigns are sometimes advertised widely, to the general public, without any specific targeting (e.g., by distributing leaflets, newspaper advertisements, posts on social media). However, sometimes community archives decide to narrow down the target group of such campaigns, focusing their action, for example, on residents of a nursing home or a veterans' union. Here, in a sense, we can witness a partial selection of potential records creators – indeed, the archive states that people in such institutions or organisations may have such valuable materials (or memories) that they would be worth including in archive collections. In this informal way, on a macro scale and a priori, they select potential donors of archival materials (or interviewees for oral history interviews).

It is also worth mentioning the key role of personal contacts in creating community archives, which has already been highlighted in the Polish literature.[17] Very often, community archivists approach some of their friends, acquaintances and family members in order to enrich the archive collections, by requesting that they provide documents or record their memories. After all, they do not turn to everyone they know, but to those whose recollections or family archives may be related to the topic area documented by the archive and may represent some value for the archive. Another criterion is undoubtedly the availability of these people or their potential willingness to cooperate.

A similar mechanism occurs when using the snowball sampling method – for example when recording an oral history interview, when the witness, after being interviewed, is asked if they can recommend other speakers.[18] Then the "burden" of selecting subsequent records creators, though clearly informally, shifts par-

16 Borodij 2007, pp. 35–36.
17 Martini / Jóźwik 2017.
18 Atkinson / Flint 2001; Cohen / Arieli 2011, pp. 426–429.

tially to the donor, which is a situation unheard of in traditional archival appraisal mechanisms.

Generally, it can be said that sometimes community archives do indeed carry out a two-stage archival appraisal, starting first with the selection of records creators. However, this is informal in nature, not fully acknowledged by community archivists and, compared with the subsequent stage of records selection, merely supplementary. Definitely, the selection of the documentation itself happens much more often, and is definitely more important for community archives, more visible and easier for the researcher to grasp.

In the case of community archives, the selection of documentation consists in choosing what the archive would like to include in its collections.

As in previous cases, this mechanism is informal and the form of this activity depends on how exactly the archive collects its materials. Interestingly, all archivists when asked about archival selection (although this term was not used directly in the question, unless it proved helpful) replied that their archive did not conduct any selection. Only auxiliary questions made it possible to establish that, of course, the selection of documentation is indeed conducted, even if the archivists are not fully aware of it.

The most common criterion applied in all the community archives examined was that the documents should comply with the objectives and theme of the archive.

So, the Miastograf.pl Digital Archives of Łódź Citizens (*Cyfrowe Archiwum Łodzian Miastograf.pl*; Miastograf translates in English as "cityographer") – a name coined to refer to its purpose of describing a city – collects photographs documenting (or describing) the city of Łódź, and therefore does not collect photographs that only depict people or photos from holidays taken outside the city.[19] Community Archives in Bronowice (*Bronowickie Archiwum Społeczne*) only collects materials related to the history of everyday life in Bronowice Małe – once a village near Cracow, now one of its districts.[20] South-Eastern Research Institute in Przemyśl (*Południowo-Wschodni Instytut Naukowy w Przemyślu*) collects materials on Ukrainian and regional issues (the Polish-Ukrainian borderland and the vicinity of Przemyśl) and on Greek Catholics in this region (although this archive, due to its limited capabilities, currently refuses new

19 Uniwersytet Mikołaja Kopernika w Toruniu, Wydział Nauk Historycznych, Katedra Archiwistyki i Zarządzania Dokumentacją: *Community archives in Poland – multiple case study (2016–2019). Project documentation* [interviews held by Magdalena Wiśniewska-Drewniak] (hereinafter: UMK: *Community archives*); Michał Gruda (Miastograf.pl Digital Archives of Łódź Citizens), interview by author, 5.11.2015.

20 Ibid., Natalia Martini (Community Archives in Bronowice), interview by author, 4.03.2016.

materials).[21] General Elżbieta Zawacka Foundation (*Fundacja Generał Elżbiety Zawackiej*) documents three main topics: the history of military service performed by Polish women on various fronts, the history of the Home Army (the underground armed forces from World War II) in Pomerania (in northern Poland) and the history of *Zagroda*, the Home Army's Foreign Communication Department (*Wydział Łączności Zagranicznej Komendy Głównej Armii Krajowej "Zagroda"*). As these topics deal mainly with World War II and the period shortly after it, and people who were usually adults (or nearly adult) at that time, the foundation primarily collects secondary materials and contacts the heirs of the soldiers whose fate is documented. That is why all new materials entering the archive are so valuable and cannot be subject to any further selection.[22] The Storytellers (*Opowiadacze Historii*) are keen to record an interview with anyone who has any recollections of Lower Town (*Dolne Miasto*), a district of Gdańsk. Ideally, they should be people closely related to the area – living, working, studying or on military service there, but respondents who just visited Dolne Miasto are of interest too. When making digital copies of photos from family albums, the criterion of compliance with the archive topic is also applied – if possible, all photos related to Lower Town lent by their owners are copied.[23] The thematic criterion is also used by Civic Archives of Podkowa Leśna (*Obywatelskie Archiwum Podkowy Leśnej*), which collects materials on the history of Podkowa Leśna (a small town near Warsaw) and its immediate surroundings, from the time when the town was founded in the interwar period, to the present day. The main topics are the actions of the anti-communist opposition and the history of the Parish of St. Christopher, the beginnings of the town and local society in the 1930s, and the everyday life of its inhabitants.[24] Also, LGBTQIA+Fem Historical Club (*Klub Historyczny LGBTQIA+Fem*) only requires that the collected materials comply with the topic of the archive (non-heteronormativity and feminism).[25]

---

21 Ibid., Bogumiła Kowal (South-Eastern Research Institute in Przemyśl), interview by author, 11.04.2017; Stanisław Stępień (South-Eastern Research Institute in Przemyśl), interview by author, 10.04.2017.

22 Ibid., Elżbieta Skerska (General Elżbieta Zawacka Foundation), interview by author, 27.09.2017; Anna Rojewska (General Elżbieta Zawacka Foundation), interview by author, 26.09.2017; Dorota Zawacka-Wakarecy (General Elżbieta Zawacka Foundation), interview by author, 26.09.2017.

23 Ibid., Jacek Górski (Storytellers from the Lower Town in Gdańsk), interview by author, 13.01.2018.

24 Ibid., Bogdan Wróblewski (Civic Archives of Podkowa Leśna), interview by author, 27.01.2018.

25 Ibid., Agnieszka Wiciak / Kamil Prykowski (LGBTQIA+Fem Historical Club), interview by author, 4.08.2018.

The selection criteria were described somewhat differently by the co-founders of Archeology of Photography Foundation (*Fundacja Archeologia Fotografii*) – an organisation collecting photographic archives documenting the work of outstanding Polish photographers. The purpose of the archive is to protect photographers' legacies from dispersion and destruction. The basic criterion for selecting materials is their value from the perspective of art history and the history of photography; it is mainly a question of artistic value as well as, to a certain extent, documentary value. As a rule, the foundation tries not to work with archives of living artists, as this is hindered due to artists' possible attachment to their materials. The foundation places tremendous value on freedom of work, and this kind of situation, as well as the heirs' lack of openness to the foundation's ways of working, could significantly hinder the day-to-day running of the organisation.[26]

None of the archives indicated time as a criterion, and some even emphasised that there are no materials too fresh to be included in their archives. Some of the archives were also involved in creating sources, not only oral history interviews (which, as a rule, speak about the past), but also, for example, by creating contemporary photographs of a changing city space like, for example, Miastograf.pl and Storytellers from the Lower Town in Gdańsk. Civic Archives of Podkowa Leśna included relatively new (only a few years old) photographs of members of the local community in their collections. This indicates a certain feeling among community archivists that nothing is too new to be preserved for the future.

Most of the archives studied did not attach much importance to forms of documents or methods of recording information that might serve to create a coherent conglomeration of originals and copies, photographs, written documents, publications, memoires, leaflets, museum objects and other various types of materials. This diversity of collections of community archives is largely highlighted in the Polish and English literature,[27] and is a characteristic feature of community archives, which care more about the thematic suitability of the materials than about following well-trodden paths by creating separate categories for archival materials, library and museum objects, or works of art.

A certain exception here is Community Archives in Bronowice, which, being an exclusively digital archive, does not collect copies of museum objects (e.g., accolades offered by donors), due to the difficulties in making digital copies of them. Likewise, Community Archives in Bronowice does not collect documents

26 Ibid., Marta-Przybyło-Ibadullajev (Archeology of Photography Foundation), interview by author, 12–13.02.2018.

27 Ziętal 2012, p. 10; Wiśniewska 2015 (2), p. 64; Sobczak / Kudosz 2016, pp. 15–17; Ziętal 2017, pp. 25–26; Flinn 2011; Gilliland / Flinn 2013; Welland / Cossham 2019; Poole 2020.

larger than A4, as this is the maximum document size that can be scanned by the equipment at the archive's disposal.[28]

The appraisal is not always made by the archive. Very often, a complete or preliminary selection is made by the document holder who decides to submit the materials to the archive, or a witness of history with whom the archivist recorded an interview and then asked to share materials from their personal archive. In such a case, the creator often independently selects whether they want to donate something to the archive, thus indicating, in accordance with their opinion, what may be valuable for a given archive. As suggested by the interviews conducted during the research, this kind of appraisal made by the donator often misaligns with the assessment made by the archivist. Indeed, the latter often notices value where the owner of the materials sees none.[29] Therefore, community archivists know from experience that in such situations it is worth asking for a presentation of the entire donor's archive and making a selection of materials together with them.

Community archives allocate archival value differently than traditional archives. According to the Dictionary of Archives Terminology by the Society of American Archivists archival value is "the ongoing usefulness or significance of records, based on the administrative, legal, fiscal, evidential, or historical information they contain, justifying their continued preservation."[30] Due to the nature of community archives (independent, grassroots, not representing any authority), it cannot be said that archival value is given due to any administrative, legal, fiscal or evidential worth that the materials might have. If we are to understand historical value as a potential value for professional historians (as sources for creating historiography), then here too it is of limited importance, because not all of the studied archives intend to collect documents for academic purposes, although some do, such as General Elżbieta Zawacka Foundation, Archeology of Photography Foundation and South-Eastern Research Institute in Przemyśl. Of course, the fact that a given archive does not aim to meet the professional needs of historians does not mean that the latter will not make use of them. This is a fundamentally difficult issue and certainly requires further empirical study to identify the purposes of community archives, whom they target, their users and how they use the information they collect. Returning, however, to the main topic of the considerations – i.e., appraisal in community archives – it can be noticed that they perceive the value of archives more locally, more practically and more emotionally.

28 UMK: *Community archives*; Martini, interview.
29 Ibid.; Górski, interview.
30 *Archival value* [2021].

Local perception of archival value consists in acknowledging what is important "to us" as valuable – for the creators of a given archive, its immediate surroundings, social group or local community represented by the archive – and what would not necessarily be of value to professional historians, state archivists or mainstream heritage institutions. What counts is the fate of ordinary people (rather than outstanding individuals), details related to the documented place, stories of everyday life and personal experiences, not necessarily great events and historical meta-narratives.

The practical perception of archival value is related, inter alia, to the collection of archival materials with a view to their potential use – e.g., for a publication, exhibition, or social media post. Sometimes community archives even set themselves this kind of practical goal (creating an exhibition, publishing a book, making an artistic installation) as the overriding objective of a project, to which the entire functioning of the archive and its collections are subordinated, rather than just the mechanisms of archival selection. This, in turn, may be related to a very important topic, which is the project management of community archives, related to their application for financing from public funds offered in grant competitions.[31] Consequently, community archives that benefit from this method of financing (and the alternative is usually no financing or limited financing from their own resources) have to meet competition requirements over other, more rational considerations affecting archival practice. This is also the case with archival selection. The creators of Miastograf had to select respondents for their oral history interviews depending on whether or not they had information relevant to the project at hand; moreover, the projects were always thematic. Indeed, it was impossible to write a project that would simply involve collecting stories from the oldest inhabitants of the city, because grant competitions always had some thematic focus. As a result, for example, a collection of oral history interviews were created on the topic of vanishing professions in Łódź.[32] Also, the quantity of collected materials and their types may be dictated by the grant requirements and the shape of the application written by the archive, and may not necessarily fulfill the actual needs of the archive.

In community archives appraisal, emotions play an important role, as indicated by examples from the literature in the field of archival science.[33] Since community archives do not seek value for great history, meta-narration, state, political and capital history, it means that they search for small, local things, often trivial from the perspective of "great history". The importance of a person, place, object or event may be dictated by emotional considerations, the organism's

31 Wiśniewska-Drewniak 2018.

32 UMK: *Community archives*; Gruda, interview.

33 Caswell 2020; Cifor 2016.

affective response to a photograph, recording, or object. Something might be particularly funny, surprising, traumatising or shocking; it may evoke a certain joy, or simply hit a note of nostalgia and, because of these emotions, be included in the holdings of a community archive, even if it does not convey any particularly valuable information. In any case, the emotional impact of community archives on the donors, archivists and end users would seem to be a particularly interesting research issue.[34] The emotional selection of materials to include in an archive is also dictated by considerations related to sharing these materials – i. e., with the assumption that documents so emotionally charged will make attractive social media posts, or be used in art projects, publications, exhibitions and so on (which is linked to in turn with the above-mentioned practical criterion).

Finally, one should look at the archival selection mechanisms in community archives from a wider, theoretical perspective. Appraisal is one of the key functions of archives, which – when viewed with a critical and postmodern eye – are instruments of power, both literally (supporting administration and oppression) and symbolically. An archivist in a state archive has limited influence on selection mechanisms, because currently the main tool for selecting records for permanent preservation is predetermined retention schedule. While it is true that a state archivist does have some influence both on the shape of the retention schedule (within the scope of consultations with the records creator and the relevant archive) and on issuing permissions for the destruction of documentation (the archivist may refuse to grant such consent). However, in comparison with these mechanisms, a community archivist has far more freedom. An archivist (in particular, a community archivist) does not find archival value in documents, but creates it. This is not an archivist as an objective seeker of historical value, but a completely subjective one, with an individual system of values, opinions, predilections and experiences – a creator of archival value.[35] As Marika Cifor rightly puts it, "Community archives literature has extended the discussion about and pushed the bounds of who has the power to appraise, how appraisal decisions are made and what is deemed to be of archival value."[36]

When looking at the mechanisms of appraisal in community archives, it is worth paying attention to the enormous significance of the "human factor" at virtually every possible stage. The interests of the archive creators influence its subject matter and the forms of the materials collected, and these may also change over time. The archivists' personal contacts often provide a path for selecting who might donate archival materials and who could give oral history interviews. Finally, the personal decisions of community archivists, their pas-

34 Wiśniewska-Drewniak 2019, pp. 400–402.
35 Cifor 2016, p. 13; Harris 2002, p. 84.
36 Cifor 2016, p. 13.

sions and opinions on what should be preserved in the archive directly influence the choice of materials for archiving (and potentially long-term preservation). But the "human factor" does not end with the archivist, because the donor also performs a kind of self-assessment as a records creator (by contacting the archive or agreeing to work together if the archive contacted them first). According to the so-called snowball method too, anyone giving an oral history interview may recommend other potential respondents to the archivists, thereby making a certain selection of people from certain circles and deciding whether someone might be a valuable interviewee for the archive. Moreover, the donor often selects which documentation to present to the archivists, deciding on its potential value for the archive. Sometimes these decisions are made in consultation with the archivists, whose selection criteria may disagree with those used by the donor. Such a situation ends up being a negotiation to form an agreement on what is important for the donor and what is relevant for the archive or archivist. Finally, the "human factor" in community archive selection can also be seen in the potential end users, who react to archival materials in different ways and whose perceptions of how an archive operates and its archival collections may potentially be a factor taken into account by community archivists when shaping their collections.[37]

However, a whole catalogue of detailed research questions emerges in relation to how community archives appraise documentation, which this chapter certainly does not answer. Who, and in what situations, gives value to records – the archivist, the donor, or maybe both together? How is the archive value negotiated? Should – and if so, how – community archives document the archival selection process? What selection criteria are used by community archives and, consequently, what features of documentation give it value, in the eyes of community archives, that justify its permanent preservation? What is the relationship between archival appraisal and the objectives and activities of the archive? And so, to what extent does the archive shape its collections in terms of how it might potentially be used? Is archival selection performed only once or is it repeated and may the decision to classify materials for permanent preservation change (as opposed to state archives where it is final)? What impact do the mechanisms of project financing of community archives have on decisions regarding archival appraisal? The catalogue of such research questions could certainly be much broader, and the above-mentioned proposals might just crack it open a little.

Archival appraisal in community archives is completely different than in public archives (for example, state archives). Community archives do not supervise the office procedures and institutional archives in their area of operation,

37 Caswell 2020, pp. 30–34.

and giving materials archival value is not based on retention schedules used in institutions controlled by the archive.

Community archivists themselves do not realise that they perform archival appraisal and selection of records creators and records. Nevertheless, certain mechanisms underpinning the selection of materials for community archives do exist and, once acknowledged, constitute a very interesting topic for future empirical research.

[Translated by Steve Jones]

Bibliography

Archival Sources

Uniwersytet Mikołaja Kopernika w Toruniu, Wydział Nauk Historycznych, Katedra Archiwistyki i Zarządzania Dokumentacją: *Community archives in Poland – multiple case study (2016–2019). Project documentation* [interviews held by Magdalena Wiśniewska-Drewniak].

Printed Sources

Zarządzenie Ministra Kultury i Dziedzictwa Narodowego z dnia 30 stycznia 2020 r. w sprawie nadania statutu Centrum Archiwistyki Społecznej, in: *Dziennik Urzędowy Ministra Kultury i Dziedzictwa Narodowego.* 2020, item 6.

Literature

Appraisal, in: *Dictionary of Archives Terminology*, in: URL: https://dictionary.archivists.org/entry/appraisal.html [14.11.2021].

Archival value, in: *Dictionary of Archives Terminology*, in: URL: https://dictionary.archivists.org/entry/archival-value.html [14.11.2021].

Atkinson, Rowland / Flint, John: *Accessing Hidden and Hard-to-Reach Populations: Snowball Research Strategies*, in: *Social Research Update.* 2001/33.

Baza archiwów społecznych, in: *Centrum Archiwistyki Społecznej*, URL: https://cas.org.pl/baza-archiwow/ [14.11.2021].

Borodij, Eugeniusz: *Potrzeby użytkowników a obecne kryteria wartościowania*, in: *Problemy wartościowania dokumentacji współczesnej – konferencja w Archiwum Głównym Akt Dawnych.* 2007, pp. 32–45, in: URL: https://www.archiwa.gov.pl/images/docs/Wartosciowanie_materialow_archiwalnych_1.pdf [14.11.2021].

Caswell, Michelle / Migoni, Alda Allina / Geraci, Moah / Cifor, Marika: *"To Be Able to Imagine Otherwise": Community Archives and the Importance of Representation*, in: *Archives and Records.* 2017/38/1, pp. 5–26.

Caswell, Michelle: *Affective Bonds. What Community Archives Can Teach Mainstream Institutions*, in: Bastian, Jeanette / Flinn, Andrew (eds.): *Community Archives, Community Spaces. Heritage, Memory and Identity.* 2020, pp. 21–37.

Cifor, Marika: *Affecting Relations: Introducing Affect Theory to Archival Discourse*, in: *Archival Science.* 2016/16, pp. 7–31.

Cohen, Nissim / Arieli, Tamar: *Field Research in Conflict Environments. Methodological Challenges and Snowball Sampling*, in: *Journal of Peace Research.* 2011/48/4, pp. 423–435.

Czarnota, Tomasz: *Archiwistyka społeczna w nauce i dydaktyce uniwersyteckiej oraz zmiany w nauce zachodzące pod jej wpływem w latach 2005–16*, in: Jóźwik, Artur / Ziętal, Katarzyna (eds.): *Archiwistyka społeczna. Diagnoza i wyzwania.* 2017, pp. 94–120.

Czarnota, Tomasz: *Komu są potrzebne społeczne archiwa?*, in: *Archiwista Polski.* 2011/64/4, pp. 15–33.

Czarnota, Tomasz: *O archiwach społecznych i ich znaczeniu dla polskiego dziedzictwa narodowego i tożsamości lokalnej*, in: *Archiwa – Kancelarie – Zbiory.* 2014/5 (7), pp. 125–143.

Czarnota, Tomasz: *Problemy polskich archiwów społecznych za granicą*, in: Mazur, Ludmiła / Łosowski, Janusz (eds.): *Arkhivy Rossii i Pol'shi: istoriya, problemy i perspektivy razvitiya* [*Аркхивы России и Пол'схи: исторыа, проблемы и перспективы развитыа*]. 2013, pp. 145–160.

Flinn, Andrew: *Archival Activism. Independent and Community-led Archives, Radical Public History and the Heritage Professions*, in: *InterActions: UCLA Journal of Education and Information Studies.* 2011/7/2.

Flinn, Andrew: *Community Archives*, in: Duranti, Luciana / Franks, Patricia C. (eds.): *Encyclopedia of Archival Science.* 2015, pp. 145–149.

Flinn, Andrew: *Community Histories, Community Archives. Some Opportunities and Challenges*, in: *Journal of the Society of Archivists.* 2007/2, pp. 151–176.

Gilliland, Anne / Flinn, Andrew: *Community Archives. What Are We Really Talking About?* 2013, pp. 1–23, in: URL: https://tinyurl.com/48ptztt5 [11.11.2021].

Giziński, Piotr: *Przegląd pomorskich archiwów społecznych – podsumowanie projektu gdańskiego Oddziału Stowarzyszenia Archiwistów Polskich.* 2016, in: URL: http://sap.archiwapomorskie.pl/wp-content/uploads/2016/09/raport-z-archiwistyki-spolecznej.pdf [11.11.2021].

Gluza, Zbigniew: *Archiwa społeczne*, in: *Karta.* 2002/36, pp. 140–142.

Harris, Verne: *The Archival Sliver. Power, Memory, and Archives in South Africa*, in: *Archival Science.* 2002/2, pp. 63–86.

Listening to the Past, Speaking to the Future. Report of the Archives Task Force, in: *Conselleria d'Educació, Cultura i Esport*, URL: https://tinyurl.com/yn6c8d4j [14.11.2021].

Martini, Natalia / Jóźwik, Artur: *Realia funkcjonowania archiwów społecznych i czynniki sprzyjające ich rozwojowi*, in: Jóźwik, Artur / Ziętal, Katarzyna (eds.): *Archiwistyka społeczna. Diagnoza i wyzwania.* 2017, pp. 62–75.

Poole, Alex H.: *The Information Work of Community Archives. A Systematic Literature Review*, in: *Journal of Documentation.* 2020/76/3, pp. 657–687.

Regulamin bazy archiwów społecznych, in: *Centrum Archiwistyki Społecznej*, URL: https://cas.org.pl/wp-content/uploads/2021/04/regulamin_baza_cas-org-pl_04-2021.pdf [20.08.2021].
Sobczak, Anna / Kudosz, Małgorzata: *Charakterystyka archiwów społecznych*, in: Ziętal, Katarzyna (ed.): *Archiwa społeczne w Polsce. Stan obecny i perspektywy*. 2016, pp. 6–18.
Społeczny, in: *Słownik języka polskiego PWN*, in: URL: https://sjp.pwn.pl/sjp/spoleczny;2523113.html [12.11.2021].
Welland, Sarah / Cossham, Amanda: *Defining the Undefinable: an Analysis of Definitions of Community Archives*, in: *Global Knowledge, Memory and Communication*. 2019/68/8–9, pp. 617–634.
Wiśniewska, Magdalena: *Archiwum społeczne – archiwum emocji*, in: Chorążyczewski, Waldemar / Piasek, Wojciech / Rosa, Agnieszka (eds.): *Nowa archiwistyka. Archiwa i archiwistyka w ponowoczesnym kontekście kulturowym*. 2014, pp. 77–86.
Wiśniewska, Magdalena: *Digital Community Archives – Selected Examples*, in: *Archiwa – Kancelarie – Zbiory*. 2015/6 (8), pp. 221–232. (1)
Wiśniewska, Magdalena: *Funkcje archiwów społecznych*, in: Czarnota, Tomasz / Konstankiewicz, Marek (eds.): *Archiwa organizacji pozarządowych w Polsce*. 2015, pp. 63–69. (2)
Wiśniewska, Magdalena: *History of Community Archiving in Poland*, in: Foscarini, Fiorella / MacNeil, Heather / Mak, Bonnie / Oliver, Gillian (eds.): *Engaging with Records and Archives. Histories and Theories*. 2016, pp. 195–209.
Wiśniewska, Magdalena: *Postmodernizm a archiwa społeczne*, in: *Archiwista Polski*. 2013/70, pp. 25–29.
Wiśniewska-Drewniak, Magdalena: *Community Archives in Poland – Multiple Case Study: Description of the Research Project*. 2016, in: URL: https://repozytorium.umk.pl/handle/item/3888 [10.11.2021].
Wiśniewska-Drewniak, Magdalena: *Inaczej to zniknie. Archiwa społeczne w Polsce – wielokrotne studium przypadku*. 2019.
Wiśniewska-Drewniak, Magdalena: *Wpływ projektowego finansowania na działalność archiwów społecznych jako możliwy problem badawczy*, in: *Zarządzanie w Kulturze*. 2018/19/3, pp. 273–286.
Ziętal, Katarzyna: *Archiwa społeczne w Polsce – prezentacja i analiza wyników badań*, in: Jóźwik, Artur / Ziętal, Katarzyna (eds.): *Archiwistyka społeczna – diagnoza i wyzwania*. 2017, pp. 14–32.
Ziętal, Katarzyna: *Archiwa społeczne w Polsce*, in: Chorążyczewski, Waldemar / Piasek, Wojciech / Rosa, Agnieszka (eds.): *Nowa archiwistyka. Archiwa i archiwistyka w ponowoczesnym kontekście kulturowym*. 2014, pp. 71–76.
Ziętal, Katarzyna: *KARTA i archiwa społeczne*, in: *Biuletyn eBIB*. 2014/6, http://ebibojs.pl/index.php/ebib/article/view/349/348 [23.04.2022].
Ziętal, Katarzyna: *Wstęp*, in: Ziętal, Katarzyna (ed.): *Archiwistyka społeczna*. 2012, pp. 7–13.

AutorInnenverzeichnis

Dr. habil. Waldemar Chorążyczewski (Nikolaus-Kopernikus-Universität Toruń)
ORCID: https://orcid.org/0000-0002-0063-0032
Historiker. Forschungsschwerpunkte: Archivkunde; polnische Königskanzlei; historische Klimatologie; ego-dokumentarische Analyse; Geschichte Polens in der Jagiellonen-Ära.

Dr. habil. Robert Degen (Nikolaus-Kopernikus-Universität Toruń)
ORCID: https://orcid.org/0000-0003-3467-9341
Historiker. Forschungsschwerpunkte: Archivkunde, archivarische Aktenbewertung und Kassation, Dokumentenverwaltung, Geschichte Polens und polnischer Archive im 20. Jahrhundert.

Dr. habil. Marlena Jabłońska (Nikolaus-Kopernikus-Universität Toruń)
ORCID: https://orcid.org/0000-0001-7189-9007
Historikerin. Forschungsschwerpunkte: Archivkunde, Dokumentenverwaltung, soziale Kommunikation und Öffentlichkeitsarbeit von Archiven.

Prof. Krzysztof Kopiński (Nikolaus-Kopernikus-Universität Toruń)
ORCID: https://orcid.org/0000-0002-4379-9217
Historiker. Forschungsschwerpunkte: Archivkunde mit besonderem Schwerpunkt auf elektronischen Dokumenten; Edition mittelalterlicher und frühneuzeitlicher historischer Quellen; mittelalterliche Geschichte; Hilfswissenschaften der Geschichte mit besonderem Schwerpunkt auf Genealogie und Neographie.

Sven Lepa M. A. (Nationalarchiv von Estland)
Archivar. Forschungsschwerpunkte: Crowdsourcing in Erinerungs-Institutionen, Fotografie des 19. Jahrhunderts.

Dr. Katarzyna Pepłowska (Nikolaus-Kopernikus-Universität Toruń)
ORCID: https://orcid.org/0000-0001-5364-684X
Historikerin. Forschungsschwerpunkte: Archivrecht, digitale Archive, Archive in der Politik der Europäischen Union, elektronisches Dokumentenmanagement.

Dr. Bogdan-Florin Popovici (Rumänisches Nationalarchiv, Kreisdirektion Brasov)
ORCID: https://orcid.org/0000-0002-7644-0446
Historiker. Forschungsschwerpunkte: Ideengeschichte des Archivwesens, Archivbeschreibung, Dokumentationsmanagement.

Prof. Aigi Rahi-Tamm (Universität Tartu)
ORCID: https://orcid.org/0000-0001-8792-860X
Historikerin. Forschungsschwerpunkte: Quelleninterpretation, Sowjetisierung der Gesellschaft, Kriegserfahrungen im 20. Jahrhundert, Beziehungen zwischen Staat und Individuum, Archivkunde.

Dr. Robert Rybak (Nikolaus-Kopernikus-Universität Toruń)
ORCID: https://orcid.org/0000-0003-2935-1982
Historiker. Forschungsschwerpunkte: Kriegskunst, die im 20. Jahrhundert in Polen entwickelt wurde, sowie Einsatzkunst und Taktik der Marine, Geschichte des Warschauer Paktes, Geschichte der polnischen Marine im 20. Jahrhundert, Militärdoktrinen.

Dr. Marcin Smoczyński (Nikolaus-Kopernikus-Universität Toruń)
ORCID: https://orcid.org/0000-0002-4111-0201
Historiker. Forschungsschwerpunkte: Geschichte, Theorie und Praxis des Dokumentenmanagements, Bürokratie im Kontext der Verwaltung und Staatsform.

Dr. habil. Krzysztof Syta (Nikolaus-Kopernikus-Universität Toruń)
ORCID: https://orcid.org/0000-0002-9466-1525
Historiker. Forschungsschwerpunkte: Geschichte der Privatarchive in den polnischen Gebieten des 16.–20. Jahrhunderts; Aktenkunde des 16.–20. Jahrhunderts; Quellenkunde des 18.–19. Jahrhunderts; Organisation und Funktion von Magnatenhöfen im 18. Jahrhundert.

Liisi Taimre M. A. (Nationalarchiv von Estland)
Archivarin. Forschungsschwerpunkte: Digital Humanities, Crowdsourcing, soziale Archive und soziale Medien.

Tõnis Türna B. A. (Nationalarchiv von Estland)
Archivar. Forschungsschwerpunkte: Estnische Bauernschaft und lokale Verwaltung im 19. Jahrhundert, Sozial- und Familiengeschichte, Mikrogeschichte, Crowdsourcing in Archiven.

Dr. Magdalena Wiśniewska-Drewniak (Nikolaus-Kopernikus-Universität Toruń)
ORCID: https://orcid.org/0000-0001-9119-1372
Historikerin. Forschungsschwerpunkte: private und gesellschaftliche Archive, neue Trends im Archivwesen, Forschungsmethodik.

Dr. Wioletta Zielecka-Mikołajczyk (Nikolaus-Kopernikus-Universität Toruń)
ORCID: https://orcid.org/0000-0001-6100-0563
Historikerin. Forschungsschwerpunkte: Union von Brest 1596; Geschichte der Ortodoxie und der Unierten Kirche; religiöse Beziehungen in der Rzeczypospolita, insb. der Diözese Przemyśl-Sambir.